Sweet

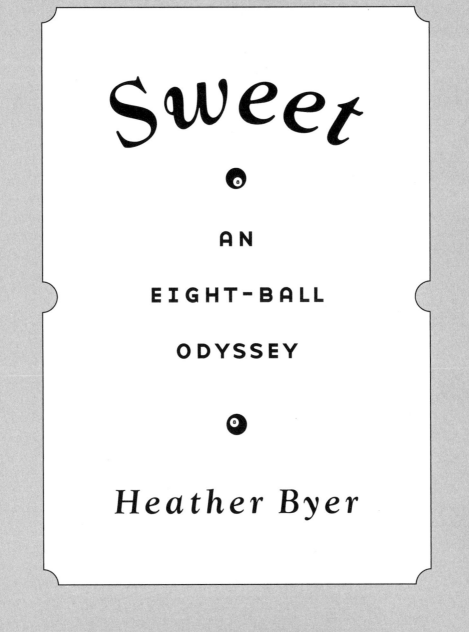

Sweet

AN EIGHT-BALL ODYSSEY

Heather Byer

RIVERHEAD BOOKS
A MEMBER OF PENGUIN GROUP (USA) INC.
NEW YORK • 2007

RIVERHEAD BOOKS
Published by the Penguin Group
Penguin Group (USA) Inc., 375 Hudson Street, New York, New York 10014, USA •
Penguin Group (Canada), 90 Eglinton Avenue East, Suite 700, Toronto, Ontario
M4P 2Y3, Canada (a division of Pearson Penguin Canada Inc.) • Penguin Books Ltd,
80 Strand, London WC2R 0RL, England • Penguin Ireland, 25 St Stephen's Green,
Dublin 2, Ireland (a division of Penguin Books Ltd) • Penguin Group (Australia),
250 Camberwell Road, Camberwell, Victoria 3124, Australia (a division of Pearson
Australia Group Pty Ltd) • Penguin Books India Pvt Ltd, 11 Community Centre,
Panchsheel Park, New Delhi–110 017, India • Penguin Group (NZ), 67 Apollo
Drive, Mairangi Bay, Auckland 1311, New Zealand (a division of Pearson
New Zealand Ltd) • Penguin Books (South Africa) (Pty) Ltd, 24 Sturdee Avenue,
Rosebank, Johannesburg 2196, South Africa

Penguin Books Ltd, Registered Offices:
80 Strand, London WC2R 0RL, England

Library of Congress Cataloging-in-Publication Data

Byer, Heather.
Sweet: an eight-ball odyssey / Heather Byer.
p.   cm.
ISBN 978-1-59448-936-5
1. Byer, Heather.   2. Billiard players—United States—Biography.   I. Title.
GV892.2.B94A3   2007   2006036907
794.7'2092—dc22
[B]

Printed in the United States of America
1   3   5   7   9   10   8   6   4   2

Book design by Stephanie Huntwork

While the author has made every effort to provide accurate telephone numbers and
Internet addresses at the time of publication, neither the publisher nor the author
assumes any responsibility for errors, or for changes that occur after publication.
Further, the publisher does not have any control over and does not assume
any responsibility for author or third-party websites or their content.

For my parents

Author's Note

Many (but not all) of the names in this book have been changed, and, in some instances, certain personal details were altered to protect identities. Likewise, some of the names of the bars mentioned in the book have been changed. Their locations were not altered, but I refrained from giving exact addresses. Again, this was done to protect the identities of some of the people described in this book. All of the pool matches I describe happened. For the sake of brevity, I condensed some of the games, but I did not alter their outcomes. I also compressed the timeline on occasion so that the narrative was not interrupted.

ACKNOWLEDGMENTS

Thank you to my parents, Howard Byer and Susan M. Byer, and to the rest of my family for their steadfast encouragement while I wrote this book. I must also thank the pool players I have met over the years—many of whom are described in these pages—for teaching me the nuances of this extraordinary game and for not allowing me to give up. Special thanks must go to Mike Shamos of Pittsburgh, Pennsylvania, who knows everything there is to know about pool and billiards, and then some. His books *Pool: History, Strategies, and Legends* and *The New Illustrated Encyclopedia of Billiards*, his articles in *Billiards Digest*, and our many conversations provided me with rich, fascinating historical information, as did the Billiard Archive, his amazing personal collection of billiard memorabilia. Robert Byrne's *Byrne's New Standard Book of Pool and Billiards* should be on the bookshelf of every pool player. It was especially helpful to me when I needed to describe a particular shot or recall an obscure rule of the game.

This book would not have been written without Bonnie Solow, who first saw a story here and whose boundless enthusiasm spurred me to tell it. Thanks to Susan Lehman for starting me off, and to the incomparable Jake Morrissey for bringing me to the finish line with his dedication, thoroughness, and wisdom.

To Beth Johnson, thank you for your friendship and for all those hours of cue balls and baseballs. To Polly Kanevsky and Justin Evans, thank you for reading and cheering, and to Ben Neihart, Alison Manheim, William Lung, Patrick Sheehan, and Lisa Cohen, thank you so much for your support.

Sweet

Shoot

BIG TONY CRAVES a cigarette, but he's trying to quit. His desire for a smoke is never more apparent than when he faces a pool table dotted with balls that aren't going where he wants them to go. A cigarette will take the edge off, soothe his impatience. But smoking has been banned from the bar, and he has taken this as a sign that he needs to give up the habit rather than work around the new rule as most players do, by running outside between innings for a quick nicotine hit, then running back inside just in time to make his shot. He doesn't like having to adjust. Quitting is easier, cleaner. It requires less movement.

So Big Tony, his eyes narrowed in concentration, his large head moving from side to side like a lumbering buffalo's, his lips parted for the cigarette that's not there, looks at what I've done to him—nicking my 3-ball in front of the corner pocket, blocking both his 11- and 13-ball. He seems mildly irritated, as if a fly has just landed on him and he's debating whether it's worth expending the energy to swat it away.

This is always how it is playing Big Tony, who's ranked a 7 and is an ornery pain in the ass if he hasn't popped a painkiller earlier in the evening (a habit he's not trying to kick). His face is passive, blank when he plays, but I know from experience that his mind is alive, his eyes picking through every available shot, every angle and safety on that table, as if he's running a sophisticated computer in his mind that calculates all of the angles for him in a nanosecond.

I've dreamed of playing Big Tony, because he's tough and rude and hard to beat; because he always insists on blow-drying his hair into a strange, glossy pompadour, about which he has no sense of humor; and because he doesn't think women are good pool players. Big Tony is pushing fifty. He hasn't evolved.

The bar where we're playing—a dank little hole in Manhattan's East Village that attracts a following every three years or so when some young fauxhemian "discovers" the place and writes about it for *Time Out New York* or *The Village Voice*, usually under a catchy headline like "Dives We Love"—is quiet, almost empty if you don't count the regulars. (It must be an undiscovered year.) A frowning dartboard, its reds and yellows faded, hangs unused on one wall. Unlike the wood-planked pubs that dot the neighborhood, this bar's floor is a dirty gray concrete that absorbs sound rather than enables it, so that footfalls—even those from heavy, weaving boots—don't make much noise. There is the occasional rough scraping of a chair, but other than that, the bar is barely a murmur. It's eerie. Even the jukebox is silent at that moment, until Ricky, a local pool player with a fondness for mixed vodka drinks, lopes over to it and announces, "I am so fucking sick of The Clash" (a bar favorite whose CD is in regular rotation) and plugs in something more hip-hoppy. There's an audible groan from the barflies. But I am at the pool table, standing across from Big Tony. I can't allow myself to care about the editorializing at the bar.

A huddle of balls—mostly mine—rests at one end of the table. Tony bends over and with a quick flick pushes his 10-ball to the rail.

He's trying to sandwich my 6, the only ball somewhat detached from this unfortunate grouping. But he taps the 10 too hard and not only does it not stay on the rail, it pushes the 6 into the whole coagulated mess, sending the balls in different directions so that there's now a lot of room for me to maneuver them.

I inhale slowly. I'm free.

Tony's face scrunches up like a baby's. "Jesus," he mutters. I can feel tension in the room now. People who haven't been paying attention to the game cast wary but newly interested eyes toward the table. My teammates hunch forward on their stools.

I look at the table and immediately see two possible shots. Then my heart rate picks up. I don't see just two shots. I see the whole game. For the first time, I feel what it must be like to be Big Tony. His bungled defensive shot has left me in the perfect position to run out my remaining five balls and get to the 8. I can actually beat him; I can topple this cranky, sour-breathed, Cro-Magnon ace.

He knows I can, too. I see it in his eyes. And I see it in the eyes of my teammates, who are afraid to speak, afraid to break the spell. But I know what they're thinking. *Do it*, they seem to be saying to me. *You can do it.*

"Come on, shoot some pool, Heather," Big Tony says, tired of my contemplation.

"I'm shooting pool, Tony. When I miss, you can shoot." I bend down and draw my cue back like a violin bow, then stroke it forward, finishing the note. The stick's path is straight and sure as it strikes the cue ball, which rolls along the table until it touches the 2, sending it gracefully but firmly into the side pocket. The shot is perfect, like something out of a dream.

Oh, who am I kidding? It is a dream.

Tony—not Big Tony, just Tony—doesn't leave me anything. He never leaves anybody anything. My one chance for a breakout is ruined when I miscue—miscue, for God's sake, in a game against a guy who's ranked a 7—and send my 2-ball not into the side pocket, as I intended, but into a cluster of balls that I don't want to break up. They scatter, and Tony has the run of the table. He finishes the game so quickly and effortlessly that he probably could've picked his Lotto numbers and talked to his mother in Florida while he was beating me.

After I lose the game, I sit on a tall wooden stool near the emergency exit and replay the final few shots in my mind, figuring out exactly how I wanted them to go—creating Tony's unexpected mistakes, adding my quick thinking and competitive zeal, imagining the attention of everyone in the bar turning toward me like a spotlight. I indulge in this fantasy while staring at the snack machine, holding a beer I'm not drinking.

I construct such scenes in my head all the time, though this is the first time I actually work in one of my favorite lines from *The Hustler*: "I'm shooting pool, Fats. When I miss, you can shoot." It's from a great scene in the film, when cynical, hardened Fast Eddie Felson returns to the poolroom to confront Bert Gordon and Minnesota Fats, to try to even the score, even though the price he's paid already is too high.

"HELLO? YOU IN THERE?"

Tony peers down at me, the linebacker standing over a crumpled running back.

"Oh, hey. Yeah, Tony. I was just off somewhere."

"Daydreaming."

"Something like that."

He blinks, gecko-like, his glittery eyes hovering over bags of mottled skin. I half expect his tongue to flick out.

"Can I buy you a drink?"

"What?" I ask.

"You played good. You got unlucky there with that two. But, you know, you made me work there a little."

A little.

"So, what're you drinking?"

I look down at my warm beer. "I've been drinking this unsuccessfully all night."

"Lemme get you another then. It's the least I can do." He smiles, somewhat fiendishly, I think.

"Okay, another one of these then," I say. "I'll just hide this one somewhere." He nods and turns toward the bar.

"You don't leave much, do you, Big T?"

"Huh? What's that s'posed to mean?"

"You're supposed to say, 'That's what the game's all about.'" He looks confused. "It's from *The Hustler*," I say. He gazes dumbly at me for a minute, then heads off to get my drink, which is what the winners always do.

I sit quietly, waiting for my beer, and observe Valerie, a pool player I've seen at pool bars around the city, banging the hell out of her rack the way she always does, swinging her sleek, dark hair off her shoulders as she watches the balls roll to unfortunate places on the table. Tonight I try to imagine her on one of my conference calls with the Los Angeles office, try to conjure her reaction to my boss's response to the script I sent him. "The ending doesn't work. Forget it. Not interested," he spits. Valerie would've said, "So change the fucking ending. You can do that, can't you?"

I, of course, say something like, "Well, I think there are ways around that, Larry. . . ." But Larry, the Hollywood producer I work for, just growls. "What else have you got for me?" His voice crackles through the speakerphone, alternately crisp and muffled, so that my colleagues and I strain to hear him, leaning forward in our seats, as if that will help. We look like a bunch of eager schoolkids, even though what we really want to do is jam a hot poker through the black box on the table. I hate speakerphones. They are without a doubt the worst gadget ever invented, especially when an irritated movie producer is on the other end.

It's mid-afternoon. We always make the phone calls then to catch our L.A. film colleagues while it's still morning on the West Coast, before they leave for their lunches and screenings and meetings. Three of us in the New York office are gathered around my desk, staring listlessly at the phone. I roll my eyes at my colleagues and plow forward with descriptions of the other scripts and books and articles we've sent Larry in the hope that he'll be intrigued enough to want to read one of them, and maybe actually turn one into a movie.

After the call is over (we strike out again), I slip into the women's room and change into straight, dark, low-slung jeans and a tight red tank top. My arms look good. I've taken to wearing sleeveless shirts after several pool players have told me I've "got some nice, sexy arms." I put my hair up, letting a few strands fall around my face. Then I head over to the bar to play some pool. And get my ass handed to me by Tony.

Now, as I wait for Tony to bring me another beer, I watch. Valerie's game is going nowhere, because she's laughing and flirting and not focusing. A plump, middle-aged man in a threadbare denim jacket totes two more pints of stout back to his corner of the bar (his fourth and fifth of the night), while his friend, who isn't drinking, peers over the brown-framed glasses balanced on his nose and chastises some poor kid who thinks he knows how to run the table but doesn't. That smarmy guy, Marty, is back, too. He tries to hit on a curvaceous woman in black leather pants who finally turns to him, moments before slicing in her 4-ball, and says, "You repulse me. Now go away." A skinny waitress crisscrosses the room, carrying a tray of empty glasses to the bar. The glasses look forlorn. So does she. Bottles clink and the denim-clad guy begins to sing along to Johnny Cash, whose voice rumbles out of the speakers. Someone must be feeling nostalgic. I am still gripping my cue; I haven't broken it apart yet to put it back into its case. I clutch it, my grip purposeful, and wait for my beer. But I notice that my waiting is starting to take a different turn: I am waiting for what will come next. I think about the game with Tony. "You made me work there a little." For the first time in many months I feel certain, strangely, deliciously sure, that I will have another chance. This is only the beginning.

Salad Days

ALTHOUGH I'VE VISITED many of the poolrooms in New York since I started playing pool eight years ago, the only one I notice before I become obsessed with the game is Chelsea Billiards. I pass the sign on 21st Street when I'm going to meet friends for dinner or when I'm headed to the movie theater on 19th Street and Broadway. As I walk by, I peer into its large, dark windows. Usually, I see young Asian men gathered at the front, playing games on enormous tables that I assume are for snooker. The balls glide across them, skimming along a wide green expanse of cloth. Sometimes I stand outside and watch, my face pressed against the glass, wondering why the balls are following their particular paths, trying—unsuccessfully—to figure out how the game is played, until invariably one of the men at the tables notices me and either grins lecherously or frowns, startled and annoyed that his concentration has been disturbed by my curious gaze.

As the men move their sticks and shoot their balls, their eyes lock onto the table, never on each other. They appear wholly engrossed, and it's easy to see why. There is something hypnotic about those colored balls shimmying around on that green cloth. In my eyes, the men who cause those balls to move—narrow-hipped guys in shabby button-downs and khakis, job IDs still hanging from their belt loops, their rough, dark hair flopped forward, covering their foreheads— seem both intense and at peace. It's an alluring paradox. Who knows what their lives are like when they aren't in this poolroom? Who cares what their stories are? I'm tired of stories.

I have not come to New York to reinvent myself. Not everyone does. I visit the city for the first time during my sophomore year of college, and the place unnerves me; it makes me feel meek and disoriented. But after I graduate, New York is the logical place for me to look for a job, since, like many starry-eyed, black-turtlenecked artistes who hungrily read Joan Didion in college, I want to work in book publishing or independent film, and Manhattan is, in the end, the only city where I receive any job offers. To top it off, through somebody's elderly great-aunt, I get a lead on a legitimately charming, almost-affordable studio apartment in a safe-ish neighborhood on the Upper West Side, within walking distance of Central Park. With a job and an apartment, it seems ridiculous not to take the plunge. So I accept a low-paying position as an editorial assistant at an audio publisher, move to Manhattan—by default, really—and wait for my-self to hate it and run back to Ohio.

But that doesn't happen. Some recessive urban gene apparently lurks in my person and is soon aroused from dormancy, because, in a remarkably short time, I come to love the city, with all of its hardships and excesses, its screaming taxis and crowded sidewalks. And the ambition that seeps out of every New York crevice and alley, wafts through every tiny gray cubicle and too-small apartment and putrid subway station, nips at the heels of every editor and banker and actor and lawyer and fashion designer, envelops me, too. And here I am, some eight years later, quite a bit of hard-earned experience under my belt, running the New York arm of a successful feature film company, and eating lunch.

This, it turns out, is the most important part of my job. Eating, talking, listening, listening, listening. It's a jabbering, noisy line of work and a relentless exercise in delayed gratification. Not one literary property I've recommended—book, article, play, scrap of paper with someone's half-remembered dream scribbled on it—has been translated to the big screen. But still I talk, and listen, and push ideas, and eat endless salads. All this noise and lettuce, and never any results. But as I'm reminded routinely by my friends, I am right in the thick of it, where it all happens, or where it *could* happen. It is the existence of the possibility that is so tantalizing. You never know what a day's lunch may bring.

To MY GREAT RELIEF, I arrive at the restaurant first. Larry is in town, and we're meeting with a hotshot magazine editor who says he has some sizzling film ideas to pitch. The guy, a "lad mag" veteran, has been named editor of the year by a trade publication that issues such awards. I scan the bar at the front of the restaurant, which is loud, obnoxious, and overpriced, full of expense accounts and rich tourists, tanned businessmen with bejeweled, heavily made-up women on their arms who look like high-class hookers but are in fact confessed "shopoholics" from Tucson. My eyes come to rest on a man sitting at the bar, a glass of bubbly water in front of him. He's wearing sunglasses, despite being inside. He wears a black suit over a black T-shirt and glossy black motorcycle boots. He is reading a magazine, on the cover of which is a man sitting on a bar stool, wearing black sunglasses, a black suit over a black T-shirt, and glossy black motorcycle boots.

As I look from magazine cover to man, I realize it's *him*, it's the same guy, the editor of the year, in the same pose, wearing the same clothes, the same sunglasses, *reading about himself.* I stare at the double image, frozen, my lips parted, clutching my nicest leather handbag, wearing one of my more chic work outfits, not knowing quite how to address him or whether I want to break up this bizarre tableau.

The man looks up from the magazine. He smiles, I smile. "You're Mitchell, aren't you?" I say. He nods.

"Interesting reading there?"

He chortles and starts to say something, but we're interrupted by Larry, who arrives explosively with one of his Armani-clad, psychotically ambitious associates—a young guy named Jared who has eagerly accompanied him from L.A.—and wants to flag down the maître d', *pronto.* I've worked for Larry for more than a year, and this frenzied search for the person who makes upscale bureaucracy move quickly is a ritual before every public outing.

Larry is not tall, but he has a towering presence, with a voracious gaze that moves over everything in its path, his eyes a steely blue, penetrating and curious, set in a jowly, rubbery face that shape-shifts into a range of forceful expressions. His hair color changes fairly regularly, too; on this trip it's an inky black, almost purple, and he pats it frequently, a rare gesture of uncertainty. (Some colorist in Bel-Air is going to pay.) Except for the hair, he is a column of gray today, draped in lush wools the color of storm clouds. Mitchell still wears his sunglasses, but something in his stance tells me he's impressed. I understand. Larry is impressive.

We're standing in a tight cluster now, near the doorway of the restaurant's large main dining room. I make the introductions and then watch Larry's face when the maître d'—not the usual one, I learn, since he doesn't know Larry by name, barely even acknowledges him—scans his appointment book and says flatly, "I don't have a reservation here, but I can have a table for you in about fifteen minutes." It's as if he's said something off-color about Larry's mother.

"What did you say?" Larry demands, incredulous.

"I said there's no reservation under your name, but—"

"My office made a reservation. They even *confirmed* the reservation today. I eat lunch here every time I'm in New York. Where's Guillaume?" (Guillaume is the owner and an "old friend" of Larry's.)

"Sir, I can have a table for you in . . . five minutes." He shaves off ten minutes, perhaps sensing the approaching thunder.

"No, not five minutes. *Now.* Now, now, NOW. I want a table now or I'm leaving!" Larry's hands clench into tight fists. He leans into the maître d's face, his sweater—soft, silvery, European—straining against his chest.

"Well, as you can see, sir, we're extremely busy—"

I have the presence of mind to guide Mitchell back to the bar and his bubbly water. I leave him there, then scoot back toward Larry in time to see him shove his cashmere coat at Jared, bellow that he's "outta here," that he and Guillaume are "through," that he will "never eat here again, ever," as long as he lives, then charge through the bustling Friday lunch crowd, out the door, and onto the sidewalk, continuing his enraged trek without stopping or missing a stride, continuing it straight across the street, in fact—right through the traffic, ignoring the blasting horns and bewildered pedestrians—and walk to another restaurant, a similarly loud, expensive, ostentatious eatery, this time Italian, and disappear inside without even looking up at its sign.

"Oh, Jesus," Jared mutters, and quickly follows, carrying Larry's coat over his arm, reduced in a matter of seconds to nothing more than a worried valet. I fetch Mitchell and say, "Bring your magazine. It looks like we're eating somewhere else."

WHEN MITCHELL AND I arrive at the new restaurant, Larry and Jared are seated at a table in the corner, facing the room. ("Mafia-style,"

Larry notes contentedly.) He's calm now but sweating profusely and already ordering his second Diet Coke.

We're able to salvage the lunch. Mitchell and Larry "brainstorm," and Larry tells amusing stories about various stars misbehaving on sets. At the end of the meal, Jared quietly takes care of the check while Larry goes to the restroom. Later, when we're on the street and have exchanged business cards and said good-bye to Mitchell, who leaves in a hired black sedan, still toting the magazine promoting his greatness, and Larry is inside his hired black sedan, talking on his cell phone, I say to Jared, "Well, that was close." He nods as he pops open his own cell phone.

"I mean, that was really insane," I prod, allowing myself a giggle for the first time.

Jared's neatly plucked eyebrows draw together. If he wasn't so young and toadying, and if his titanium cell phone wasn't so small, he would actually look stern.

"These things are important to Larry. *Commitment* is important to Larry. Loyalty. He worked hard to get to where he is, you know."

"Jared, we would've had a table in five minutes. He had a tantrum back there. In front of our guest."

Jared sighs, as if I'm hopeless. "I hear what you're saying, Heather, but you have to understand, Larry is a very proud, passionate, dramatic man. It's why he's chosen to tell stories for a living. He's a risk taker."

One of the "stories" Larry told grossed half a billion dollars worldwide. I suspect there are other reasons he's chosen this career.

"It's true that Larry tends to create drama in unusual places," Jared adds. "But, hey, that's what makes him Larry."

ALL WEEKEND I THINK about how I can't take another scene as silly and immature as the one I'd endured with Larry and Jared. I also contemplate Mitchell's reading about himself in front of his hosts and wonder if he will continue this routine until the next issue of the magazine comes out and he's booted off its cover. I think that my job is meaningless, wonder how I can live in this thrashing, exciting city and yet feel completely empty. I can't remember when I started to feel this way. And worse, I can no longer remember *not* feeling this way. It's a thoroughly unoriginal predicament, I know, but I have what I think might be an original way out of it.

We have a three-day weekend coming up because of Columbus Day. On my free Monday, I take the subway from Brooklyn, where I live, into Manhattan. I get out at 23rd Street and Sixth Avenue and walk two blocks to Chelsea Billiards, the poolroom with the big windows and the intense, peaceful players.

I seek out pool at first because the activity strikes me as asocial. I want to lose myself, not find myself. I have no need to come out of my shell, or so I think. I'm searching for a temporary retreat from the Larrys and Jareds in my world, looking for something private, unusual, elegant—all elements that seem to be missing from my life. The last thing I want to do is meet more people, engage, be noticed. I'm not quite ready to give up my careerist, fast-track life, no matter how much it frustrates me. But I yearn for another life, too. What I think I want, though I can't articulate it, is a double life—a parallel existence in which I can relax and be someone else.

And so in the fall of 1998 I walk into Chelsea Billiards on Columbus Day, shy but determined. I've never been inside a pool hall before. This one is almost empty. The place has a hushed feel to it, the air cool and still. It's the middle of the afternoon, but natural light cannot seem to find its way inside. Then I notice that the room's only windows, which bracket the entrance on 21st Street, are tinted. The lights that hang above the tables are not turned on, so the hall is dark, as if resting before dinner. The tables fill the room—there are dozens of them, each spaced exactly the same distance from the next, lined up in neat rows, creating the atmosphere of a ward. I notice a puny bar on one side of the room, near the doorway to the restrooms. There are no chairs or stools hugging it; it's just a counter with rows of bottles behind it.

The wiry blonde standing behind the bar doesn't look up when I approach. She continues to look through what appear to be accounting records, a sheaf of papers with columns of numbers on them. I clear my throat and ask if there's anyone there who can teach me to shoot pool.

"You can come to pool school," she says, her voice clipped. She sticks a flyer, Xerox on pale green paper, under my nose. "Mondays from six to eight, five dollars an hour." She forces a tight-lipped smile.

"I'm not very good. . . ."

"They all say that. That's why you come."

"No, I mean I've never played." Which is the truth.

"Doesn't matter. We take all levels. There are a lot of beginners." She looks back down at her papers and at a calculator I hadn't noticed before. I am being dismissed. She's imparted the necessary information, and it's clear we're not going to chitchat. It's about 3:30. I don't feel like waiting for two and a half hours, and I'm starting to feel uncertain about all this. I leave with my pool-school flyer. I return the following Monday before six, having resolved to try pool school at least once. I don't know it, of course, but the grinning, middle-aged man who greets me, a pool instructor named Mark Finkelstein, who stands about five-two and wears short, wide, pointy ties and gigantic square-framed glasses that make him look like a bug, is about to change my life.

Chelsea Billiards's pool school usually employs three instructors on Mondays, local sharks in various stages of glorious ascent or downward spiral. They receive free table time in exchange for their teaching services. We take our lessons in the basement, which, unlike upstairs, reeks of cigarette smoke and dust. When we collect there, each of us is assigned to a pool table. They're regulation tables, which means they are nine feet long and four and a half feet wide, and each also has an automatic ball return. The Chelsea Billiards tables are in good shape, as are the balls, but not all of the cues are. I soon learn you must examine the cues closely before you select one, since many need to have their tips replaced, the original ones worn down to the nub and therefore useless.

Most of the students, I discover, are either regular players who have a lot of bad habits they're trying to break or beginners, people who've recently played in a bar, smashed, and had fun, and thought getting better at the game might be a good way to meet people. These folks come for a few Mondays and then disappear, to be replaced by others just like them.

The students barely interact. Pool school is about drills, about learning a technique and then practicing it over and over, a hundred times in a row. The ennui is often excruciating, though I end up finding that sort of fierce, myopic focus strangely relaxing. Nothing else penetrates my brain—not my work, not my family, not my social life. It is, more often than not, two hours of heaven. I emerge as if I've just woken up from a two-hour nap, fully refreshed.

Even though the woman behind the bar told me that pool school was for all levels, it's clear I am the class anomaly.

"You've never played pool?" Mark is incredulous.

"No, not really," I say. "But I want to learn."

Mark is delighted. "Well, we're gonna teach you. This is great." I don't realize it, but for a player as superb as Mark, I am a dream candidate, a tabula rasa, a child he can mold into a champion.

"Let's start with the basics. Here, hold this." He thrusts a pool cue in my direction. "You're little, like me—that's gonna work to your advantage, by the way—so I'm guessing you won't want a stick that's longer than fifty-seven inches."

I clutch the pole as if it's a baton I'm getting ready to twirl.

"Let's see whatcha got." Mark puts a cue ball in the center of the table. I glance at the square panes of plastic perched on his nose, then at his tie; its knot has been loosened, and it seems to spread across his chest like a dinner napkin. It's flat, a bit shiny, with thick brown and gray stripes—comical, really, like something from *The Carol Burnett Show*, something Tim Conway might wear in a skit.

"What're you waiting for?"

I'm still gripping the cue, paralyzed.

"What do I do?"

"Whaddaya mean what do you do? Hit the ball. Here, you bend over"—Mark leans over the table—"and just make contact with the ball. I want to look at your stroke. Well, you don't have a stroke yet, but you will." Mark slides his arm back and glides it forward, the cue stick clicking softly against the white ball, sending it in a perfect line to the other side of the table. It bounces against the far end (the sides are called rails, I learn later) and slides back, ending up exactly where it started. Simple. Beautiful.

I am thirty years old, a high-school valedictorian, an Ivy League graduate, a holder of a master's degree. I have lived alone for eight years, know that Cincinnati Reds outfielder George Foster hit fifty-two homeruns in 1978, and am a runner, a solo world traveler, and a vice president at a feature film company. I speak passable French. I know how to drive and how to cook. I can program a VCR, install a phone jack, or hook up a stereo system by myself, and have even assembled the sixty-seven pieces of an IKEA dresser without bursting into tears.

And I miss the cue ball.

Completely.

I lean over the table like Mark did. I try to imitate his fluid gesture, swing my right arm back, my right hand holding the cue at the end of the fat part, the part closest to me, then I thrust it forward, aiming (I think) for the cue ball.

The cue stick lunges off to my left, missing the ball by a good six inches and dragging me forward, where, if I do not put my hand out to stop myself, I will fall across the table and the stick will fly, like a javelin, from my grasp. To my relief, I manage to hold on and the cue just flops like a fish, cracking against the side of the table a couple times until I steady it. The cue—and I—are at a bizarre angle. My body is curved to the left, the cue thrusting into the air. I'm leaning far over the table, as if I'm about to heave. It's an incredibly uncomfortable position, but I'm not sure how to straighten up without hitting Mark or the lamp that hangs above the table.

"*Wow.* That was *terrible.* You really have never played, have you?"

My face burns. I stand up slowly, without hitting anything, and force a smile. "No, I told you. I wasn't kidding."

Mark looks at the table thoughtfully. "Don't worry. You're gonna be fine. You come here every week and you practice and you listen to me and"—Mark scrunches up his face—"in eight or nine months you're going to be playing good pool."

"Really?" This is encouraging. I thought he was going to say something like two years.

"You gotta practice, though. And you gotta listen to me, but yeah, eight months. I'm serious. I've seen it before."

Mark grins again, thoroughly delighted by my horrible first stroke. He can't wait to get started.

I COME BACK TO Chelsea Billiards, just as Mark advised me, every Monday (except holidays) for the next fourteen months.

Mark's method is to assign me a drill and then say, "Do that fifty times." He sets up the shot, demonstrates it, watches me do it, tells me the twenty things I did wrong, makes me watch him again, makes me do it again, tells me the ten things I did wrong, makes me set it up again, and then leaves me to my work.

"You pissed off yet?" he calls from another table.

"Yes."

"You bored and frustrated yet? Are your eyes glazing over yet?"

"Yes."

"Good! Then do twenty more."

Mark is so warm and genial, so thrilled with the game and anyone who wants to learn it, that he makes a wonderful teacher. He is articulate, good at explaining complicated concepts. A lot of pool players talk in the ether. They describe shots and strategies the way they appear in their heads, and for the uninitiated, it's like listening to someone speaking a foreign language. Fortunately, Mark is bilingual.

Mark is married and has two kids. They're grown now, but sometimes, he tells me, they "shoot pool with the old man." Mark is an administrator at a hospital in Queens and has a relentlessly sunny disposition. Energy and intelligence crackle behind those giant glasses. There is no one else I'd rather have showing me the ropes at this tender, early stage.

One cold night as I'm heading to the subway after class, I run into Mark on the street. I've never seen him "out in the open" like this, since he's usually shooting practice balls in his shirtsleeves when I arrive every Monday. To me it's as if he belongs to Chelsea Billiards, perhaps lives in a locker or sleeps in the basement underneath a pool table.

We stop and chat. He has his cue case slung over one shoulder. His smile isn't so easy anymore; it even strikes me as a bit furtive. There's an awkward silence, the kind that springs up when you don't know how long you should stand and talk to someone whose real life you've just impinged upon.

"You going to the F train?" I ask.

"Nah."

"Well, you going that direction?" I figure we'll walk together. Talking is usually easier when you're walking.

"Nah, I'm going this way." He gestures vaguely, somewhere in the vicinity of the Empire State Building and Mars. "To Twenty-eighth Street," he mumbles.

"Is there a poolroom there or something?"

Mark shifts uncomfortably. "No. There's a place, a bar. I shoot there sometimes. Thought maybe I'd try to earn a little money." With this he grins, but his eyes are dark.

In an instant I see it: the little guy, friendly, big smile, goofy glasses, pointy tie, a day job, *helping people.* He gets a game going and then shreds his opponents, one by one, without them knowing it. He makes it seem hard. He makes it seem lucky. They won't know what hit them. But I know. I have a picture in my mind now of Mark walking out of a bar and stuffing a wad of bills into his coat before heading for the subway to Queens. He'll make it home in time to watch the 11:00 news with his wife.

I am surprised again by this strange, interesting man. I know I can't tag along. The idea even scares me a little. "Good luck," I say.

He waves cheerfully, as if unburdened, and walks off, a small, bobbing figure amid the parking lots and forbidding buildings that loom along the street like judges. I watch until he disappears, then turn and head for my train.

AFTER I'VE BEEN WORKING with Mark for a few months, he starts pestering me about buying my own cue stick. "Your game will improve ten percent just from playing with the same stick every time." It isn't that I don't believe Mark. I know he's right, yet still I resist. He and Ruby, another pool instructor at Chelsea, argue about what cue is the best size for me.

"I'd say fifty-six inches, if there even is such an animal," Ruby declares, her voice rich and twangy, from somewhere deep in the South. But Mark feels my cue should have some extra length, since the longer shots can be tough on people who are our height. "Nah, I'd say fifty-seven minimum, maybe even fifty-eight. Yeah, I'd go with fifty-eight inches."

Pool cues are, for most players, intensely personal items. The same way that a tennis player gets used to a particular racket, or a golfer selects her favorite club for a certain shot, or a baseball player finds the bat that is the perfect weight and length for his body, so it is when a person finds the ideal pool cue.

I enjoy listening to Ruby and Mark talk about my cue—and me—as if I'm not standing right there. Ruby is a mystery, a former professional pool player approaching the far side of middle age, who shows up at Chelsea Billiards periodically, then disappears for weeks—sometimes months—at a time before showing up again, cheerful, vague about where she's been, laying on that Southern charm, covering up a weariness and heartache that I sense have solidified long ago. Her eyes are bright, her hair thick and wavy and gray, kept short and no-nonsense. She wears boxy, short-sleeved blouses untucked—they hit well below her waist—and straight, sensible pants that give her room in all the right places. I can't decide whose advice to follow about the cue, hers or Mark's.

"You have a stick yet?" Mark asks, week after week. "Go to Blatt. I'm telling you."

And so, after several weeks, I finally follow Mark's advice. I go to Blatt Billiards, which has been on lower Broadway, at 12th Street, since 1923. It's one of those old New York places, commonly referred to as an "institution." There's an old cranky guy behind the counter who barks at the young guys who work there. The place is narrow and musty and cluttered, like somebody's attic, with high ceilings and bad air and no room to walk without bumping into something. It's packed with every kind of pool paraphernalia—tables, cues, balls, gloves, racks, cleaning equipment, old billiard catalogs from the dawn of time—everything shoved together haphazardly, making it difficult to find anything.

Fortunately, the people who work there know pool and they're eager to help. Ryan, slim and soft-spoken, wears his hair pulled back in a silky black ponytail that hangs all the way down his back. It's immediately apparent that he knows what he's talking about. He pulls out several cues for me to hold and scrutinize. He even lets me try them out on one of the tables. I'm nervous about making a decision, worried I'll pick the wrong one. But Ryan gently nudges me this way and that. The cue I finally choose—a fifty-eight-inch McDermott—costs $100. This seems like a lot of money to me, but Ryan assures me it isn't.

"Heck, you can have cues custom-made," he explains. "It's not unheard of for them to cost thousands of dollars, especially if you've got all that inlaid wood business and leather grips and artsy designs and fancy wood." Still, I get the cheapest case there, a red canvas one (called a "soft" case) for $25. I'm not sure why I feel I have to be frugal. It's as if I don't yet deserve anything better.

Pool cues, unless they're bar cues, usually come in two pieces: the butt, which is the wider piece you grip while shooting, and the shaft, the narrow piece that culminates in the leather tip, the part you chalk. ("God, how woefully phallic," my friend Alison says when I describe my purchase to her.) The two pieces screw together at the joint. I decide to try the longer, fifty-eight-inch cue, to help me with those long shots, which, when you are unable to lean very far over the table, can be excruciating to execute. The risk, of course, is that if you're short and the cue is long, the stick could end up waving around the table when you don't want it to, like a spastic conductor's baton.

I solve that problem by getting a fairly lightweight cue—eighteen ounces. Cues weigh from sixteen to twenty-two ounces, though sixteen is awfully light and twenty-two is, in my opinion, a little like playing with a garden shovel; something that heavy is typically used for the break, which requires a lot of power. When someone asks me how big my cue is, I always say "eighteen." That's how you answer such a question; the pool-savvy inquirer wants to know the weight. I learn never to say "It's a fifty-eight" unless someone specifically asks me how long it is.

MUCH APPLAUSE AND ATTENTION greet me when I show up the following week with my purchase. "Very nice," Mark says, screwing the two pieces together and then rolling the conjoined cue in his hands, examining it with great seriousness. It's a simple stick, two-tone with a black grip, the shaft a light-colored wood. "It's you," Ryan says when he sees me handle it at Blatt. I can tell Mark is pleased I've sprung for the fifty-eight-incher. Ruby, despite being overruled on the issue of length, gives me a similar stamp of approval, Southern-style. "Damn, it's just dandy."

ONE DAY I COME into Chelsea Billiards and Mark assigns me to a table next to a woman I've seen there before. She has always struck me as an ice princess, aloof and entitled, her gaze wintry, her sleek jeans and blouse effortlessly casual. She's around my age and has long blond hair, smooth and straight, the color of chardonnay, always falling just so.

Despite its incorrigibility on rainy days, my hair, too, often gets admiring stares. It's thick and soft, turns wavy in hot weather, and has been streaked with silver since I was eighteen. It's also hair that, much to my outrage, is strikingly similar to the hair the girl in the movie has *before* her big makeover. I go to great lengths to keep it out of my face during pool practice, yet nothing works. It's constantly distracting me, falling across my cheek, my neck, my forehead, always blocking an eye at the worst possible moments. But this woman's hair always seems to behave, to lie across her shoulders like an obedient pet, one enticing tendril occasionally falling forward but never getting in her way.

In contrast to the cold set of her face, her skin gleams, golden and luscious, not even a freckle, and as she leans over the table, I can't help noticing that her body is exquisitely sculpted, the work of many hours at a high-end gym. She doesn't look like a chiseled bodybuilder or a ropy athlete. She has the smooth, supple body of someone who wants to be in front of a camera, a body conceived by a well-paid professional.

Her name is Melanie.

She's good. Not just at playing pool but at completely ignoring me. She doesn't make eye contact if we happen to pass each other going to our respective tables. I smile at her in recognition on occasion and she keeps walking, her eyes without expression, focused somewhere far away from me. She doesn't appear preoccupied as much as she appears haughty, and maybe a little worried, as if she doesn't want ESPN's senior management to leap from behind an imaginary curtain and catch her talking to me—a fumbling amateur who actually dares to look eager and interested. It's humiliating for me; every time I pass her in the pool hall, it feels as if I've been caught with my youth group by the kids who smoke cigarettes by the bike racks. These days I always look down when I see her.

"Hey, Heather, this is a perfect example of what I was talking about when you showed up that first day. Melanie here"—Mark jabs his index finger in her direction—"started coming to pool school, what, six months ago?" This is about the same time I started. He looks at Melanie for confirmation. She's bent over a shot and pays no attention to him, which never really stops Mark.

"Yeah, it's been about six months and the improvement has been remarkable. She's playing real games now, and winning. She's entering tournaments. So you think that's right, Melanie? I told Heather if she comes here for about six or eight months and is really devoted, she'll be really good. What do you think?" (Mark ignores the fact that I'm not anywhere near "really good" yet, even with my new cue.)

By calling us out of our roles in the childish social structure we've constructed, Mark breaks some sort of poolroom taboo. I find myself curious about what she will say—and a little frightened.

Melanie keeps her eyes on the multihued balls spread out on her table. She bends over for another shot, doesn't look up, doesn't look at me or at Mark. Then, in a quiet, silky voice laced with ice and condescension, she says, "If you practice." Melanie comes to Chelsea Billiards almost every day. I'm averaging about twice a week—pool school on Mondays, then maybe one lunch hour, and occasionally a weekend visit.

It's a terrible moment for me, because, while her aim is to swat me away, the person she really embarrasses is Mark, who has not realized until this moment how little regard Melanie has for me—or for anyone else who isn't on his or her way to professional pool stardom. I feel as if I've just been dissed by the snooty head cheerleader, the blonde goddess who, I find out later, is married to a catalog model.

The Chelsea Billiards basement becomes thick with silence. I say nothing and fumble around, trying to think of a shot to practice. Mark finally says, "Okay, why don't we work on speed control today." I feel like a fraud.

That moment—and that woman—haunts me for a long time. It's strange how a seemingly innocuous barb can have such a powerful effect. Oddly enough, I think of Larry then, my neurotic, voracious, bicoastal boss. *"What've you got for me?"* Nothing yet. But that is clearly about to change.

Coming out of
the Closet

THE MONDAYS COME and go. I'm no longer whiffing cue balls, and I feel little surges of improvement. Then one day, a few months after Mark tries to inspire me by using Melanie as a role model, I am invited to play in a pool league, on a bar team.

I've been coming to Chelsea Billiards for nine months by this point, and one of the other instructors there, a guy named Wally who's a member of a Monday-night eight-ball league, tells me that his team desperately needs another player, preferably someone "lower-ranked." You can't get further down the ladder than me. I don't even have a rank, having never played on a team before, and I'm not yet skilled enough to hope for any rank but the lowest.

The thought of actual competition terrifies me. I'm content to just bang the balls around by myself for the next thirty years or so. I tell him I'll think about it.

The following week Wally's on vacation, but a guy shows up asking for me by name. He's an emissary from the pool team in question. He's been sent to persuade me to come and play. Tonight is the last night his team can sign up a new player. Bar league teams have eight players. This team has seven.

His name is Leo. He's about forty, pasty-faced, and tense, with a few sparse blond hairs spread out along the crown of his head like a lady's fan. He has watery blue eyes and a formal manner, even though he's wearing shorts.

All I can think is *Leave me alone.* This is what I love so much about my Mondays: I am utterly alone with myself. I'm quiet, I don't wisecrack, I concentrate. Nobody knows what I do for a living and nobody asks. Nobody knows where I live and nobody asks. Nobody knows how old I am or where I grew up and nobody asks. It is utterly tranquil, blissfully anonymous. And this guy with a comb-over is about to shatter my peace.

He asks if I'll play a quick game with him and I freeze.

"Well . . ."

"Just to warm up, and so I can see how you play."

Wait, am I being auditioned? I pose this question to Leo. He backs off. My manner hardens. He becomes supplicant. "Just one game. I won't say anything while you shoot. Please?" He's beginning to look anguished. I sigh, say, "Okay, whatever," and agree to play him—I'd shot a few games in pool school, at Mark's goading, with some of the other students, but I hadn't been happy about it, especially since I'd lost most of the time.

Leo asks if I want to break, and I decline. So, using the pricey-looking twenty-ounce cue he brought with him, a fifty-nine-incher with a brown-and-black diamond pattern along the joint, he rams the cue ball into the rack of balls and sends them zinging around the table. One plops in—a striped ball. He studies the table. His face is drawn. He sinks two balls in a row, then misses. "Your turn." I notice him glance at his watch.

I'm nervous and annoyed. I shoot too quickly, jabbing my cue stick toward the 5-ball. I think I've ruined the shot, but the 5, as it rolls down the table, knocks into another ball and falls unexpectedly into the pocket. I shrug at Leo and smile. I miss the next shot, a long one on the 7, but not by much. The 7-ball ends up near the correct pocket, so I don't look like an idiot, just someone who needs to work on her aim.

We continue in this manner, polite, talking very little, until the game is finished. Leo beats me, of course, but I don't totally embarrass myself. I have three balls left on the table, which means I sank four others. It's enough for Leo.

"Is there anything I can say that might persuade you to do this? We really, really need someone. Tonight."

"I'd have to play *tonight*?"

"Well, yeah. But don't worry. It doesn't matter if you win."

I am taken aback by Leo's remark. Although I have not exhibited any competitive spark so far—in fact, I'd been trying to figure out a way to avoid joining Leo's team—I have also been shooting balls at a pool hall for nine months and am not a total imbecile at the table. It's clear Leo's telling me it doesn't matter if I win because he thinks I won't, and he also senses that I don't want to humiliate myself, that I won't find it "fun" to be the least accomplished player on a pool team. It's simultaneously insulting and perceptive of him. I realize I've sold Leo short. He's not the Droopy Dog character that I've pegged him as. He's intelligent, good at pool, and perhaps something of a schmuck.

We stare at each other. Leo waits. I hear the faint clicking of balls from some of the tables in the back of the room. It finally penetrates my brain that I've been coming to Chelsea Billiards for nearly a year, and that ultimately, the goal is to play. What's holding me back? I think it may be as simple (and as arrogant) as: I'm used to succeeding, and I don't think I will succeed at this.

I had been a superior student all through school. Tests and papers and projects and presentations—all that came easy to me. When I would get tests back with, say, a 98 in red ink at the top, I'd immediately look for the one I'd missed, not angry but curious—and surprised. I always thought I got them all right. And most of the time I did.

I didn't care that much about how my classmates performed. My competitive drive was not fueled by other people. I wanted to do well because I liked how it felt, because I was ambitious and knew that doing well in school would send me places, and because, I suppose, a high bar had been set for me at an early age by my parents, and I loved trying to leap over it.

It's true that part of the initial lure of pool for me was the game's nuance and its delicious, dangerous connotations, the stuff I'd gleaned from movies and from the shady characters I'd seen slouching in and out of poolrooms like Chelsea Billiards, their faces shifty, the moods that followed them dark and foreboding and electric.

But something else was at work here, too. I am, when you get right down to it, a perfectionist, and another aspect of pool's appeal is the players' constant strive for perfection. There really is such a thing as a perfect shot in pool, and that shot's success is determined, achingly, by mere millimeters. For a perfectionist, the game is sublime torture.

But perfection and excellence are two very different things, and I have often confused the two, to my detriment.

I had a clear sense of my strengths and weaknesses early on, which is why, for example, despite my love of baseball, I never tried out for the girls' softball team in high school. I knew I was lousy at sports, even if I did hit the occasional long ball. Instead, I wrote for the school newspaper, excelled in foreign languages, and was always cast as the lead in school plays. It's why I got an after-school job at the one art-house movie theater in town. It's why I had a lot of brainy friends but few dates. My confidence rested in my cerebrum, in my wit and my often sarcastic mouth, not in my physical self.

When I felt the first tug toward pool, I ignored the fact that it touched me somewhere physical. Rather, it seemed like the perfect puzzle to solve with my A-student brain. The cogs would click into gear as they always did, as I was convinced they did for legends like Ted Williams, whom I was certain was the first and only man to actually *figure out* how to hit a home run. I had no doubt that I would enjoy similar success with pool.

I should have known better.

ALTHOUGH IT IS New York City and the silent, soothing tableau of Asian men playing snooker that beckon me into my first pool hall, my attraction to this peculiar drama goes back a long way, to the baseball diamonds of my youth, both the backyard variety and the ones on my television screen.

I'm young when the romance starts—five years old at the most. And who can blame me? It's the 1970s, a time of weird mustaches, crazy sideburns, and giant afros, baseball caps perched precariously on top of them looking small and jaunty, like paper umbrellas in fancy drinks. It's learning funny and exciting words: spitball, knuckleball, shortstop, balk, foul tip, grand slam, the windup, stolen base. It's baseball, it's Cincinnati Reds baseball, and I'm in love. My unbridled passion is not for the game's grand tradition or eccentric rules, however—that will come later. No, I'm in love with a player. I'm in love with Johnny Bench. Not in love-in love, I'm too young for that, but in love the way that kids who are taken with something or someone are filled first with awe and then with utter devotion.

I live in Columbus, two hours north of Cincinnati, and I'm seven years old when I see my first game in person at Riverfront Stadium. The Reds are playing the Philadelphia Phillies. We sit far from the field, near the bleachers, so that the players seem like ants to me, zipping around on a green-and-brown lawn. The game lasts fifteen innings, until Ken Griffey—who at the time was not yet known as Ken Griffey Sr.—breaks the tie with a solo home run.

I watch baseball, guided by my dad and my older brother, Andrew, on the big, square RCA television in our family room. I understand home runs immediately, as most kids do, but I also quickly comprehend singles, doubles, and the ever-rare triple. I love gravity-defying catches in the outfield, the fielders stretching across the wall like unfurled flags; I love the acrobatics of the shortstop (the graceful and underrated Dave Concepcion), and I'm thrilled at the delicious prospect of a stolen base (Joe Morgan—"Little Joe," as my dad, and the whole country, calls him—never lets me down).

But I quickly deduce that something else is at work underneath this obvious drama. My brother and father are always talking about certain "plays" and pointing to the screen: "If he's smart, he'll bunt." "Think he'll go for the hit-and-run?"

I ask questions, and concepts are explained to me, most of the time to my satisfaction. I learn the rules; I learn that the managers have strategies, that they perform other tasks besides screaming at umpires. My dad teaches me how to read box scores—and this is before the newspapers did all the math for you. The early box score reader had to figure out for herself how many games behind or ahead a team was. It was a great way to learn fractions.

In my opinion, there cannot be a better team from which to learn the perplexing, addictive minutiae of baseball than the Reds of the 1970s. And always, there is Johnny.

Johnny Bench is special. He wears glumpy equipment that makes him look like a crab scrunched up behind home plate. He squats down, his face invisible behind a dangerous-looking mask. He gets to trot out to the mound and talk with the pitcher. He gets to bean balls to second base—throwing right at the pitcher, or so it seems—and save that base from the likes of Lou Brock and Davey Lopes. He sees the whole field spread out in front of him, the only player besides the batter with that perspective. He knows weird sign language, which he uses to communicate with the pitcher, their own secret code through which they choose what pitch to use. He acts like the boss, directs the game, seems to know great secrets. He gets to wear his hat backward. He gets to slide his mask up to his forehead and peer out during breaks in the game, his large, round glove hanging like a giant paw at his side, a lion taking a breather before pouncing again.

In short, he stands out. And he has a great name, *Johnny Bench*, a name both carefree and sturdy. And although I am fascinated by his defensive work, I'd be lying if I didn't admit that what I really love is how he hits home runs. And for a brief period, I actually think I have something to do with them.

When Bench, number 5, comes up to the plate, if I'm not nearby (a rarity), my dad or my brother will call out to me that Bench is up, and I come streaking into the room, flushed with excitement and fear. I watch him crouch there, looking completely different without all of his bulky gear, and sometimes I just can't take the tension. I mutter that I want him to hit a home run (even if my dad says, "All we need is a single here"), and one day I announce that it's all too much, I can't take it anymore, I'm going to watch from inside the closet. No one pays much attention to me as I slip into the grown-ups' coat closet. Our snowsuits and windbreakers and rubber boots are crammed into the "kids' closet" on the other side of the utility closet. These important closets line the family room, the most-used room in our two-story, aluminum-sided house on Stanwood Road. The closets all have louver doors. I don't know what a *louver* is, but the important thing is that the doors have slats and you can peek through them, a distinct advantage when hiding—or when praying for a home run.

So I crouch in the closet, among the leather boots and umbrellas, draped in my mother's soft, sweet-smelling coats. By ducking my head at a certain angle, I'm able to find the right slat to peer through so I can still see the TV. I poke my fingers through the slats and hold on. I don't make a sound. And then, after a few foul tips and a few balls, Johnny cracks one over the wall. Much commotion on the couch from my dad and my brother. "Heather! Get in here! Bench hit a home run! Andy, where's your sister?"

"She's in the closet."

"What? What she's doing in there? Heath—"

At this point, I fling open the door and leap out, screaming, "I can't believe it! I can't believe it!" and jump up and down. Johnny has come through.

That I've witnessed this home run from inside a closet amuses everyone, including me. The next time Johnny comes to the plate, my dad suggests I go into the closet again, and I happily oblige. Johnny Bench hits a double into the left corner.

So for a while, depending on the situation (it must be a tense one, where the Reds really need a run), I retreat into the closet whenever Johnny Bench is at bat. "Heather, get in the closet! Do your stuff!" my dad commands, and I obey. My percentage turns out to be pretty good. More often than you'd expect, I leap from the closet in triumph, in time to see Bench rounding the bases. We all seem to believe that I have some mystical connection to the man, that somehow I am *causing* his home runs, or at least contributing in some small but meaningful way.

This leads to another discovery. I begin to sense, at age seven or eight, that glorious power-hits are not *random*. They can be anticipated, even planned. There are different pitches that go with them, different situations that call for them. Players don't just amble to the plate and hope for the best, banging away at any ball in their path. I'm not one hundred percent sure how this all works, but in the solipsistic way of little kids, by placing myself in the center of the drama, I begin to intuit the elegance and intelligence of this game. As fun as it is for me to imagine, deep down I know I'm not pulling Johnny Bench's strings, or anyone's strings. He's doing it himself.

My fascination with catchers and my fixation on Johnny Bench only intensify. I am no longer satisfied with being sidelined, mute and in awe. I want to play. So my dad and my brother and I play Whiffle ball on the weekends, with the familiar yellow plastic bat and the white ball with holes in it. We set up a makeshift stadium in our backyard. But soon it becomes too easy.

When I'm ten, I am finally old enough to join a summer softball league for girls. I arrive for the first practice somewhat shy. The other girls are huge. I'm small for my age, a tiny kid with long, dark hair and big eyes whose years steering the Big Red Machine from a coat closet evaporate the minute the tallest girl in my class, the sloe-eyed and inscrutable Jennifer Fate, whizzes a ball past my ear into the waiting glove of Stacy Goodall, who has a boys' haircut and is built like a truck, thick and broad-shouldered—even her teeth are big— and who ignores me, even though I know more about baseball than she does. These girls are athletes. They are tomboys, tan and taciturn, with complicated athletic shoes. They wear baseball caps year-round.

At the other end of the spectrum resides a group of bored girls who've been forced by their parents to join the team as a summer activity. They're irritated at having to show up twice a week and play in the thick, humid air under a blazing Midwestern sun. Worse, some of these bored, blonde, ponytailed girls are natural athletes. They move with grace, catch on early during our drills, mechanically throw the ball in perfect arcs, and scoop up grounders with ease while rolling their eyes.

I have some grace, too, I suppose, and I am brilliantly fast, but my throwing arm is pathetic. Instead of shot-putting across the field toward a stunned, wide-eyed ten-year-old, like the balls thrown by Jennifer Fate, my balls flail in the air, straining for a distance that is never achieved, then dribble morosely to the ground, finally rolling into the glove of my throwing partner, who squats down, neither stunned nor wide-eyed, just wilted from standing in the heat for so long. Occasionally, the balls I throw soar up—straight up—and then fall straight back down with a soft thud.

"Heather, we're throwing overhand," Miss Holloway, our mannish, unsmiling coach calls out to me, her voice tinged with exasperation.

"I *am* throwing it overhand," I call back. Does she think I'm an idiot? I know how to throw a ball, I'm just terrible at it.

My fielding is only marginally better than my throwing. I run over ground balls, then have to run back for them; I flinch at line drives; and in the outfield, while charging toward one of the few balls ever hit out there, I extend my arm, glove upturned, eager, only to watch the ball plop down about a foot in front of me, where I scramble to grab it and hurl it back into our practice game, watching it bounce twenty times before reaching the disgusted girl on third base.

Despite my awkward, confused athletic style, there is one thing I can do: I hit. I've imitated the batting stances of enough Reds in my backyard to know how to hold a bat firmly, to bear down but not choke up. I swing hard and all the way around, flinging my bat to the side and taking off the second I make contact. I'm surprisingly powerful for being just a slip of a thing, and while I never hit anything truly momentous in practice, I am one of the few who regularly makes contact with the ball.

One day, as our first game nears, Miss Holloway gathers us into a circle, the ground hot and brown beneath our feet, the sky overhead an unflinching blue. A lawn mower buzzes in the background—the eternal sound of an Ohio summer. Miss Holloway tells us it's time to pick positions and get our jerseys. It isn't very scientific: "Who wants to play first base?" Little hands shoot up like spears. When she gets to "Who wants to be catcher?" no hands rise in the air, which surprises me. I guess it must seem a boring position. You just squat behind the plate, fielding easy balls and tossing them back to the pitcher's mound. There's no glamour. I raise my hand.

Miss Holloway looks at me in disbelief, no doubt thinking about how I often shrink from the balls in practice. (It wasn't fear, it was pure mortification.) "Heather? You want to be catcher?"

"Yeah, I'll do it."

"Are you sure?" She eyes my sixty-two-pound frame, my two long braids, my little sneakers covered in dust. "Jennifer's going to pitch. Do you really want to catch all of those balls?" She's probably worried I'll be knocked flat after the first strike and there will be a lawsuit.

"I wanna do it," I say. I'm a hitter. And catchers are hitters. Johnny Bench is both a catcher and a hitter. In my mind, there is no room for discussion.

"Okay," she says, smiling for a change.

Our jerseys, oversized T-shirts that say *Bexley Recreation* on the front, are red—red!—and we wear matching red baseball caps. The following week is our first game. My parents, grandparents, and brother are all there, as are the families of the other players, sitting either in the narrow bleachers that have been set up or on lawn chairs they've brought from home. I'm nervous, my stomach fluttery. I'm using an old baseball glove of my brother's that looks ridiculous over my small hand. We're the home team, playing a bunch of girls dressed in royal blue.

The game starts at 1:00 sharp, the sky a warm, milky blue, coated with sunlight. I squat behind the plate, dropping most of Jennifer's pitches, but not in an embarrassing way. It isn't nearly the disaster Miss Holloway has anticipated.

Soon it's our turn to bat. I'm third in the batting order. When I get to the batting circle, no one has made it safely to a base yet. The first couple of pitches are terrible, and I watch, unblinking, as they fall off to the side, nowhere near the plate. Then I swing at one that's reasonably close and miss. I notice the royal blue girls inch forward. This makes me angry. *Oh, yeah?* I think, digging my feet into the dirt. *What've you done up here?*

And then, while waiting for the girl on the mound to scratch her nose and pull on her shorts and wind up for her next pitch, I have what can only be described as a vision. I see just where I want to put the ball. In fact, for a split second I see the rest of the game stretch out in front of me, see myself swinging, running, moving. I crouch down, stare hard at the girl facing me, who looks like she'd rather be at home watching TV, and when the pitch comes, I swing long and full and hear the sound—*that sound*, the crack of bat hitting ball— and feel it all the way through my arms, from my fingertips to my shoulders, and hear a gasp from the crowd and see, just for a second, the ball arc up and out, disappearing as it sails over the sea of blue baseball caps. Someone cheers. I fling the bat and run, my arms pumping, my head down, thrilled and terrified, running as fast as I can, a streak of red. I can hear people yelling. I run so hard and so fast and with such determination that when I finally turn, in a graceful curve so I can take what I'm sure will be two more bases—this is at least a triple—it takes me a moment to realize that people are no longer screaming at my hit, they are screaming at me, calling my name, gesturing wildly. I search for second base and finally stop where I think it is. Only then do I realize I'm in the outfield.

I have run so hard and with such joy and gusto after my bat cracked that ball that I've shot past first base and then arced so wide when I made my turn toward second that I am now in center field. The ball, which has landed somewhere far away and has been bob-bled about by the frantic girls on the blue team, is making its way toward the infield. My team shrieks at me to go to second base, but I can't find it. My eyes rake the field and finally spot the base about twenty feet in front of me, just as the other team's third baseman is lobbing the ball to second. It's a race against time. I run toward the bag, but the ball gets there first. It bounces once, the girl grabs it and holds it out as I charge to her, tagging me and screaming, "You're out!" And I am. I hit the longest ball anyone on our team has ever— or will ever—hit. And I got lost on the way to second base.

There is a loud "Ohhhh" of disappointment as I walk dejectedly to our bench, my face burning. I can't meet the eyes of my teammates.

My brother, normally mild-tempered and encouraging, leaps from the bleachers and runs up to me, shouting. "What were you doing? Are you *blind*?" From somewhere that sounds very far away I hear my dad say, "Leave her alone." My brother stalks off. I sit down on the bench.

The incident does not leave terrible scars on my psyche, though it certainly lingers for a bit. I blame myself, cleanly, and want only to learn how to not make the same blunder again. I am not turned off from baseball, or from catching, or from my beloved Reds. Quite the contrary, I am thrilled that I gleaned something from staring through those louvered doors, that when I was standing at the plate in that one glorious moment, I knew ahead of time where I wanted to put that ball and just how hard I needed to hit it to get it there. It wasn't random.

But this is not my only epiphany that summer. I begin to consider the possibility that I might never improve as a player, at least not enough to earn the prominent place on a softball team that I've hoped for. My love of the game is not enough. It will never be enough. It will never, for example, give me a throwing arm. I am not the second coming of Johnny Bench. I am a kid who will decide to take a pottery class the following summer. (I make a beautiful glazed turtle that sits on a bookshelf for years, gazing solemnly at our family room from its perch in front of hardcover copies of *All the President's Men* and *The Making of the President: 1968*.) The class is not anywhere near as exciting as hitting a ball or flipping my hat backward in my role as catcher, but I excel, which is, it turns out, more important to me than pure excitement. I don't know yet what a burden this will prove to be.

I don't start playing pool for another twenty-one years, but many of the elements that make pool, at least inside my head, such a natural fit for me are the same ones that made baseball seem like such a natural fit all those years ago. Like baseball, pool is deceptively complex. It's a game with no clock, carved into innings, units of time that can stretch into the next day if necessary. And both are games often determined by millimeters. By this I mean that how a pool player strokes a ball, or where *exactly* the pitcher throws one over the plate, can determine an entire game.

Batters, like pool players, hit with an idea in their minds, a plan they are trying to execute. Fielders try to anticipate this plan. Sometimes it unfolds like a stage play, with exits and entrances marked, but sometimes, if a swing is just a little off, if the pitch goes slightly farther than it was supposed to, everything is altered and you have to improvise. The quicker you are at improvisation, the better baseball player you will be. This same art applies to pool.

You could argue that *chance*—and the creativity that accompanies it—is a facet of all sports, but I'm not sure I believe this. In baseball, and in pool, this room for creativity has to do with the speed—or, rather, the lack of it—in the game. You have room; you have time. Judgments are made, then rethought, then rethought again. I believe that these games are not about physics, despite the diagrams you may find in instruction manuals. They are about executing and adjusting in small increments and remembering certain situations and how to get out of them. If you've got a good memory—and I do—both games can provide hours of fun and torture.

But although the elemental connection is there, after I am no longer simply watching pool, hypnotized from a distance by its complex geometry and quiet beauty, and begin to play it, some of the connections to baseball, the game of my heart and my youth, start to crumble until they disappear altogether, as if they've never been there at all.

Which is the bittersweet transformation that occurs when you make something your own.

WHAT IS INITIALLY SO stunning to me as I flail about the pool tables at Chelsea Billiards those first few months is that successful pool, while being connected to intellect, is also heavily reliant on pure athleticism, on a physical grace that brings to mind the velvety movements I associate with baseball players, on an inner balance that is wholly related to the body. Pool players, I learn, are not just hucksters and smart-asses and self-taught physics geeks. They are not merely poets of the profane, finding the most colorful and shocking and offensive ways of describing their particular art. They are athletes, in body and in temperament, and I am not, just as I was not twenty-one years ago when I entertained fantasies of being a major-league catcher. But I've gained confidence in many other areas of my life since my short career as a children's summer-league power-hitter. And so, since I grasp the strategic part of pool quickly—the notion of playing for position, of not always focusing on sinking the ball, of acting preemptively and defensively against your opponent—and because I so very much want to excel at the game, I assume that I will take to it instantly, that I'll be—what else?—the class star.

But I am not, it turns out, a "natural" at pool. And so for nine months I hide in the basement of a pool hall, completely at sea, feeling invigorated and, at the same time, utterly destabilized as I try to decide whether to commit to something I'm not good at.

Now, from out of nowhere, some guy from a local pool team, without even knowing it, is coaxing me into the sun. The recognition of my limitations is now inevitable, and the prospect of pursuing this new passion anyway, of undoing a part of my identity, is completely intoxicating. I feel, as I square off with Leo at Chelsea Billiards, both defeated and victorious.

"Okay," I say. "I'll do it."

Nice Rack

LESS THAN AN HOUR LATER, I follow Leo into a garishly lit Irish-style pub on Third Avenue and 19th Street called Paddy McGuire's. The place is loud and aggressively air-conditioned, with two pool tables in the back, placed next to each other like twin beds. I walk slowly through the place, shy and unsure. The bar is surprisingly crowded for a Monday. Loud, obnoxious music blasts from somewhere. I see a tray of amber-filled shot glasses go by, balanced on the hand of a harried waitress. People laugh over their beers, some too loudly. A woman in a body-clinging tank top gives me the once-over, her eyes outlined in thick, black eyeliner that does absolutely nothing for her except make her look like a pudgy raccoon. Butts in tight jeans push out from under the bar as their owners lean forward, looking for an errant bartender to *take their damn orders already*. I stand in the center of all this activity, feeling a little helpless.

The pit in my stomach is breaking apart, starting to flutter and groove, crossing the line from fear into excitement. My mouth goes dry, but for some reason I am terrified to order a drink, as if even a glass of water will somehow ruin any pool skill I might possess. That I am even thinking about trying to win this game, that I am taking it seriously—as a player, not as some sort of billiard dilettante—is entirely new. What I'm feeling is a sense of possibility—the same possibility that my friends find so tantalizing about my film-industry lunches, the same feeling I lost somewhere among the endive and arugula but am feeling tonight, in a cheap, too-bright pub on the East Side. My gaze travels to the twin tables again. One is empty, waiting. Some guys in ratty T-shirts are banging around on the other table, laughing, bending, shooting, throwing exaggerated winces at every shot. Their faces glow.

We arrive just in time, it turns out. The team from Paddy McGuire's has been getting impatient and is appeased only when Leo walks through the door with his new young charge. I'm quickly introduced to the other team members: a jovial fellow from Australia named Gareth, with glasses and a thick, messy beard that he will shave off the following week; Delores, a curvy, sun-streaked woman with a son in the military who informs me she's a "swirl"—half Puerto Rican, half German—and her fiancé, Eddie, high-cheekboned and handsome, with a rich, chocolatey voice that he uses to entice. He works for a cable television conglomerate. "I'm in distribution," he says, shaking my hand. Eddie works in the mailroom. His smile is sly.

Two other team members will show up later. In the meantime, Leo, looking worried (which I will come to learn is his perpetual expression), is pulled into a team conference. The opposing team just put up their best player, a cocky guy named Simon who's from somewhere in Northern England. He wears an ugly gold chain and has big, square teeth. Simon is a 6—a high rank. No one on Leo's team is likely to beat him. My new compatriots huddle together, murmuring. I stand off to the side and watch the woman with raccoon eyes in the tank top try to flirt with a guy at the bar.

"Heather, you're up," Leo says.

I'm going to play. Right now. They've decided to use me as cannon fodder. My stomach returns to its previous leaden state. I pray that I won't get sick. I imagine myself running to the women's room, my hair flying behind me, one hand clamped over my mouth, all of the league players forming a little half-circle around the pool tables, staring after me, slack-jawed, wondering who invited Barf Girl in the first place. Eddie would come up with that. Barf Girl. "Man, could she toss." Leo would probably have to be sedated. No, getting sick is not an option.

I peel open my red canvas case and slip out the two pieces that, when joined, make up my cue. It's been three months since I purchased my cue stick, and it still feels somewhat new, the linen grip still a pleasant surprise each time I wrap my hand around it. I notice that everyone on both teams has their own cues, the cases lined up neatly against the walls. I place my case at the end of the row, next to a mean-looking black leather one that's supposed to look as if it's made out of alligator skin.

Simon introduces himself and mock-gallantly kisses my hand. I smile dumbly and follow him to one end of the table. He puts two balls in front of us and immediately shoots one across the table. It rolls back to him like an eager puppy, and he does it again—practicing, I assume. What I don't know yet is that every game starts with something called the *lag*. The two players simultaneously shoot a ball from behind the first diamond (a mark stenciled on the table), banking it off the opposite rail and back to the head of the table. The closest ball to the head rail wins, and its shooter gets to break.

"You ready?" he asks. I nod, bend down, take a few practice strokes, then shoot the ball just the way he did, having absolutely no idea what I'm doing or why I'm doing it, but I'm too frightened to ask. I hear Leo say, "She's new, this is her first match."

Simon winks at me. "No worries, love." I lose the lag, which means he gets to break and I have to rack.

I set up the balls in their triangle but worry that I might not have done it quite right. I've never had to do this in a real game. Simon shrugs and says, "It's all right, it looks nice."

"Gee, no one's ever told me I had a nice rack before," I say. I am becoming saucy.

Simon grins, chuckles to himself, and proceeds to kick my ass. He breaks and pockets the 2-ball, then sinks the 6-ball, the 1-ball, and the 3-ball in quick succession. Next he walks around the table, says, "Aw, will you look at this?" and stops. He chalks his cue, winks at me, then, drawing his thick eyebrows together as if he's extremely worried, bends down and pockets the 4-ball. Each time he makes a shot, the cue ball ends up somewhere fortunate, a place on the table that enables him to take another shot. I don't understand how he's doing this, how he's getting the cue ball to move like that. I have nothing to do while he prances around the table, so I stand there and try to keep my posture aloof, my face blank. I don't know if I'm pulling this off, but I see Gareth grin beneath his furry beard and give me the thumbs-up sign.

Simon finally misses a ball. I approach the table, select a shot, take a few practice strokes like I've been taught in pool school, try to summon Mark's voice—"Stroke through. Don't snap the stick, *stroke it*"—and then make my first shot in a real pool match. The cue ball hits the 11-ball, which rolls energetically to a rail and stops. "Aw, almost, love!" Simon says. The 11-ball is nowhere near the pocket. Simon is an ass. It's his turn again. I've had about twenty seconds at the table so far.

And so we press on. At one point during this lopsided contest, which will span a total of six games, the trouncing is so bad that Simon actually calls a time-out to order a pizza. It's delivered during the third game of our match, and he turns his back to me while he eats it, not even offering me a slice, though that might've been even more insulting. By game six, I've accepted my fate. I'm not even demoralized. I do a bit better this game—I've sunk four of my balls, and I notice Simon's getting sloppy. He's got one striped ball left to pocket, then the 8-ball, but he can't seem to finish it. He's had a couple of beers and is bouncing around like a kid, talking loudly, flirting with me, giving me patronizing encouragement.

The situation on the table is miserable. My three remaining solid-color balls are nestled against the rail, and the cue ball is in a place so preposterous I can't believe I'm really expected to use it to try to sink another ball. I am permitted to take a quick time-out to consult with Leo. There is only one shot I can try, he says, but he doesn't look too confident when he suggests it. I follow his advice anyway and go for the billiard equivalent of a Hail Mary.

For a moment, the bar seems to stop moving, the faces around me frozen in a range of exaggerated expressions, the colors blurring together, the voices and laughter and music collapsing into a buzzing background noise, staticky and distant. I look at the spot on the far rail that Leo tells me to aim for. My hand is shaking as I try to form a bridge through which to slide the cue. I stop, straighten, take a breath. I have to steady my bridge hand. I shake it out, wiggle my fingers, then I bend down and try again. *Better.* My cue stick feels light to me, like a toothpick. I look at the cue ball, then at the spot on the rail, then back to the cue ball. I stroke my stick several times. I notice it's curving to the left at the last second, which means I'm not stroking properly. *Goddamnit. Goddamn these people. Why am I even here?* I stroke more slowly this time and the cue stick levels. I'm ready. I pull the stick back, rock it forward, and then watch as it smacks the cue ball and sends it down the length of the table, watch as that ball sails stormily across the green cloth, plowing breathlessly, miraculously toward the opposite end, where it hits the rail and slices all the way back, coming toward me like a lost, scampering child—and hits the 3-ball, knocking it cleanly into the corner pocket.

There's a stunned silence. Then the bar erupts. I hear Delores shriek, "Oh my God!" and someone else exclaim, "Jesus Christ!" I am enveloped by noise and sweat and adrenaline and the whooping sound of cheers. Simon doesn't move. He continues to chomp coolly on his slice of pizza. What he should've done, what most stand-up players do, is say "Good shot" or "Nice shooting," but he refuses, perhaps because he knows it was luck, not skill, that sent the 3-ball into the pocket. Yet I am the one who kept my nerves in check, who had to absorb Leo's instructions and carry them out, who lined up, stroked the cue stick, and sent the ball flying. Something stirs in me. I cock a hip, brush my hair back, and hear myself say, "Turn around, asshole," or something equally Clint Eastwood. And he does turn. And finally gives me a nod. He also beats me—puts his 10-ball in the side and fires the 8 so hard into a corner that it bounces up and plops back inside the pocket—but it doesn't matter. I barely watch him make the shot.

AFTER THE MATCH, I'm engulfed by my new team, lots of backslapping and hand-pumping and "You *go*, girl." I earn major points for being such a good sport about being sacrificed to a better player, and for bringing Simon down a notch with that one magnificent shot. I chat with my new comrades for a while, but I don't want to hang around—it's late, I'm tired and hungry, and I want to savor the moment in private. I played pool tonight. I even stood up to a brute and made a killer shot that brought down the house. It was just like in the movies. Just like when Johnny cracked one over the wall. True, I hadn't actually beaten Simon, but winning didn't matter tonight, just as it hadn't mattered if the Reds won, as long as Johnny Bench came through for me.

I pack up my cue, say good-bye, and ease my way through the crowd. I push open the door and stand on the sidewalk for a moment, getting my bearings. The door shuts behind me and the bar noise magically vanishes, as if sealed in a Ziploc bag. New noises replace the old ones, but they seem softer, kinder, the night changing, no longer young but far from over. I cross 22nd Street and amble down Third Avenue, not thinking yet about where the closest subway stop might be, just letting the summery city air brush my face. I have a slash of blue chalk on my pants. I reek of cigarette smoke and somebody else's cheap perfume. I am dancing. I am dark-haired and powerful. I am lovely.

I am hooked.

Kiss Shot

THE EVENING OF POOL at Paddy McGuire's changes my life. I have a new Monday routine now. If I'm wearing clothes that are corporate-looking or constricting—because I have a meeting with an editor or an agent, say—I change my clothes at the office at the end of the day, slipping into jeans and whatever shirt seemed flattering when I packed my "poolwear" that morning, usually something dark and sleeveless that hovers just above my waist. I leave the office at 5:45 p.m. and arrive at pool school at 6:00 p.m., although after over a year, I no longer think of it as "school," I think of it as my "warm-up." My game has improved the more I've played, though I have yet to win a league match.

I say hello to Mark, my steadfast instructor, then, after no more than a minute or two of conversation, I select a table and start setting up long shots, just to get my arm loose, my stance correct. If I don't make four or five in a row, I won't allow myself to move on to the next exercise. I swear a lot, cussing as floridly as my grandfather, who was the grand master of colorful language. This is not necessarily conducive to a "winning mind-set," so Mark always makes me practice an easy shot before I leave for my match—a shot I will always make and that I will not have to curse over—to build up my confidence. He often makes me use the 8-ball for these shots. "Don't be afraid of it," he'll say. "Get used to seeing that thing go in the pocket."

Then I leave Chelsea Billiards at 8:00 p.m. for my league match, which will be at some bar in the East 20s or teens, occasionally lower and farther east, near the river. There seems to be an endless supply of these places, each with pool tables and players in various states of disrepair.

These bars, no matter how dingy, are connected to the APA—the American Poolplayers Association, the governing body of amateur pool. I'm now a card-carrying member of the APA, which means that I, along with all of the other players on APA teams, pay seasonal dues: $22 in the late spring, the fall, and the winter—the three seasons of amateur pool. The teams in my area (downtown Manhattan) are under the thumb of the Manhattan league administrator, the enigmatic Tyrone, whom I have never met or even seen, although I've been assured that he does exist, and who, I'm told, is paid $30 per team per week for his services. Somewhere between fifty and seventy bars in downtown Manhattan participate, meaning Tyrone makes a fortune. There are APA leagues in the Bronx, Brooklyn, Queens, and Staten Island as well. Nationally, the APA boasts 250,000 members.

I love having the APA card in my wallet—it's white with blue lettering, made of flimsy plastic, with a bar code across the top as if it were a discount card for a drugstore chain. It says, in white block letters on a blue band across the middle, *Official APA Member*. I have to sign it or it's not considered "validated." I'm not sure what happens if I'm not validated. I doubt I'll be snatched from a pool bar and thrown into the back of a car. I've never had to show the card to anyone, yet I still feel it gives me some credibility.

In addition to the card, I now carry a rank. I'm ranked a 2 most of the time, though during one glorious season I'm bumped up to a 3. The number always appears next to my name on the score sheet, as do the rankings of my teammates.

The teams in these bars consist of eight players, five of whom are tapped each week by the team captain to play. And here's where the numbers come in: The choice of who plays is not random; there is a strategy involved. Each player is ranked between 2 and 7; a 2 is the lowest—and usually greenest—rank, and a 7 is a tournament-level player, a cool customer who is rarely beaten and who does stunning things on the cloth. In pool's typically sexist fashion, a woman always starts as a 3 when she first joins the league and a man always starts as a 4. Your first match determines if you'll be bumped up or down. If players started as 2's, there'd be no downward bump, hence starting at a higher rank. The fact that men start *two ranks* higher than the lowest rank, rather than one rank higher, has always irked the women who play in the APA, and there have been rumblings—even a petition—to make a change, though to date there's been no indication that these complaints have been heard.

Some teams have a preponderance of high-ranked players, and others have a glut of lower-ranked ones. To make it fair, the rankings come with their own handicapping system. The rankings of the five players picked to play on a particular night cannot equal more than twenty-three (thus, three 7's and two 6's won't be able to play, should a team be so lucky as to have such a skilled group). In other words, a team needs 2's and 3's and 4's or it won't be able to exist. These rankings add a sense of egalitarianism to the game. They turn amateur pool in New York into the great equalizer. For that night, you are not your job, or your pedigree, or your level of education, or your ethnicity. You are your rank. You are not a Harvard degree, you are a 3. You are not a busboy or an unemployed computer IT specialist, you are a 6, and you rule. You get to shed your everyday skin and exist only as your ability, as your passion. When the ranking system works—and most of the time it does—it is a remarkable, even beautiful, thing. When I shoot pool, the reassuring fairness of these ranks leaves me calm and content in a city that isn't.

The rankings are not tallied only by wins and losses, however. The score sheet, which a group of reprobates is responsible for tallying each week (Eddie or Leo on my team—whichever one is in charge or sober enough that night to hold a pen), is a complicated affair that keeps track of what happens to each player in every game of all the matches. When both opponents have shot until they are unable to sink another ball, it's called an "inning." The number of innings is marked for each game, and the total number of innings for the entire match is recorded at the end. Defensive shots are also tallied, as are the number of "coaches," or time-outs to consult with a designated coach about a sticky situation—those ranked under 4 are allowed two of these; those ranked 4 and above are allowed only one.

At the end of the night, all of this is tabulated and compared with the opposing team's statistics, the score sheets are signed by both captains, and each sheet is sent along to Tyrone, who then inputs the numbers into his computer and figures out the teams' respective positions in their divisions as well as the players' individual rankings, based on how they've fared over their last ten games. It is the quirky, personal stats—innings and scratches and defensive shots—that, along with wins and losses, determine a player's rank.

In the upper-left-hand corner of the score sheet is a little grid that shows the handicapping scale for matching one rank with another. For example, if two 5's play each other, it's a four-four race, meaning that whoever wins four games first wins the match. The match could stretch out for as long as seven games if the players are evenly matched and really going at it. If a 3 is playing a 4, the 3 has to win two games, the 4 has to win three. If a 3 plays a 6, the 3 has to win two, the 6 has to win five. This means that if a 6 does something unfortunate, like scratch on the 8-ball in the first game, giving the 3 an unexpected victory, said 3 now has to win only one more game to take the whole match, while the 6 must win five in a row. More often than not the 6 will win, but it can get tense. Sometimes a captain will put a 2 up against a 6 or 7 if he thinks even his best players can't beat this particular 6 or 7. The 2 is, in effect, sacrificed (which was my role in my first league match); the other players on the team are thus saved for the matches that they are more likely to win.

The team gets a point for each match won, so if a team takes three out of the five on a given night, it has prevailed for that evening and gets three points plus a bonus point. (This extra point is awarded to the team if it has paid its seasonal dues on time, if it did not have to forfeit any matches that night due to a shortage of players, and if it turns in its score sheet by Wednesday.) At the end of the season, the team with the most points takes first place in the division. Tyrone keeps track of this, too.

Division winners play other division winners in the playoffs, and those winners are sent to the city finals. The team that wins the city finals (there are two rounds) goes to the regionals, and then, if it remains hot, the team ends up in the promised land—the amateur nationals in Las Vegas—along with all of the other APA regional winners. Once there, that lucky team has the opportunity to win $25,000 (for a first-place finish) and get its picture in *The American Poolplayer* magazine.

I NO LONGER LEAVE Chelsea Billiards by myself for these league matches. I have an escort now: Wally, whose children's-book name fits him perfectly: He's cheerful, often bewildered, and even, on occasion, a little loopy.

Wally is country, which is a rare quality to find in a citizen of New York City. He's authentically country, not the kitschy, affected version you find on small liberal-arts campuses or the rich-boy, faux-swaggering versions that end up running for political office, attempting to appeal to NASCAR dads and oilmen. Wally looks as if he's ten feet tall and weighs one hundred and fifteen pounds. (His true proportions are almost as absurd: He weighs one hundred and fifty pounds and stands six-foot-three-and-a-half inches—"And I'm very particular about that half-inch," he tells me. "No rounding.") He has a lovely head of thick brown hair that, planted on top of his long face, thin neck, and swaying, toothpick limbs, brings to mind a palm tree. Wally tells me he moved to New York from West Virginia ten years ago. I never understand why he came or why he stays, he seems so befuddled and out of place most of the time. Except, of course, when he's playing pool. At a table he is startlingly proficient and sure of himself. It's where he kicks back, relaxes, and fits in like a native.

I meet Wally at Chelsea Billiards's pool school. He's the instructor there, the one whose pool team was in need of a lower-ranked player. (It's now "our" pool team, along with Leo and the rest of the crew.) When Mark, my original guru, feels he can push me out of the nest a little, Wally begins to amble over and take a look at my game, offer helpful pointers, suggest different practice drills. He doesn't pry, doesn't ask me any questions about my life outside of pool. He's gentle, sometimes funny, and charmingly self-deprecating. He even tells hillbilly jokes.

"You know how you know if you're a hillbilly?" he asks me one Monday, when I'm practicing stop shots with minor success. (A stop shot is when you hit below the center of the cue ball to stop it in the exact spot where it hits the object ball.)

"No, how?" I reply, not looking up from the table. I'm trying to concentrate. Wally stands behind me, a lanky tree offering shade.

"You know you're a hillbilly if anyone in your family has ever died after uttering the phrase, 'Hey y'all—watch this!'"

I giggle and turn around. Wally is laughing, too, smiling crookedly, looking silly and pleased with himself.

I see Wally at Chelsea Billiards every week without fail. Sometimes he offers me a few suggestions on my game, sometimes we have no interaction at all—he'll watch my table silently from across the room, not coming closer, perhaps because I don't make him feel welcome. I get like that sometimes, staring at the table, not sure why I keep missing the pockets but too exasperated and proud to ask for help. I don't really notice Wally most of the time, even when I'm not frustrated with my game, and I certainly don't notice that he's noticing me.

Mondays are long evenings now that I'm part of a pool team and, despite my initial quest for anonymity, meeting new people. The students and teachers at Chelsea Billiards know me now, and when I walk into pool bars on the East Side of the city, my red pool case hanging from my shoulder, I get subtle nods as I walk by, heading to the back where the tables are usually located. When I stand on the subway on Mondays, rumbling to and from work, people stare at my cue case—and me. Their stares, for once, are not crude or hostile or blank but curious, even aroused.

I am learning an entirely new way of carrying myself. I learn how to stalk a table. I learn how to get people to take me seriously—or playfully—without uttering a word. Pool players pretend to ignore each other but are, in fact, reading every twitch, cigarette puff, beer swig, or grin flashed at a teammate for a sign of their opponent's game. You have to be close, intimate, alive to notice these things. You think, aim, shoot, smile dangerously, taking as long as you want.

Eight-ball, despite its outward simplicity, is not necessarily an easy game. It's full of subtleties, even though the rules are straightforward. To prevail in eight-ball, you have to sink all of the balls lower than 8 or all of the balls higher than 8 (depending on which set you've ended up with after the break), and then you have to conclude this succession by—what else?—sinking the 8-ball itself. Of course, you won't have to do any of this if you sink the 8-ball on the break, which gives you the win (unless you also happen to sink the cue ball, in which case you've lost the game by scratching on the 8). You must hit your balls first, whether they are high balls (stripes) or low balls (solids). It's okay to hit your opponent's ball as long as you've struck one of yours first. If, as you try to shoot your own ball, you nick your opponent's ball along the way, that's a foul and your opponent gets *ball in hand*, meaning he can plunk the cue ball down anywhere on the table to make his next shot. He also gets ball in hand if you scratch while shooting.

After each shot, a ball must hit a rail—either the ball you're aiming for or the cue ball. If that doesn't happen, it's a foul and your opponent gets ball in hand again. And in the 8-ball that's played in many of the New York bar leagues, you'll often hear someone explain that "slop counts." It's an indelicate expression for an important rule: If you try to sink a ball but miss and sink one of your others instead, it counts in your favor. Regular bar rules are different; you have to call your shots in advance—and make them. If you sink something else, it's a foul. "Real" players scoff at the "slop counts" rule, but I love it, not only because it favors the player but because your accident, your excess, is sweet.

I discover all of this with Wally hovering benignly in the background. He's a gentle, reassuring presence. I usually leave the bar where we're playing before he does, because he likes to stay until every match has been played, which sometimes means slumping out of the bar at 1:30 or 2:00 in the morning. I can't face my workday— or Larry—on so little sleep, so I try to cut out by 11:30. But occasionally the matches finish early, usually because one of the teams is getting trounced. When a team collectively falls apart, the matches don't take much time. In these instances, Wally and I leave together and take the subway home, since we both live in Brooklyn.

One night in the middle of the summer, while we're waiting an interminable length of time for the F train, both of us wilting on the humid, airless platform, Wally says, "Can I ask you something?"

"Sure," I say.

"Is there, like, some really big guy that I'd have to move out of the way if I wanted to ask you out?" He gestures widely, stretching his arms out to indicate a big bruiser of a fellow.

Wally's inquiry takes me completely by surprise. How could I have not seen this coming? My mind scrambles to come up with some sort of sign that I missed. Then I decide it doesn't matter. I look at Wally's stringy frame, planted firmly on the subway platform. His shirt is sticking to his chest in the heat. His face is calm, but his chin tilts upward just a little as he waits for my response. I smile as I remember his hillbilly joke.

"Well, no, actually. There's not," I say. "I mean, you know, there's no one serious."

"That's some good news," he says. I find myself agreeing. We're both quiet. He smiles awkwardly but winningly. "So does that mean we can have dinner sometime?"

"Yes. I guess it does."

"ISN'T THIS LIKE DATING your personal trainer?" my friend Alison, who lives in Los Angeles, asks, scolding me when I tell her over the phone of my upcoming plans. She seems both thrilled and slightly horrified.

"No, it's nothing like that." I'm feeling mildly defensive. "We simply met doing something we both like. But if you insist, why don't we say it's like dating my . . . professor?" This sounds more romantic to me. And less tacky.

Alison scoffs. "I'm sorry, but it is nothing like that. I just don't want you to become a cliché. Next he'll want you to come back to his place to see his pool table. Instead of his etchings."

According to Wally, his apartment is too small and dumpy to accommodate a pool table, but I do not volunteer this information. I just ignore Alison.

Wally and I have our first dinner at a self-consciously hip coffee shop not far from where we play pool. He informs me he's wearing his "date clothes," which, at his own admission, are pretty sorry: a limp, white collarless shirt that makes his neck seem especially long and thin, navy blue pleated pants, and pointy black shoes. The clothes accentuate his gangliness rather than his sweet face.

As we munch on our salads (Wally will order one only if ranch dressing is on the menu, he tells me), I ask him if he dates a lot of pool players.

"Well, no. Not really. I think you might be the first."

"Really? That's surprising."

"No, it isn't. Most women pool players are either ugly or lesbians." He states this matter-of-factly while digging into a ranch-covered crouton. "At least, that's been my experience," he adds, a bit sheepishly, no doubt in response to the look of horror now frozen on my face. Wally is a wonderful teacher, but I realize he's going to need some outside instruction of his own.

I decide to steer clear of the topic of lesbians and the women Wally doesn't feel are attractive enough to date. "So why'd you come to New York anyway?" It's something I've always wondered.

"I ask myself that sometimes." He takes another bite of his salad. "Good," he says, indicating the lettuce, which he's chewing vigorously. I'm eating some sort of organic, hipster meat loaf. It's rich and delicious. It comes with garlic mashed potatoes, which Wally refers to as "taters," but with a wink.

"You haven't answered the question," I prod.

He takes a sip of his beer, swallows. "Well, my story isn't that original. I came here to be an actor. Which means actor-slash-receptionist. I got a job answering phones. I've got a good phone manner." This I believe. Wally has charm, and he's very polite.

"So are you still doing that? Trying to be an actor?" The potatoes are divine.

"No. But I was in an actual play once. The show was in Brooklyn. On a real stage. And people had to buy tickets. The whole shebang." He smiles at the memory. "But it's really competitive out there. And after a while, well, the paycheck becomes more important." Wally works at a computer company now. He's good with people and machines, it turns out. "Not a bad combo," he says.

We don't talk much about me. This is nothing new when dating men in New York, but this time it feels different, less like I'm across from someone self-absorbed and not interested in my thoughts and more like I'm facing someone who's being asked personal questions for the first time in a long while. It's a pleasant dynamic. I'm sick of talking about my résumé, about my goddamn ambitions, about what movies I've seen. We talk about geography for a while— Wally spent some time in the Midwest growing up, when his dad was transferred there—and we talk about West Virginia and southern Ohio, and I ask him if he likes baseball (he doesn't), but I start talking about the Reds' current team anyway, and he stares at me with this smitten look on his face while I hold forth on small-market teams vs. big-market teams and why I think the designated hitter is bullshit.

"That's so cute," he says, his country drawl released by the beer he's been drinking. I wrinkle my nose.

"Cute?" Now I'm ready to get into an argument.

"Aw, I didn't mean anything by that. Just that seeing a woman so interested in sports, well, let's just say that outside of women talking about pool, it's a sight I'm not all that familiar with. Perhaps I should've chosen a better word."

I relent. Wally is sincere. He's wearing date clothes and treating me to meat loaf, at a restaurant in Chelsea, no less, which I now realize is almost entirely filled with gay couples. He's refreshing, and I'm enjoying myself.

"No," I say. "It's okay. I am cute." And this time I wink.

———

DESPITE WALLY'S NARROW WORLDVIEW on female pool players and a few other differences that make a romance between us seem unlikely, we start dating, and continue to do so for a few months. (No, we never do it on a pool table. But that doesn't mean the thought doesn't cross my mind.)

No one on our team says a word about us, which surprises me. They are so inscrutable that I begin to wonder if they even know we're dating. I ask Wally one night and he says, "I think most of 'em know, just because they're not dumb. I mean, we do always seem to leave at the same time. And I know Eddie knows, because I mentioned it to him, and Gareth, too, I think." Pool romances can sometimes cause friction or awkwardness on a team, Wally tells me, such as if the captain favors his girlfriend when it comes to choosing who plays a match. But the league-wide attitude seems to be not to make too much of it, outside of a minimalist confirmation: "Yes, those two are dating." End of subject. This suits me fine.

Wally and I often end up playing pool when we go out, though "pool dates" with him are neither the first nor the only for me. The first such date is with an Irish man I meet in early 1999, not long after I start attending pool school but before I'm invited to join Wally's pool team. His name is Mark O'Toole, and he is fascinated by my learning the game so late in life. He professes to be "mad for the game" himself, says he used to play all the time as a university student in Dublin. Our first date is at Chelsea Billiards and about four minutes into the evening, not long after breaking the first rack, as I'm studying the table, contemplating the best shot to take, Mark leans in, as if not wanting to embarrass me, and says, "You hit the white one first." He points at the cue ball.

I stare at him, unblinking. "Excuse me?"

"This white ball here. You've got to hit it first, to hit the others."

"Thanks, Mark. I think I got that."

Mark O'Toole is small and bright and wiry, with little wire-rimmed glasses and dark, captivating eyes that light up when he speaks. He has full, pink lips, but his other features are sharp, almost pointy, even his forehead, which is high and narrow and seems to give his hair gravity, pushing his dark curls upward. He's opinionated, and he speaks in caffeinated, rabbity bursts in a tone that's good-natured but always insistent. Mark and I play pool only once. We go out several more times over the next couple of months, but then he's sent to Montana for work, some sort of "information technology project." Wally makes his move on the subway platform at about this time, so Mark and I never get to play the much ballyhooed rematch that he hounds me about before his transfer. His concerns about my knowing what to do with a cue ball are allayed rather quickly that first night when I beat him four straight games. He makes endless fun of himself afterward and complains that he "played like crap" and "wasn't worth shite anymore."

But Mark O'Toole's brutal defeat at my cue-wielding hands doesn't keep us from getting together again before he moves out West for good, which is not the case with Matthew, a man I meet at my first job in New York, years before I start playing pool. I was an entry-level assistant at an audiobook publisher; he did something exotic involving "foreign rights" and "transatlantic publishing deals." He had a nasal New York voice that sounded perpetually amused. I would hear him talking, look up from my cubicle, then watch him covertly as he glided among the offices, making wisecracks, his shoulders broad and athletic, his gait confident, his dark, glossy hair all the more striking when viewed against a backdrop of gray, corporate walls. I had a secret crush on him while I worked there, the kind where I was always nervously dropping things when he walked by—pencils or staplers or paper clips—or else tripping over invisible stairs, or jamming the copier even if I was making only one copy of a single page. He made me goofy. We never exchanged more than three sentences the entire year we worked on the same floor.

Over a decade later I run into Matthew, this time without dropping anything. He's still at the same job, but with a more exalted title now. I'm working for Larry's film company. E-mails are exchanged and a date is set. The "cute" aspect of our finally getting together after all of these years makes the evening seem particularly promising, in a movie-script sort of way. He's the one who suggests playing pool, though he apologizes ahead of time for "generally sucking." Matthew claims he's one of those on-or-off players, meaning he either can't miss or else he doesn't sink a single ball. I tell him not to worry, I'm just learning myself. "Good," he says. "Maybe you can give me some pointers."

We meet at Corner Billiards, on 11th Street and Fourth Avenue, and have to wait forty-five minutes for a table, which enables us to drink a beer and catch up on a decade's worth of what he terms "professional and emotional strife."

Matthew is tall and cynical. His face seems too small for his body, round and rosy, with a dainty nose and smooth skin, almost cherubic, but his eyes are dark and mischievous, as if aware of the incongruity. He can be—and is this night—side-splittingly funny. He's in his early forties now, gray at the temples, a paradoxical combination of dashing and neurotic, the kind of guy television executives build sitcoms around. He is also, unfortunately for him, "off" that night as far as his pool game goes. And I am, as I had been with Mark O'Toole, completely "on."

Matthew wins the first game and I win the next five rather handily. I don't apologize or tell him I never play like this, that it must be some kind of fluke. He knows I take lessons, am a member of a team, and play a lot more often than he does. He takes the losses in stride, making jokes at his own expense.

After a couple of hours of my throttling Matthew on the felt, we decide to get some sushi in the neighborhood. The merriment continues until it's late enough that we both have to get home. He walks me to my subway stop and says, "Well, glad we got to do this after ten years," and then makes a comment about my "superior" pool playing. I thank him and smile and say something inane about the subway to Brooklyn. There's an awkward pause, and then he says, "See you." And that's it. He turns and walks off into the night, leaving me standing on 14th Street without even a vague "Let's not wait ten years next time." I'm thoroughly baffled as I trudge down to the Q train.

I never hear from Matthew again. I send him a chirpy e-mail a couple days later, thanking him for the nice evening and suggesting a movie or something in the future, and get no response. While I am hardly in despair, I remain confused and a bit humiliated.

I relay the story to Alison in L.A. "What were you wearing?" she asks.

I describe to her in minute detail my Vivienne Tam "day to night" shirt, a filmy blouse in vivid greens and blues, with a hidden front zipper that zips from both the top and the bottom so that you can show as much skin as you like. "I feel great in that shirt," I say, somewhat defensively, as if it's my clothing choice that turned Matthew off.

She sighs. "Did you beat him?"

"Huh?"

"When you played pool in the barrio, did you beat him? Did you win?"

"We were playing near Union Square, and yes, I won. Mostly. Maybe five games?"

She sighs again, with audible exasperation this time. "Have you learned nothing?"

"What do you mean?"

"Well, of course you'll never hear from him again! You beat him *five games*. Are you insane? You've basically ruined any chance he might have for getting an erection in the next week. Or with this guy, probably the next month."

"Oh, for God's sake, Alison. This isn't finishing school. I have to act like I can't play well so he feels good about himself? Did you go to Wellesley in the fifties or something?"

"I bet if he had won even two more games, you would've heard from him again. I'm just saying. This does not mean I am endorsing that sort of behavior. You can't go out with a guy who is unable to lose to a woman. I could, of course, since I hate sports and any game that is played in a bar. I'm just offering this as an explanation for this loser's behavior."

I'll never know if Alison is right. I choose to believe she is not.

It seems rather Stone Age to think that in the twenty-first century, a man can't date a woman who occasionally beats him at pool, but competition is a strange animal. The evening with Matthew and the subsequent conversation with Alison prompt me to recall one of my early league matches. I'm playing at a dreary, windowless pub near First Avenue, a cramped, dark place full of people—mostly men—who feel that life has served them a raw deal and are taking it out on the sixteen balls that roll around in front of them on the bar's nubby, shopworn table. I find myself facing a handsome, smooth-talking guy named Mo, who tells me at the beginning of our first game, all creamy-voiced and Barry White, to "relax," that we're "just here to have fun."

Mo wins the first game and, relaxed, thus grossly underestimates me in the second game. Since the second game is often where I come alive, I find myself slowly gaining momentum and then prevailing. It isn't even close, which doesn't go over well with Mo. The more shots I make, the more rattled Mo becomes, which causes him to start missing easy shots, ones I'm sure he could have made in his sleep. I pound him, and he's right: It is fun. When it's over, he doesn't say a word to me. He packs up his cue stick and his other belongings and walks out of the bar, his mouth pressed into a hard, thin line, his teammates calling after him, wondering where he's going. I just shrug and continue to revel in my victory. My teammates shake their heads, chortling. They think it's funny that I beat Mo and remark that he's behaving like a "big baby," though some of their laughter comes from sympathy. They've been where Mo is; they know how he feels, wince in recognition, then cheer me on.

This is not to say that I've never exhibited Mo-like behavior. Although I am hardly a pool-playing force, I do play with intensity. That's the one observation I hear from people consistently. And because I cannot seem to master pool as easily as I mastered my classes in high school and college, I am, for a long time, extremely sensitive when I feel I'm not playing well. It isn't about the win so much as it is about not looking foolish. If you have any fears about looking foolish, then you shouldn't play pool, because it makes fools of everyone, even the best players, a truism, I suppose, of any activity requiring dexterity, physical grace, and an unwavering focus. No one can be dexterous, graceful, and focused all the time, and yet I'm invariably furious with myself when I bungle one or more of these requirements. And since pool is a two-person tangle, the other party often gets the brunt of this frustration, at least until I become more comfortable with losing.

For a while, if I lose a match the way Mo lost to me, by letting my opponent get under my skin and by making amateurish mistakes, such as trying to sink every ball, even those out of my reach, instead of studying the table and thinking of ways to lock up my opponent, I become snappish. I take exhortations to "have fun" as condescension and take well-meaning advice as personal criticism. I am adolescent, impossible to please or console, unable to let go of a bad game. And the easiest target for this behavior is, not surprisingly, the person with whom I'm most intimate at the time, a boyfriend or a lover. This is why pool and romance have never been a good mix for me.

Sometimes, of course, I am genuinely provoked. I go out once with a man I meet in my league named Malcolm, a witty, cosmopolitan fellow with a nonspecific European accent and intimidating black shoes. He's smart and worldly and unemployed. He smokes and slouches and says clever things about pop music and international politics. He plays a nice game of pool, too.

We decide to meet at SoHo Billiards, on Houston Street, after my workday is over. He buys me a beer and is loose and flirty and unconcerned, and thus makes all of his shots. I, on the other hand, do not acquit myself well, making one boneheaded shot after another. I keep my irritation quiet, but my face is tense as I approach the table, and, being the smart, worldly, European, unemployed, observant sort, Malcolm notices and remarks on it.

"You're awfully serious about this."

"I'm just pissed that I missed that shot. I've been practicing how to send a ball along a rail from an angle. I read about it in this book I have—"

"You read books about pool?" he asks, incredulous.

"Well, yeah. You know. I mean, yeah, I have some instruction manuals. They're pretty good."

"God, that's so"—he searches for a word—"wormy."

"Wormy?"

"Yeah, you know, it's just . . . well, odd and . . . wormy." He pretends to be repulsed by my reading habits. His jeans hang loose, sliding down his skinny hips. He's smiling, his eyes mischievous. Limp spirals of brown hair fall across his face. He brushes them back, tries to tuck them behind his ears, but they aren't long enough yet. His face is wide and flat, shaped like a skillet, his skin stretched tight over his cheekbones. I want to say something juvenile, like, "Well if I'm wormy, you're a skillet-head," but I quash the impulse. I'm pretty sure he means "geeky" rather than wormy, and that he's just trying to flirt, but I'm annoyed. I don't like being called wormy. And I don't think it's weird that I own a pool book or two.

Malcolm, when he isn't critiquing my reading selections or finding ways to stretch his severance pay, is an aspiring photographer. He lives downtown at a hip address and has had some of his photos featured in a gallery as part of a showcase for "emerging artists." I ask him what he likes to photograph and he says, without even pausing to think, "Urban archaeology." When I press him, I learn that he takes pictures of the sidewalk.

He orders another beer for himself, and we play a couple more games, and then he feels compelled to say, "You know, it's only a game. We're just supposed to have fun." Malcolm is all about fun. He has his own website. On his home page, a huge photo of him wielding an ax and looking deranged greets the visitor. He's quite the merry prankster.

I'm being overly simplistic here, linking my pool game to a mediocre date. But I think the problems arise when pool becomes performance, when you or your partner are playing to impress. I never feel the need to impress someone this way until I get addicted to pool. I then become very conscious of myself, *self-conscious* in the literal sense: aware of myself, my being. And the weird, acting-out behavior arrives not long after. It's a phase I go through, like puberty. Fortunately, I grow out of it, but it's a shame that I don't mature sooner, when I'm first getting to know Wally.

For all his loping, gangly awkwardness, his creaky country twang, his bizarre, powder-blue high-top tennis shoes, his scrawny legs teetering out of a pair of ridiculous summer shorts, his tales of a Southern-style, born-again baptism in a giant tub of water out in the middle of nowhere, surrounded by earnest members of a youth group he'd been corralled into as a teen, his fervent, myopic opinions on salad—all qualities that combine to make him seem like someone who can't tie his shoe unassisted, let alone woo a woman—Wally has presence. And it emerges when he's playing pool.

At the table, Wally is both graceful and steely. He has beautiful hands. Something seems to fall off him when he plays, his outer coat. His essence comes through, as I think mine does. We have this in common. It's what sparks the attraction between us, which never seems to last beyond a night of pool, but for a while, for a few months, at least, it's enough.

Although pool is our initial connection, after many evenings of shooting at different rooms around the city, Wally suggests to me one night that we "not play socially anymore." He seems a little nervous when he says this.

"What do you mean?" I ask.

"Well, I'm just thinking maybe that's not the best way for us to, um, to spend time together. You know, while you're still learning and . . . uh . . . taking it so seriously."

Oh. Right.

Admittedly, I have some issues.

Wally is a 6, a high-ranked player, good enough to be a pool instructor. He enters regional tournaments pretty regularly and, when pressed, admits that his fantasy would be to turn pro some day. And while I have no trouble receiving advice from him at pool school, I become extremely prickly about it when we play on our own. This is understandable, I suppose—no one likes to feel patronized, even if it's all in her head—but I take these feelings a little too far.

Wally and I often go to a basement poolroom on the Lower East Side that smells of mildew but is never crowded and is cheaper than most joints.

We'll get a Coke and play a "practice game," then I'll insist on playing him without any handicap, which is ludicrous since Wally is so much better than I am. Wally makes most of his shots, but the harder I try, the more I miss, and I become visibly perturbed with myself. Wally will try to console me, which only makes matters worse. Or he'll offer an astute insight about what I'm doing wrong, and I'll grumpily try to adjust my stroke or my stance or my bridge hand; I know he's right and is just trying to help.

This teacher-pupil dynamic is not a good one for a couple, because one person always feels he or she is lacking, not up to snuff. I find myself compensating for my pool inadequacies by telling stories in harried tones about my fast-paced career, or by bringing up current political issues when I know Wally doesn't read about such subjects and will be uninformed. He always ends up trying to appease me, tries to pull me out of these post-pool moods as if he's a children's television host or a kind but stern uncle. Sometimes he's afraid to challenge me, which makes him appear silly and nervous in my eyes, and thus less attractive.

Perhaps as a Band-Aid solution, Wally teaches me how to play nine-ball. I've seen parts of such tournaments—the women's finals, usually—on ESPN when he firsts suggests we give the game a try. There's a reason nine-ball can be found regularly on TV: Of all the pool games there are to play, nine-ball is probably the most fun to watch, at least for the novice, and the easiest to follow—and to film. It's played, as the name would indicate, with nine balls (handily numbered 1 through 9), which are arranged in a diamond-shaped rack rather than the triangular rack most people are familiar with.

In nine-ball, the cue ball must always hit the lowest-numbered ball first, so if the player breaks and no balls are pocketed, her opponent must hit the 1-ball first. If the 1 is pocketed during the break, the player who executes that break has control of the table and must now go for the 2. If the 2 is also pocketed on that same break, she must start with the 3, and so on, until she reaches the 9. However, the balls do not necessarily have to be pocketed in numerical order. If you hit the lowest ball on the table—say, the 3—and as a result, the 5-ball also goes into a pocket (this is called a combo), you get to shoot again and try to pocket the 4-ball. (The 5-ball stays pocketed.) And if you make the 9-ball at any point during the game using a legal shot—say, a combination in which the lowest-numbered ball is hit first and the 9 goes into the pocket as a result, or by sinking the 9-ball on the break—then you win (unlike in eight-ball, where you have to sink all your balls and then the 8). This means lots of gritty maneuvering and sly defensive shots from the two players. Because if you can't sink the low-numbered ball, then you need to think about how to shoot so that the cue ball is not left in a place where your opponent can pocket the lowest-numbered ball or, God forbid, use it to pocket the 9-ball.

What this means is that you have to be an artist. You have to excel at long shots and curve shots and be unafraid of bank shots, since this will most likely be your arsenal for pocketing anything. (A bank shot is when you sink a ball by banking it off the rail *opposite* the pocket you're aiming for.) But nine-ball is even more about defensive play. You have to be devious when it comes to masterminding safeties (defensive shots meant to block your opponent from pocketing his ball), and excellent at executing them. You also have to be innovative about escaping from the traps in which your opponent will no doubt ensnare you. The pros even use the glorious, gasp-producing jump shot in the name of screwing over their opponents. (When executing this shot, the cue ball is hit from above in the center with a great deal of force, causing it to jump over the ball blocking its path.)

When I've watched nine-ball on TV, I've noticed how the players use the rails as much as possible. I once saw world champion George Bustamente sink a shot in the side pocket after making the cue ball carom off of not one, not two, but three rails before hitting the lowest-numbered ball and sending it effortlessly into the pocket, much to the consternation of his opponent, Earl Strickland, and much to the audible delight of the crowd.

Nine-ball forces you to think about your next shot like no other game because of the rules about the numbered balls and the "I win!" bonanza that is the 9. And just to make things even spicier, the penalty for fouls is ball in hand, meaning you can put the cue ball anywhere on the table if your opponent doesn't hit the lowest-numbered ball first, or if he scratches or commits some other foul. And three fouls in a row means loss of the game. In other words, there is very little room for making mistakes in nine-ball, hence the need for expert, creative defensive play.

There is one other quirky rule, a strange little nut called the *push*, or the *push-out*. If the first player breaks and makes one or more balls but, despite this, doesn't like what's left on the table (perhaps the lowest-numbered ball is impossible to reach from where his cue ball has ended up), then he's free to push, meaning he can shoot the cue ball anywhere he wants. He's not trying to sink a ball here, he's trying to move the cue ball into a place where the lowest-numbered ball is within reach for his opponent but still difficult. The second player might be able to sink the low-numbered ball, but the shot will leave him in lousy position for his next one. The reason for choosing a push is not whimsical. It's a risky move that the player uses because he doesn't have a legal shot he can make and he doesn't want to risk earning one of those three dangerous fouls, or because his one legal shot will leave him locked up for the next shot and in danger of being safetied by his opponent. Likewise, if, after the break, the first player doesn't sink a ball but leaves his opponent in a lousy position, that opponent can call a push. It's like saying, "Right back atcha, babe."

Once one of the players pushes the cue ball (and this option exists only after the break shot), his opponent can accept the new position and shoot, or decline and force the first player to shoot again. That's why it's risky, because it's the *second player's* choice. If nothing drops on the new break, the second player is allowed to decline shooting again. It's a game of cat and mouse, with neither side wanting to give, and it can become agonizing, which is why it's not used lightly or frequently.

I'M HONORED THAT WALLY wants to introduce me to a new pool game—and the one played by the pros, no less. This placates me for a bit, until it occurs to me that perhaps Wally suggested nine-ball because it's also a fast game—you can play a race to 10 and still have an early evening, maybe even grab a snack afterward. The plan ends up backfiring, because now a pool night might end with Wally beating me 10–2, the gap in our abilities glaring at us like a don't-walk sign, and I'll shuffle out of the poolroom with my head down, frustrated, complaining that I'm not improving. Wally will then remind me that we are out for the evening to have fun, and that I need to lighten up. He's right, of course, and I soon agree to his proposal of keeping our pool playing only to the bar league and pool school.

This works well and keeps us from getting snippy with each other, except that now we don't have anything to talk about. Without a pool table between us, I realize that we don't have a lot in common, and that Wally's rigidity over crucial issues like salad dressing extends to other areas as well. For example, he lives in Brooklyn like I do, but in a horrible apartment with a partially caved-in ceiling. He won't move because he has it in his mind that he should live somewhere "nice" only if he's living with a girlfriend or a wife. So for ten years he's lived with one, sometimes two roommates in a noisy, water-logged apartment in a drug-infested neighborhood even though he can afford to move somewhere better. We feel differently about our domiciles. I need to enjoy coming home to a place; it doesn't have to be big or luxurious, but it can't be dangerous or dirty. Wally views his apartment simply as shelter, a roof over his head and nothing more. So he always comes to my place.

Wally keeps his money in a savings account in West Virginia, even though he's been living in New York for a decade. Investing in the stock market is certainly not for everyone, but Wally keeps his money back home because he doesn't trust keeping it anywhere else. Wally takes three trips a year—two to West Virginia to visit his family (at Christmas and in June) and one to a music festival he enjoys in upstate New York. He has friends in different states—on different continents, even—but he won't visit them. When I ask him why, he just shrugs. "I don't really know."

Wally's inertia begins to grate on me once the pool table is no longer the central part of our relationship. He doesn't have to be sophisticated or worldly; I just wish he'd be more curious, less fearful.

I soon realize that while he is a nice man with a sunny disposition, Wally doesn't really stimulate or excite me, and thus, I assume, I can't possibly stimulate or excite him. I think more and more about Rita, the girlfriend who preceded me. She's nineteen years old—thirteen years younger than Wally—and a cashier at a store uptown. She's quite sexy, according to Wally, but "doesn't have much to say." Wally broke up with her because she was "too clingy" and was also seeing other men, which is not as paradoxical as it sounds. These both seem like valid reasons to end a relationship. Yet Wally has not gotten up the guts to tell Rita he's seeing someone new. I ask him once, when we're on the way to see a movie, if Rita even knows they are no longer a couple. "Well, yeah, I think she's figured it out."

"What?" I am dumbfounded.

Wally never really told her he was ending their romance, it turns out, he just "sort of stopped calling her."

"How long did you go out?" I feel a tightness in my chest.

"About a year," he says. I am incredulous that a man in his thirties can behave like this. I don't say anything. Wally hangs his head a little, gives me a dopey grin, shrugs. It's endearing for a moment. But only a moment. I start to think that maybe a clingy nineteen-year-old is more Wally's speed. She will not press him about the state of his ceiling or his old-fashioned savings account or current events.

So I decide, after about three months of dating, to end our relationship. This seems logical to me, to be simply "pool buds," friends who share a love of pool. I try to be as sensitive and positive as I can, try to resist the usual platitudes, to keep the conversation amicable without being glib.

It does not go over well. I'm surprised at how disappointed Wally seems, and I feel terrible about making him feel bad. His eyes fill with tears. "I knew it," he says bitterly. He gets up from his chair and exits the small bar where I asked him to meet me, not wanting to hear me say nice things about him or explain what I'm thinking. He leaves me sitting there, his unfinished beer on the table. I stay awhile, sipping my glass of wine gloomily, hoping the situation will be better when I see him at pool school the following week.

It's not. Wally avoids me and looks insecure, as if he's in pain. I've certainly felt the same way when I've been in his shoes, but I am taking a rather coldhearted view because I don't want my pool-school classes or my new status as a league player to be affected by his moping, hangdog countenance.

I complain about the situation to Alison, who doesn't have much sympathy. She feels that meeting someone through playing pool is insane, that this world is beneath me, or, perhaps more to the point, beneath her. "So, what's next?" she asks me over the phone. "The gun range?"

I sit once again in defensive, slightly confused silence.

"I mean, you'll probably have to give up pool after this and find a new hobby, so I assume the next stop is target practice? Hey, I'm sure there are plenty of hearts to be broken there. Only that might not end so well. Guns use bullets, you know."

"No, I am not going to the gun range. And I'm sure things with Wally will blow over. Christ."

Indeed, Wally ends up having the last laugh.

After a few weeks, I begin to have second thoughts about ending our affair. He is, after all, an extremely kind, thoughtful guy. I won my first match playing for his team. He was there when my final 8-ball rolled into the pocket, and he picked me up and swung me around as if I was a 1940s ingenue on a train platform.

When the clouds finally blow over with Wally, when he really does start to get over me, I begin to miss his attention; his twang; his slow, slender walk; his pool. I approached this all wrong, I think: I acted too hastily. So I call him at home and get his answering machine. I leave him a message telling him I've been thinking about him. I ask if we can get together. When he calls back, he tells me that he played my message about twenty times, that his heart was in his throat. "But I'm leery," he says. "You gotta know, I'm leery."

"I would be, too," I say.

WE MEET A FEW days later and go on a walk in my neighborhood. He's a bit standoffish, doesn't want to kiss me hello. He's wearing a rumpled jean jacket, and he looks sad.

"I just don't know if I'm up for this," he says. I tell him I'm sorry that I acted impulsively and hurt his feelings, that time away from him has enabled me to appreciate him more. He looks down at me from his spindly but impressive height. He swallows. I notice what a large Adam's apple he has, and that he hasn't shaved in a few days. Then he smiles. He's relenting, I can tell.

We start to spend time together again, and we play pool together again, and I behave perfectly this time, not like a petulant child, and so we do, briefly, reunite. We start by exchanging chatty e-mails, talking on the phone, going out on chaste dates to movies and restaurants, as if we are just getting to know each other. Wally is cautious at first, but his ardor grows. His earnestness returns. He even buys new clothes, with the help of a friend who's been dying to take him shopping. He wants to impress me again, and I don't nitpick: I am pleased and flattered by his attention, not annoyed by his quirks. I am extremely proud of myself—for my introspection, my maturity, my bold action in picking up the phone when I realized I had made a mistake.

Wally waits, biding his time. He's in no rush. Then he turns everything around. After a few weeks, he takes up with someone else behind my back and dumps me, hard, right outside of Chelsea Billiards, in the middle of 21st Street, with our pool and billiard compatriots walking in and out of the entrance as I scream at him on the street. This is right around Thanksgiving and Wally has, uncharacteristically, not returned several phone calls and e-mails, so I go over to Chelsea Billiards, knowing that's the place he's most likely to be. I find him there and drag him outside. When I see his guilty face, I know immediately. I hadn't suspected a thing until this moment. He's obviously much more wily than I ever gave him credit for. I ask him tearfully what the hell he's doing, why he's done this to me. To us. I've never yelled at anyone in the street before. It's horrible, and rather thrilling.

Wally says to me, too confidently, "You're not the one."

"The *one*?" I explode. "Since when were we talking about 'the one'?"

"Well, I am looking for the one, as it happens. And you're not it. I don't feel relaxed around you."

I feel as if I've been kicked in the stomach. A sheepish look passes across Wally's face. He has hazel eyes. Our eyes are the same color.

"When were you going to tell me this?" I ask, my voice rising to a shriek, my face now wet with tears.

"Well, I was going to take you to dinner—"

"Oh, really? And this generous invitation was going to come when? And how? Through telepathy?"

"No, I was going to call you. . . ."

"You're a fucking asshole."

Wally never says his abrupt change of heart is about revenge, about reclaiming some sort of masculine dignity that I had taken from him, but I think that's what made him do it. I hurt him, despite my efforts not to. It's true my reasoning may have been skewed by a misguided sense of who I thought he was and who I thought I was, but I had been straightforward with him. I had not been a coward. I had tried to consider his feelings, though when you break up with someone, it's ultimately your own feelings you're considering the most.

People passing by start to stare less covertly at the ugly scene, the ugly coda to something that has been, for a while, rather lovely. I remember the time Wally called me when I had a cold. He offered to bring me soup, and I declined. But he persisted. He really wanted to help, to make me feel better. He also just wanted to see me, even though I warned him that my nose was red and I looked like hell. "Maybe some soup from that Thai restaurant?" I said girlishly. He was at my apartment in less than an hour. The soup was delicious.

I sob harder and my nose runs, perhaps in solidarity with the soup memory.

Wally leans against the pool hall's big front window, blocking the silent snooker players from my view. He can't look at me, just stares at the sidewalk. He starts to say something and stutters, trying to find the words. I turn and walk away. I don't want to hear any more. I wipe my face as I walk, feeling empty, wondering how I've gotten here, to this desolate place.

I head west, searching halfheartedly for a subway entrance. New Yorkers leave you alone on the subway. Whether you're crying or giggling or muttering, no one pays you any mind. I crave this anonymity right now, but I'm not sure which train to take. A homeless man shuffles ahead of me, dragging a filthy bag that appears to be stuffed with smaller bags. He has a tangled, bushy beard that I see in profile as I pass him, a flame shooting from his face. The sun disappears beneath the horizon, leaving the sky deep gray and streaky. The early-evening air feels cool on my face. It's gentle, soothing. I hug my coat against me as I walk and marvel at what has just transpired between Wally and me. But despite my sadness, I decide not to feel any regret about my time with him. For, as I have just begun to learn, slop counts.

BUT IT'S NOT SO EASY, the no-regrets part. Wally makes that really difficult, which I find out during my next pool-school session at Chelsea Billiards, where he is still an instructor and where I am still showing up before my Monday-night league matches to work on my game. He gives me a curt nod when I walk in and then finds the youngest, most attractive woman there and wildly flirts with her, cranks up his "aw shucks, I'm just a country boy" routine. I feel as if I'm in eighth grade again.

His behavior is even more childish during our league matches. He grins and winks at the waitresses, invites his women friends to come by the bar and watch him play. One night, one such friend, an olive-skinned woman with a tiny rhinestone stud in her nose, looks over at me, stares unabashedly for a few seconds, then says to Wally, "So that's her, huh?" That's when I know I'm going to have to leave. I realize I am going to have to give up this team and this great, majestic game because of a man who's pathologically devoted to ranch salad dressing.

I don't want my teammates to see me feeling so vulnerable. I hate being exposed, and I feel that way often, as if my jealousies and insecurities are always on display. This is why it took me so long to join a team in the first place. I prefer to be cocooned, protected by pool's arcane rules and elegant angles, lulled by the gentle clicking sounds coming from the table. If I stay on this team, I'm convinced that my loneliness and misery will be out in the open for everyone to see. I will no longer be a woman learning to play pool; I'll be a woman who was dumped by a pool player. I've come so far, and to be perceived this way is unbearable to me. It's better to give it all up.

I am heartbroken. But not over Wally.

———

I QUIT MY FIRST pool team because of our breakup, though I tell my teammates it's because of my job, which has become "too demanding" (a lie). They're sensitive to my plight and play along, wish me well, tell me to be sure to stay in touch. I don't.

I am morose for a while, the absence of pool tugging at me like a far-off black hole. But after a few self-pitying months, I realize that it's naive of me—just plain stupid, really—to think that the end of Wally means the end of pool. If this had been a severe disappointment in my job, I would never have walked away. I would've stayed and figured out a way to make it work.

By spring I know what I have to do: I have to find a new pool team, one that's in a different division—there are several divisions in the league—so I won't have to worry about seeing Wally. But no matter what, I have to find that team. And I also have to make a solemn vow, a rather easy one, I think, which is never to become romantically involved with a pool player again. It's asking for trouble.

Drama in
Unusual Places

My search for a Wally-free pool team, a quest that spans several weeks, eventually takes me to a bar in a desolate part of the East Village, near Avenue C.

The East Village used to be, and I suppose to some extent still is, the scruffy cousin to the leafy, winding-lane West Village—the cousin who still smokes and is always in a bad mood. It's a place, like most neighborhoods in New York City, with a rich, fabled history, in this case one that involves avant-garde theater, radical poets and artists, urban pioneers, people who don't need dappled sunlight or charm, who need energy instead, who thrive best at night, which is when the East Village comes alive—restless and exciting and ultimately exhausting.

But the East Village's rough edges and iconoclasm and art deco buildings, even its housing projects and drug corners, have been packaged and sold to young, aspiring hipsters working in "creative fields" like advertising and magazine publishing, so that the cramped, boxy apartments in six-floor walk-ups with no light now rent for thousands of dollars a month, and the cold, spacious artists' lofts have been renovated and sold for small fortunes to those eager to acquire an edgy persona. Pricey cocktail lounges and crowded sidewalks awash in expensive European boots and black leather jackets push up against old crones who have lived in the neighborhood for decades, who pull wheeled carts with sad bundles of groceries. It's a complicated place, a little at war with itself. And with that kind of tension, it should come as no surprise that the East Village is home to more than its fair share of pool bars, ranging from the trendy to the downtrodden. It's the strange dualities of this sulky, gritty section of New York—the inauthentic mixing with the authentic—that draw me to play pool within its confines, since the notion of a dual existence is beginning to feel more and more familiar to me, and more comfortable.

I AM INSIDE THE bar near Avenue C. It's called the Ace, and I've shot there before. I appear out of the gloom on a ferocious rain-soaked night wearing a blinding, lime-green windbreaker that stands out in the dank bar like a lightning bolt against a black sky. The back room, which contains two pool tables, gets quiet when I approach. I look wild and windswept, with my voluminous, wet hair and bright, shiny jacket, my cue, in its red canvas case, slung over one shoulder. I imagine myself as some wry, knowing stranger from a Western.

One of my favorite American billiards tales is a Western, come to think of it. It involves none other than the violent Earp Brothers, five of whom fought at the O.K. Corral. Morgan Earp, the youngest of the pack, died in 1882 at age thirty while shooting pool. The story goes that after the famous gun battle at the O.K. Corral (Morgan was shot in the shoulder but survived), the Earps nursed their wounds and bided their time in Tombstone, Arizona, knowing full well it wasn't over yet. They were right. One night at Campbell & Hatch's Billiard Parlor, about five months after the gunfight, Morgan was in the middle of a game of pool, and as he bent over to stroke in a ball, a loud shot shattered the glass of the door behind him and a bullet sliced through him, followed by another that missed and lodged in the wall beyond. As reported in *The Tombstone Epitaph*, outlaws bent on revenge after the O.K. Corral had tracked him down. He collapsed onto the pool table, his body splayed across the felt, bleeding. Four of his brothers—including Wyatt—were there, and they carried him to the card room in the back. According to the *Epitaph*, several doctors were summoned, but it was hopeless; they declared the wound "mortal." The only thing to do was try to ease Morgan's pain in the time he had left. The men and women hovering around him tried to help him sit up or stand, thinking he'd be more comfortable, but he cried out, "Don't, I can't stand it." He whispered something in Wyatt's ear, then said, loud enough for a few to hear, "That's the last game of pool I'll ever play." And with that, he died.

In my head, the line is delivered in a voice like John Wayne's.

THE PLAYERS AT THE Ace aren't so friendly at first, except for a tall, angular guy named Ricky who reminds me of Big Bird. He wears a knit cap pulled down low over his forehead, straw-colored hair defiantly poking out on either side. I suspect there's a lot of hair under there but, with the hair forced into submission by the fuzzy wool hat, the emphasis is now placed unavoidably on his nose, a fantastic appendage shaped like a root vegetable, with a bump on the bridge that, if it were drawn to scale, would be a perfect mogul for downhill skiing. He smiles crookedly, then curiously, his head cocked slightly, and when I inquire about joining the team, he points to the team's captain, a guy called Paul G., who's in the middle of a match. I sit quietly off to the side, waiting. There's one other female there, a square-shouldered woman with deep, dark brown eyes and an impassive face, who I think might not be pleased about my intrusion.

After winning his match, Paul G. saunters over.

"So, I hear you're looking for me."

He really says this. I haven't seen anyone approach him, so I don't know how he knows I'm looking for him. His manner is not threatening, it's even amiable.

"Um, yeah. I'm looking for a pool team to join. I heard you were the guy to talk to here." I sense that this sort of macho flattery—"the guy to talk to"—will go over well.

He nods, one hand gripping his upright cue, rocking it nervously back and forth like a windshield wiper. Paul G. is a fidgety guy. He's giving me a headache. I try to focus my gaze on the wall behind him.

Paul G. asks me questions about where I've played, how long I've been playing, if I live in the neighborhood. "So you really just walked in here? You've just been walking into bars?"

"Yes." I act as if I do this all the time. I've been trying to slip away from work early, avoiding, if possible, those end-of-the-day calls from the West Coast. Not that I'm shirking my responsibilities; I've had several pleasant but unproductive lunches this week. I simply don't have much to report to my Los Angeles colleagues, other than that I've noticed the Cobb salad is making a comeback.

I tell Paul G. that I tried to find a new team last week, too, at Barfly, at Antarctica, at Lucy's, but none of them had an open spot.

"You know, it's sort of dramatic," I say. "Me coming in out of the rain, out of nowhere. Maybe it's destiny." I attempt a winsome Ingrid Bergman expression. He chuckles and nods and adjusts a baseball cap that I will never see him take off. (He's self-conscious about losing his hair.)

Paul G., it turns out, is not the captain of Ace's team, but of the visiting team that's playing against them, from a pool bar I've been to before called The Wrong Side. He's a slight fellow, maybe five-seven, slim-hipped and spindly-armed, fond of baggy khakis and even baggier short-sleeved shirts, his elbows poking out like little coat hangers.

They swing back and forth as he moves his cue stick around the table. He has a drug problem, which I don't know about yet, and a not-knowing-when-to-stop-talking problem, which I will also become acquainted with, as well as a short fuse when it comes to pool and to managing a team. But he also has a sweet smile and sad brown eyes, and at that moment I want only to join his team. They call themselves Dawn of the Dead.

Paul G. says he'd like to play a game with me, which makes my stomach tighten, but his team keeps distracting him and we never get around to it.

A few minutes later, a guy named Roger walks into the bar, soaked but grinning. "Sorry I'm late, man," he says to Paul G., who rolls his eyes in disgust. "I had some things I had to take care of. Cut me some slack, I'm drenched here. I walked over from the other side of town with no umbrella."

Paul G. feigns indifference. "Whatever, Rog."

Roger glances at me and shrugs, enacting a "Who, me?" pantomime. Then he bounces off to the bar to get a drink.

"That guy," Paul G. says, shaking his head. He turns back to me, refocusing his attention, realizing that he needs to come to a decision about my presence on the team. Finally, he says, "Show up next week at The Wrong Side. I got a good feeling about you."

"You mean that's it? No audition?"

"Yeah, you're on the team. I'm not worried." I thank him eagerly and think it polite to stay for a few minutes to watch his team play, and to watch him watch his team play. Then, when I determine the moment is right, when a frozen ball is being argued, I leave, slipping past the silent, gloomy bar and disappearing into the rain, which is still coming down like the world is going to end.

Underbelly

PLAYING FOR PAUL G.'S TEAM is a little like sitting in an airport watching the planes take off and land, expelling one set of passengers and vacuuming up another.

There's a revolving-door quality to most of the teams in the league, I soon learn, with two or three core members that hang on for years, and a rotating posse of players that join, stick around for a season or two, sometimes several, and then move on, because of either getting a job or getting evicted or getting married or getting divorced or getting banned from the bar for unpaid tabs or a propensity to start fights, or sometimes none of the above, sometimes because of simply wanting a change, a new plan for Monday nights. They come and go with little fanfare, often not giving the team captain a lot of notice.

I play for Paul G.'s team for about three months before the other players, who are a bit guarded at first, start to get comfortable with me, to look forward to seeing me every week, which only makes the pool more enjoyable. I'm becoming friends with Liz, the other woman on the team, and am routinely drawn to Roger, since he has such a knack for putting people at ease.

Paul G. was the team's founder, before it was known by its ominous moniker Dawn of the Dead, and yet rather than function as a magnet, drawing everyone in, he's more like a dull, heavy stone dropped into a pond, sending everyone rippling away from him. The main reason for this is that Paul G. will not shut up. His incessant talking is a nervous tic, without content or goal, functioning the same way nail-biting does for those, like Paul, who are cursed with an excessive amount of nervous energy. His nonstop chatter is anxiety-driven and unconscious; he does it out of habit, and he simply cannot stop. Since he's in sales, the subject of his monomaniacal diatribes is usually work-related, some dull product he feels the need to discuss ad nauseum, or else the equally stultifying tale of how he successfully sold that product, how much he made on commissions, how he's headed for a big payday, you better believe it, how he has all these ideas for making the product better, for selling it more widely. The unlucky recipient of this earful will cut Paul G. off at a certain point and say, "That's great, but the thing is, Paul, I don't really give a shit," and walk off in search of the bathroom, the jukebox, or anyone else to talk to, even if the choice is between an ashtray and a bag lady. Yet this never fazes Paul G. Although he perceives slights everywhere, people blatantly ignoring his monologues or walking off in the middle of them never seems to offend him. He is willfully blind. I guess he has to be.

Despite this, Paul G. has assembled a pretty decent lineup of pool players—he's a skilled player himself and has the eye to spot it in others—but his cardinal rule is that no matter what, he has to play each week. The team is to revolve around him. This drives Gary and Trevor and Ricky crazy. Roger, being Roger, doesn't care.

"Christ, does the guy have even an ounce of humility? Could he maybe not think about himself for one goddamn second?" Gary, who's a mediocre pool player but fond of—and rather expert at— throwing punches, asks this question, sometimes more colorfully, regularly. He is met with supportive mumbles and jibes from Ricky and Trevor, but no one ever goes so far as to attempt a coup. That's because Paul fulfills an important function: He is the negative, deviant force against which people rally; his irritating personality serves to unite everyone else. No matter how different we are when it comes to our work lives, our sexual partners, our weekend activities, our beer choices, we're bound together by a mutual disgust, laced with pity, for Paul G.

Gary is probably the most vocal critic. There's very little about which he isn't vocal. More often than not, he's scathingly funny. He works from his home in Queens, doing freelance Web design. He's short, maybe five-six, with thick, corded arms and bulging shoulder and neck muscles. He clomps around in stiff biker boots and wears only black—including, of course, the requisite leather jacket. Tattoos crawl menacingly up his arms, and he slicks his hair back in a gleaming pompadour, his long sideburns slash marks on his face. He is instantly recognizable, a comical and dangerous figure hunched at the bar like a bulldog or prowling around the pool table like a mean alley cat.

Gary is of the "You gotta problem with me?" school of conflict resolution. Once someone rubs him the wrong way, there's no turning back, as I observe firsthand one night at a bar on lower Third Avenue when he lands a punch square on the jaw of a guy from the opposing team, some ninny in pressed khakis and Birkenstocks who's been pissing Gary off ever since he waltzed into the bar with a Zagat restaurant guide.

"Look at this guy," Gary says as soon as Birkenstocks walks in. He takes a swig from his beer bottle and glares at the guy, who appears oblivious. "What's this idiot doing here?" He keeps at it. "Oh, now look, he's already contesting a shot and it's not even his fucking match. Jesus Christ."

Gary pushes himself off his stool and clomps over to the pool table, around which stand a few members of the opposing team, along with Roger and Paul G., who don't seem bothered by anyone.

Gary doesn't say anything at first but keeps staring at the guy with the sandals and khakis. Liz and I can't hear Gary, but it's soon clear from the way he's cocked his head and shifted his body that he's finally said something. The guy looks at him, confused, then gestures, asking if there's a problem. Gary says something else and I hear the guy say, "Don't be a dick, man," and then Gary's arm swings out, the guy goes down, there's a scuffle of feet and sounds of protest, and then Liz and I watch as Gary is dragged out of the bar by his head. The bartender is over the bar and has him in a half nelson in about two seconds. I hear Gary call out, "Later, guys!" as he's shoved out the door. We wait for a few minutes, let the situation cool down, watch the sandal-wearing guy get helped up by his teammates, then rub his face and try to look tough—he'll no doubt be telling people later about how he "got into it" with some leather-clad idiot at a pool bar and that the guy ended up on the street, refining and embellishing his story each time he tells it.

Liz and I finally go outside and find Gary about half a block away, smoking a cigarette.

"I know, I know, that was dumb. But honestly, I was done. I just didn't want to be there anymore, and I knew I'd get thrown out if I did that, and I also knew how unbelievably satisfying it would be to belt that guy, so . . . what can I say? One-stop shopping." He grins. He seems more teenage delinquent than psychopath. He's thirty-four, but he'd be the first to admit he has no plans to grow up.

We stand outside with Gary until he finishes his cigarette and wave to him as he heads off for the subway. Liz looks at me, shakes her head, and smiles.

LIZ HAS THE MOST interesting, soulful, impossibly dark eyes, round and deep, almost black, like onyx against her pale skin. Her build is square and straightforward, and she's got a loping, easygoing stride that reminds me of home. She is quiet and gentle, the kind of person about whom I've heard people say, "She has such a nice . . . aura." I think what they mean is that she comes across as completely authentic, centered, present in herself, which can be particularly soothing if you are not.

When she's shooting pool, and, come to think of it, even when she's not, even when she's just walking or sitting or drinking a beer, Liz tucks her straight, dark brown hair behind her ears and lets it spill carelessly over her shoulders. She favors cargo pants or nameless, unadorned jeans, the occasional flannel shirt, and no makeup. We meet for the first time that rainy night at the Ace bar, where, until I came along, she'd been the lone woman on Paul G.'s team. It takes a while for us to become friends. At first I think she's completely indifferent to me, even annoyed, maybe irked that she's no longer the only female on Paul G.'s team. But I discover pretty quickly that I'm wrong, that it's my own initial insecurity, the kind that comes when you're trying something new, that's clouding my perspective.

What I learn soon enough is that Liz has a pointed, deadpan wit and a generous heart; that she's shy and tomboyish and incredibly curious; that she has a wonderful, creative mind for pool; that she loves baseball, finds it as beautiful and agonizing as I do; and that, like many Midwesterners who live in New York, though she endures, even indulges, the complex neuroses of others, she keeps her own in check. I'm handy at this, too, though not nearly as good at it as she is. We go out and are not neurotic together. It's a relief, like getting a seat on the subway after standing for ten stops.

We live close to each other in Brooklyn, it turns out, but our friendship develops slowly. It's quiet and comfortable and unflashy. It takes probably a year before we start spending time together in non-pool environments. We begin by sharing cabs home after our matches, going over every detail of our games, one usually comforting the other about a boneheaded decision or a bungled shot that cost one of us a win.

Liz and I really don't belong here, in a world where guys like Gary throw punches and get tossed out of bars because they're annoyed by someone's shoes, and yet we stay. Week after week we shake our heads and smile tight-lipped smiles, and laugh sometimes, staring at the ground or the street or a dartboard or an 8-ball, then catch each other's eye but never really say it out loud: that we are in control, that we have our lives in some semblance of order, that we will probably continue to get raises and interesting jobs and better apartments, and that our families will want us home every year for the holidays. We come each week because we love pool, and we stay because we love pool, but also because we are secretly thrilled to get a glimpse of this dark world, where a guy who looks at you wrong gets smacked and the smacker gets tossed onto a city sidewalk. It isn't "slumming," it isn't a social experiment, it's exciting, a world where people regularly push limits that we are afraid to push in our own lives. Crossing these lines, or being around those who cross them, has an interesting, often liberating effect on our games, sort of like the artist who goes to Paris with an easel instead of enrolling in art school. Liz and I have in common an unspoken attraction to this world, and slowly we form our own unit within a unit, the sort of friendship I haven't had in years.

Our fascination with this other life is not, however, a secret. Everyone else is aware of it, but they don't care, since they, too, are there because they love the game, and because they thrill to things that are different. And Liz and I are different, so we count; we contribute to the cause. There's no pretense, no artificial glossing over of different backgrounds. The differences are, in an odd way, celebrated.

For example, I am always encouraged in my pool playing—praised when I do something right, gently reprimanded when I do something dumb. But the way I know that I am finally accepted by that mangy, prickly team from The Wrong Side is when I start getting teased—regularly—for the way I speak, for my vocabulary.

It starts one night when I'm finishing a game, one I'm probably going to win, and as I bend over to take my shot, Gene, a ruddy-faced English guy on our team, a recovering alcoholic who has a brilliant eye for the table and a vicious, near-perfect stroke, says to me, as I lean over, adjust my stance, and take aim, "Would you like a coach?" I stop myself mid-stroke and say, "Well, no, not unless I'm about to do something egregious." Gene stares at me blankly for a moment, then says, truly baffled, "What the hell did you just say?" Liz convulses with laughter and Gary calls out, "Hey, Heather, are you using those forty-dollar words again? Jesus, talk down to us, all right?" I blush and laugh at myself, and ask Gene if I'm about to make a really dumb shot, a shot that will wreck the rest of the game, and he says, "Well, no," and I tell him a coach isn't necessary then, but thanks for offering. This little scene breaks the dam, and a torrent of good-natured abuse follows.

"I understand maybe two out of every thirty words you say," Gary announces. "Liz translates for me." Roger asks how many syllables I think I use in a given day and tries to start a betting pool among the bar patrons to guess the number.

The ribbing among teammates is mostly good-humored, except for certain nights when Paul G. is particularly annoying or Gary is particularly obstreperous. For the most part, though, it's a low, entertaining thrum: The better you tease, the more you are respected.

There's been and empty place in my life, and it becomes clear that pool—and the off-color jibes and prickly personalities that accompany the game—fills it. This is not what I am expecting to learn after joining a pool league, but it has become an unignorable fact now that I'm stalking into an East Village pool bar every week, almost growling in anticipation as I unzip my cue case, one high-heeled boot cocked, eyes darting around the room, wondering who I will face across the table that night. My teammate Roger watches this transformation with amusement and affection—and recognition. His own transformation occurred a long time ago, far from New York City, though not so far from pool.

The Keeper of
the Peace

Roger's tab is hefty once again. He buys three beers for Gary (Bud in a bottle, "none of that fancy imported shit"); four pints of Brooklyn Lager for Ricky; a Stella for Liz; two rum-and-cokes for the giggly, frizzy-haired woman with the toy-poodle face who looks as if she goes to a lot of happy hours and who enjoys drinks with maraschino cherries; a cranberry and seltzer for me (I'm abstaining that night); a vodka and cranberry for somebody's whiny girlfriend; and several shots of Jack Daniel's for the beer drinkers, so they have something to chase. He sticks with his usual Stealth Bombers (a pint glass with gin, cranberry, and lime), three or four of them, which he drinks with a straw, as if they're milk shakes. He keeps a cigarette lit and dangling, and laughs with Maura, the lithe, silky bartender who moves like a cat in a small space, elegant and cornered.

The total, with a generous tip for Maura, comes to $90, which Roger is now trying to count out on the bar, pulling crumpled bills from his various pockets, unfurling them to find out their denominations, and tossing them on the bar like Kleenex.

This is a ritual for Roger, buying everyone drinks. He's jovial about it, always arrives with plenty of cash, rarely allows anyone to buy him one back, unless it's the bar itself, which floats him free rounds all the time since he's such a good customer and doesn't pull stunts like disappearing to go to the ATM and then never returning, leaving the tab unpaid.

Roger's generosity is completely sincere. He doesn't buy rounds to be a big shot or because he's just a big, dumb sheepdog. He has money—he's a lawyer, meaning he has a regular salary, not exactly a common occurrence at The Wrong Side, the bar on East 3rd Street where Paul G.'s team is based, and he inherited some money unexpectedly several years ago and bought a sweet apartment in a desolate pocket of the far West Village, near the Hudson River, a place now worth a small fortune due to the newfound hipness of its once marginal locale. But he knows what it's like not to have money, and he knows how much some of the regulars at The Wrong Side and on his pool team need a drink or two at the end of the day, and so he acts the bon vivant, hams up his role as the loud-laughing idiot, so that he can buy his friends and acquaintances drinks without making them feel indebted or patronized. He spends probably $250 a week at The Wrong Side and just shrugs it off. "You're not being taken advantage of if you know it's happening, if you do it willingly."

Roger's style of pool playing is much less eager and tail-wagging, however. He's friendly, true, rarely contests a hit or a rule, his body loose, relaxed, boyish, his stroke so easy and sure it's like walking for him. But there's a steeliness underneath.

His girlfriend, Shelly, a small, tense, unhappy woman with a variety of hang-ups (a thing about stairs, and about leaving the three-block radius of her neighborhood) and many demands, works at a chic SoHo clothing store, so Roger often shows up wearing expensive, odd-shaped shirts and amusing shoes. ("Shelly gave me these. They're Bruno Magli. Do you know how much these normally cost?")

She never sets foot in the bar, but she isn't about to let him out of the house without what she considers the proper attire. He's gained weight, he tells me, so he doesn't look as good anymore in just jeans and a T-shirt.

What Roger looks like is a cartoon character: large head; brown-green eyes framed by bushy eyebrows; perfect, shiny teeth; thick, matinee-idol hair brushed into a square. "I used to be really handsome," he says more than once. "I mean, I'm a handsome guy, but you shoulda seen me a few years ago, when I used to go to the gym every day and was all stressed-out and thin and muscular. I was a hunk, man." Then he chuckles and slices in the 2-ball and says to me, trying to impart some wisdom, "You know why I did that? Because now I can screw him on my next shot." He sucks on his cigarette, then adds in a low voice, "Not that I care about winning. Who cares, right?"

So Roger lumbers around the table in his Bruno Magli shoes, puffing on his Camels, sipping gin through a straw, but his eyes are sharp, taking in the spread of balls like a general surveying the battlefield, and he never lingers. He's a fast, smart player, utterly calm and confident, not the big dope at the bar buying everyone drinks.

Sometimes—a lot of times—he drinks too many Stealth Bombers, and he gets loud and frat-boyish and not so funny. "I'm an idiot, aren't I?" he'll say, shaking his head at his own drunken imbecility. "You want another? Jesus, what sissy drink are you having? How come you never drink?"

"I drink, just not as much as you."

"Do you have a boyfriend?"

"No. Not right now."

"That makes no sense." Long drag on a cigarette. "Shit, I'm up. Hold this." And he shoves the cold, sweating pint glass at me while he saunters to the table, giving his opponent a chance to underestimate him. That never lasts long.

After I join Paul G.'s team, Roger goes out of his way to be friendly to me, as if I'm the new kid at school and he's the student council president. It's clear he's the backbone of the team, which bugs Paul G. to no end. *He* wants to be the backbone of the team. But since Paul G. is insecure, lonely, often coked up (if his long trips to the bathroom and his jittery nose-wiping are any indication), and still lives with his mother, he is never the man in charge. During the day, he's a salesman—high-end copier products maybe, or software systems. No one ever really knows, or cares. He must answer to the consumer, coaxing, seducing, cajoling, flattering, but never acting as if he's the boss. His client is always the boss, or at least must be made to feel that way. So Paul G. can't quite muster the authority when he's at the pool bar, no matter how hard he tries. The role just doesn't fit. At the table, he bounces on the balls of his feet, grips his cue, and sucks nervously on a cigarette, demanding to see the score sheet.

"This is my team. I decide who's up. I've got a strategy here. Shit, I've only been doing this for years." Paul G. will then stare fixedly at the clipboard as if he's trying to split the atom. When he carries on like this, Roger casts me an amused glance and shakes his head. "Okay, Paul, whatever."

ONE NIGHT, as we're hanging around between matches and Paul G. is "consultating," his word for trying to figure out who to put up next, Roger beckons me over. He's grinning, exuberant.

"So, you like all this?" He gestures to the bar. "You glad to be on this team?" I can't tell if he's drunk yet, but I don't think so.

"Of course," I say.

"Siddown a minute." He pats the spot next to him. I sit.

He smiles at me, his marquee face a mixture of curiosity and earnestness. "So here you are, you're sweet, you seem really smart, you're sexy—how come you don't have a boyfriend?" We're back to this again.

"Well, I don't know, Rog. I just don't right now. It's not so easy."

"Oh, come on. I find that hard to believe. Are you now gonna tell me how the guys you date are all assholes?"

"No, because that wouldn't be true."

"I don't really see you dating an asshole." He smiles. He and Shelly have been together for almost ten years. Roger likes being a boyfriend. He likes taking care of people, except for himself.

"Okay, well, that's all. I was just wondering, and I thought you should know how completely shocked I am, and appalled with my own gender, though maybe your standards are too high. You ever think of that? You need a nice guy, like me. But the thing is, we're usually below the radar. Okay, well, not *me* maybe, especially when I was handsome, but you know what I mean."

"That's nice of you to say. I'll keep it all in mind."

Paul G. is in the process of picking a fight with Trevor, a teammate who is much bigger than Paul (most men are) and who is particularly loud and angry and drunk tonight. Their voices rise above the din from the jukebox.

"Jesus, now I gotta go deal with this. I'm like a goddamn corrections officer." Roger gets up, flashes his high-wattage cartoon smile, and sidles over to the other side of the pool table to try to keep the peace.

ROGER IS FROM CALIFORNIA, from the bad side of a small, unremarkable city. He and his brother grew up the only white kids in a mostly black neighborhood. "I'm white trash, and I grew up in the hood. Makes no sense, does it?" Roger says when he feels like telling stories. "I was one of the few kids at school whose family lived in an apartment. All my friends were black. Yeah, that's right, 'we all got along.'"

He liked to cut class and go to the beach and mess with girls and drop acid. He had to take two buses to do this, he reminds me, and admits that he and his friends terrorized the other passengers with their loud laughter and rough language. Sometimes he'd stay all night at the beach, burrowing into the sand, his hair ruffled and wavy from the sea, his skin golden, like a kid with a future, his body curled around beer bought with a fake ID and drugs bought with no ID.

Although he was bright and funny, he was incorrigible and was eventually expelled from school for squandering his many second chances. He learned to play pool then, to fill his days, but thought nothing of it. He wasn't overly attached to any pool halls and felt no tug toward the game—he'd rather be at the beach—but it killed time and it exercised his brain, as he tells it, keeping him nimble. He'd bang the balls around and attempt trick shots and smoke Camels, quiet and sullen, until his friends picked him up and they scraped together enough money for another night on the beach, where they could forget who they were.

Roger's dad died when he was young, from something awful and unexpected, a brain aneurysm or a tumor; Roger's vague on the exact cause. His mother sounds nasty: She smoked and drank and yelled. I imagine her as a hard, drawn woman, with a taut neck and limp, cranky hair, furious at her predicament. Her boys ran wild. What could she do?

Lots of people on Roger's family tree died young, riddled with early, virulent cancers, emphysema, cirrhosis, or were hit by trucks, cut down by stray bullets. And so Roger, not surprisingly, suffers a bit from the Mickey Mantle syndrome—another good-looking, talented, hard-drinking guy whose father and brothers and uncles never made it to old age. Mickey assumed he'd have the same fate, so he lived twelve days for every one, thinking what the hell's the point, it could be his last moment on Earth. Roger seems to have a similar sense of doom about himself, which he covers up with smiles and compliments and wisecracks and Stealth Bombers, but it's there, lurking under the surface. It fuels a lot of his behavior.

Roger wised up when it was time, earned his GED, and was accepted to a great university in California, one of those "from out of the projects" stories that admissions officials love. With only a minimum of application on his part, he earned straight A's. Then he decided he wanted to move to New York, to a big, exciting, bustling city where he could lose himself, so he applied to law schools here, got accepted, and moved his life east, leaving behind his acid-tripping friends, his bleeding-heart professors, his harsh mother, and his whacked-out brother ("who's certifiably insane, in case you're wondering, and movie-star handsome, makes me look like an extra"). He had just met Shelly, and she came, too, her myriad urban phobias soon to follow.

Roger aced law school but was turned off by the tony, white-collar firms that were courting him. "I didn't fit in. I wasn't even blue-collar, I was no-collar. They wanted me, but I knew it wouldn't work. So did the big partner dude who eventually interviewed me. He was just like me. He told me I'd be happier downtown. That he would've been, too, if he had to do it over again."

So he got a nine-to-five job as an attorney at a small personal-injury firm. They were ambulance chasers, and they were successful. Now Roger reads case law all day, except when he's sent out to take pictures of a restaurant's sidewalk or sneak into a construction site to snap a photo of the safety lock on a crane. Sometimes the firm gets a real case, one with a social message, like the one against a foster-care agency that was rife with abuse and negligence. Roger likes to think he helped clean it up.

Nervous immigrants come and go through his office every day, a few looking for an angle, but most with heart-rending stories that inevitably end with some unspeakable injustice that Roger wants to correct, and that his boss will allow him to if he can get some cash out of it. These people, with their broken English and frightened eyes, gravitate toward Roger, who would do everything pro bono if he could. (He does quite a bit of work that way and hides it from his boss, sometimes contributing his own money instead but saying he extracted it from the clients.)

Meanwhile, Shelly gets the job at the boutique; the inheritance—from a great-uncle—appears out of nowhere (infuriating Roger's mother), and so he buys a place for them, paying for it up front, with no mortgage. The timing could not have been better, since Shelly has become increasingly anxious about their most recent rental: She's convinced that a guy in the building is a drug dealer and that she and Roger might be murdered. The new apartment makes Shelly feel safe, she can walk to work, and it's around the corner from an ancient, scruffy pool bar, which Roger discovers not twenty-four hours after moving in. For the first time since coming to New York, he feels at home.

THIS ALL HAPPENED years ago, of course. Roger's tiring of his job now, and maybe even of Shelly. He plays pool three or four nights a week, to "unwind." And he goes on lots of trips, taking Shelly to Italy, to Prague, to France, to Costa Rica. Roger likes architecture. Sometimes he drives around New York and looks at buildings, and he likes to do the same in foreign cities. He enjoys going to museums and staring at paintings, too. "I hate reading—I've done enough of that to last me. Shelly reads constantly, she's in some book group, but I tell her I read all day, I'm not joining some group with a bunch of wannabe literary scholars." Roger doesn't like movies much either, because they're so "unrealistic." And he hates plays. "I'd rather wash dishes for five hours than see a play. They're so stupid. I hate how actors talk, I hate sitting and listening to that shit. It means nothing to me."

Roger is not a philistine or a buffoon. He's simply very clear about what speaks to him and what doesn't. He prefers the quiet, the visual.

He likes the unpredictability of looking at a painting and seeing something different each time, and he likes the grandeur and solidity of buildings, how they look against a skyline or next to other buildings, what went into their conception. They awe and calm and inspire him, like, I think, a pool table does.

Roger, more than anyone I know, is his own man, and he keeps it together for a long time. Just not long enough.

A Painful Case

WITH ROGER STRUGGLING so hard to keep his life buoyant and carefree, to stave off his sense of doom, it makes sense, I suppose, that there would be, on the other side of the hill, a person who's always kicking rocks and dirt down the slope—the intense, angry counterpart to Roger. This role on our team is played with great passion by Trevor, who, when he starts showing up regularly again, rips a hole in the fabric that Roger has been trying each week to keep stitched together.

Trevor is magnetic—brooding, sexy, unrestrained. Women watch him when he walks down the street, their covert gazes a mixture of admiration and fear. He inspires both in people. He acts like someone who is meant for more—and he was, I think, a long time ago, in a different life.

"Listen to this, you have to listen to this." It's Roger, calling me at work, something he's taken to doing once or twice a week. He wants me to hear a message left on his cell phone. It's from Trevor, who, like Roger, is one of the original members of the team—he's been on it since Paul G. assembled it a few years ago. His attendance is sporadic: Trevor disappears and reappears with no warning or explanation. No one seems to mind. Such behavior is hardly uncommon in the league, even if Trevor is the only person on our team to exhibit it. Roger gives me his access code and tells me to call his cell phone.

Trevor's message is there, rambling but not wholly incoherent, for those who know him. He's upset with Roger's being "part of the system." It's a familiar rant, and I've been on the team for only three months. I can't imagine listening to it for three years.

"Okay, first of all, don't try to put any of your slick lawyer moves on me. You hate yourself, man, but that's not my problem. I've made sacrifices and, yeah, maybe my life hasn't worked out so great, but I can't even imagine being you. Okay? That's number one. And also, I don't need you to settle my arguments, and when I want to, I can play better than anyone on this team. Anyone. And I just feel sorry for you, man. Don't you condescend to me, or think you can. . . . You can't buy me. I don't need your money. You like to think you're Mr. Nice Guy, and want everyone else to think you're Mr. Nice Guy. But I know the truth. And you know, I mean, fuck this shit, I don't need this shit, I don't need this team, I don't need your money, or your attitude, or your money, or any of this crap. I've got my art, and I am true to myself, and I don't need anyone to tell me how to live my life. And I'll make my own decisions, and play the way I want to play, and don't interfere. And I mean . . . it's just over. I don't want you in my life. Do you hear me? You represent everything about the system I hate. I feel sorry for you, man. You can just keep your fucking money. That's all you care about. Fucking lawyer. You—" And then finally, mercifully, the message is cut off.

The real issue, which reared its head during the team's most recent pool match, is that once again, Trevor has no place to live. He hasn't had a construction job in a few weeks. He has no money and an unquenchable thirst for whiskey, right out of a James Joyce short story.

Roger gives him a couple hundred dollars in the hope that Trevor can bribe some friend of a friend into letting him crash on his floor. Shelly tells Roger *no way* can Trevor stay at their place, not even for one night. So Trevor accepts the money—he always does—but then proceeds to start a fight with his next pool opponent, some meek, oblivious guy from a meek, oblivious team, which then metamorphoses into picking a fight with Roger, who is the person he's wanted to fight with all along. Roger bails him out all the time. And Trevor leaves insane messages for people constantly—not just for Roger, for others as well—but this particular one seems to carry more venom, delusion, and desperation than usual. It gets to Roger, enough that he saves it, and now he needs me to listen to it. What can I say?

"Trevor's an unhappy guy, Roger. I mean, you have to dismiss all of this."

"But where does this come from? What the fuck did I do? I am nothing but nice to this guy—all the time."

"I think that's part of the problem, Roger. I think your generosity makes him feel terrible. He needs you, but you remind him of everything that's wrong with his life, everything he can't do, and how he can't be similarly generous to people. It doesn't excuse that ridiculous, crazy message, which was mean and unnecessary. But it sort of explains it, you know?"

"Yeah, I know."

There is almost constant friction between Roger and Trevor these days, instigated entirely by Trevor. He's a contradiction, because despite his role as instigator, he's also dashing and handsome and can actually be quite charming at times. He reads a lot, follows politics, tells entertaining stories, and carries around his head shots, as if maybe some casting director will stop him on the street. He thinks of himself as a director-playwright-actor-producer, but I've yet to hear about anything theatrical he's been involved in, other than renovating a theater in New Jersey. And of course the daily drama of his own life.

Trevor likes to stare at people, to make them feel uncomfortable. He hits on women with a decent level of success. He says to me one night, after I've been on the team for two weeks, lowering his eyelids seductively, tucking a curl behind his ear and rubbing his sexy, sandpapery stubble, "I want to be your lover." He's completely serious. I'm so flabbergasted I have no response at first. "I'm just putting it out there," he adds. Then, stating the obvious: "What can I say? I'm direct." I politely decline his offer—which I find myself doing repeatedly—though I can't say the solicitations offend me.

Trevor's hair is soft and lush, an inviting thicket that wafts romantically behind his ears when the wind blows, as if he's some swashbuckling hero from the eighteenth century. He has deep brown eyes framed by long lashes that curl up at the tips. But the sensitive features stop there: His face is tough, Irish, unforgiving, his neck thick. Years of construction work have helped cultivate rippling muscles that he shows off in tank tops and ripped T-shirts. He's a dark, compelling character, but I enter his life at the tail end of its unraveling. I never knew Trevor when he was the exuberant, fast-talking ad man full of promise, with a young family and a golden life in some other part of the country.

Trevor's from Texas, though his twang has been smoothed over the years into a deep, husky purr. He never speaks of his family there; no one knows if there are any siblings or grandparents or cousins, or even parents, for that matter. It's as if he emerged, fully formed, from the piney woods, where he walked straight to the nearest baseball diamond and hit a ball so far that it was rumored to have landed in a parking lot in Arkansas. He's a glorious athlete—football, cross-country, basketball—but baseball is his true gift. He has major-league scouts looking at him when he's a teenager, and eventually a small Southern college gives him a four-year scholarship in exchange for consistently dazzling his coaches on the field, until he messes up his knee, twists it cruelly during some gravity-defying dive into a fence or a base or home plate—the story tends to change—and spends his final year on the bench, his knee now crisscrossed with surgical scars, his temper stretched to the breaking point as scouts come to watch the newest crop of Jesuses to emerge fully formed from the piney woods somewhere, with free rides of their own.

So Trevor leaves the sleepy South in a rage, determined to change his luck, to be the golden boy again. He ends up in a big Midwestern city where he talks his way into an ad agency and a year later is running a whole division. He earns a huge salary, gets invited to parties at the boss's house, which has a swimming pool and a gazebo, meets a beautiful woman from a wealthy, prominent family, and marries her. They soon have a son. His life is perfect. The only trace of the raw deal he still sometimes feels he's gotten is the scars that are now fading to a soft, bumpy pink on his leg.

But here's where the story gets confusing, because something goes terribly awry with Trevor, and it's hard to figure out exactly when it happened or why, but it certainly can't be blamed solely on the premature end of his baseball career. First, he gets fired—not laid off because of budgetary reasons but escorted to the door by a hulking security guard for much darker reasons. He says it's because he looks out for his people, not himself, that he won't lie to them, won't capitulate to The Man. Then his marriage ends, badly, and his wife's influential family gets involved, and it's ugly and public and he loses all privileges regarding his son. He isn't even granted visitation rights—again, because of some "conspiracy" that's been designed to undermine his strong will, his streak of iconoclasm.

Trevor makes it seem as if he's been run out of town by the sheriff. He comes to New York to reinvent himself and becomes hell-bent on expressing his peculiar, angry, self-serving vision of the world in the theater. He will be an actor (he's certainly charismatic enough), and he will finally explain it all. He will rehabilitate his tarnished image, and his genius will be revealed. But except for the head shots and building a few stage sets, that hasn't happened. It's been five years since he came to the city, five years since he's seen or talked to his son or his family. He writes letters to his son, who's eight years old now, he says, but he suspects they're never given to the boy, they're probably intercepted and most likely burned.

He runs out of money and loses his apartment. He's able to get sporadic construction work, and, through his web of offbeat friends and the women who've fallen under his spell, he's managed to find floors to crash on and beds to sleep in for almost a year. He has some books and some clothes and a beautiful pool cue, which he brings with him to each new tenement. He drinks and he picks fights and he plays pool and he seems to take up for every fired bartender or kicked-out band member in town. He is for the downtrodden, always.

He's also now thirty-eight years old. And if it wasn't for Roger buying his drinks and slipping him a couple hundred dollars when he's between construction gigs, I really think Trevor would be sleeping on the street.

He's not without grace. I see flashes of the man he once was, we all do, and they usually appear, fleetingly but memorably, during a game of pool.

Trevor's a good pool player who is occasionally brilliant. He can come up with tournament-level moves when he wants to. But his play is so erratic and so dependent on his mood and the amount of alcohol in his system that his league rank—he's a 4—will probably never go up. He's stuck in pool, just as he's stuck in every other aspect of his life. But somehow he doesn't see this as his fault. Rather, it's the fault of the world for misunderstanding him.

He brings to my mind a line from *The Hustler*, when George C. Scott, playing the role of sinister stakehorse Bert Gordon, says to Fast Eddie Felson, "All you gotta do is learn to feel sorry for yourself. It's one of the best indoor sports, feeling sorry for yourself. Sport enjoyed by all. Especially the born losers." Eddie sets out to prove Bert wrong, but in the end, though he returns and beats Minnesota Fats, there's something sad and Pyrrhic about his victory. A similar pall falls over Trevor's games. His expertly crafted wins, when they occur, provide only a flicker of pleasure. They seem merely to remind him of everything else he's lost.

What do I have in common with a tormented guy like Trevor? Or guys like Paul G. and Gary? Why do I desire, at age thirty-two, to surround myself with human wrecks who exhibit occasional bursts of beauty?

As I get to know them, the pool players I meet strike me the same way the East Village strikes me: as a contradictory presence. They appear to need no one and yet also seem unbearably lonely. When I think of my own loneliness—my feeling out of place in the jabbering, fast-paced New York circle I'm in—I realize how private it feels, how embarrassing. I also realize, after I join Paul G.'s pool team, that what I feel when I play alongside someone like Trevor is a strange kind of kinship. I revel in this unspoken solidarity while I'm with my dark-souled teammates, but I leave it at the door on my way out, using it—and, if I'm honest with myself, using them—to fortify myself. This is why I don't find myself leaving anguished messages on people's cell phones.

There is no question that for Paul G. and Gary and Trevor, pool, and where it is played, serves a much more vital purpose than just recreation. Pool bars function as their offices, as their relationships, as their connections to the world or their buffers from it. This is an entirely new landscape for me, both physically—dark and small and cramped and dangerous—and psychologically (also dark and small and cramped and dangerous). That landscape can change quickly, which is the other magnet that draws me to pool, and to the lives of pool players. Every Monday, when I enter a bar with a pool table in the back, my teammates sprawled on bar stools or slouching near the rack of cues, Liz raising an eyebrow and giving me a nod and a smile as I make my way toward the inner sanctum, feeling just a little superior as I pass the non-pool-playing patrons, I feel a sense of anticipation, a tingling apprehension. *Anything can happen tonight. Anything.*

Is this the real appeal? Do I secretly want to step into my own downward spiral, sleep with "rough trade," become an unwitting participant in shady drug deals, learn how to hustle and cheat and identify "marks," make strange, late-night calls from pay phones to mysterious friends in far-flung places, live my own Elizabeth Wurtzel, tragi-chic dysfunctional existence until a kindly therapist, who bears an uncanny resemblance to Robin Williams or Whoopi Goldberg, pulls me out of it?

No. I don't think so.

I am not an adrenaline junkie, nor do I have a particular desire to associate with "bad characters." But the distance between fear and joy is, not surprisingly, quite short, and the journey from one to the other is, more often than not, quite thrilling, no matter which direction you're heading.

Melissa Holbrook Pierson addresses this sensation in her intelligent, passionate, and eccentric book *The Perfect Vehicle: What It Is About Motorcycles.* The risks associated with motorcycle riding are obvious and real: One mistake, one wobbly turn, or one slick, badly lit road can cost you your life, or at least your limbs. In trying to present for nonriders the reasons that sane human beings find themselves caught up with these machines, Pierson tries to break down the components of danger, of risk. She starts by addressing the work of Michael J. Apter, who wrote *Dangerous Edge: The Psychology of Excitement.* He points out that "anxiety and excitement produce the same physiological response." The chemicals that course through us when we are faced with these emotions make us either want to run from the cause or embrace and enjoy it, depending on the situation.

The application to motorcycle riding is obvious. The application to my frequenting pool establishments is no less so, I think.

The pull for me is not the scruffiness of certain players, or the hair-trigger aspect of certain situations, though on occasion both qualities contribute to my anxiety and excitement levels. Rather, it's the rush of being able to emerge from a dark corner—both literally and metaphorically—and live inside this elegant, sexy, often maddening game, this strange, subterranean world where my background is meaningless, my voice, even my posture is different, to stand front and center, forced to draw from another part of myself, a part that's less sure but perhaps more interesting, to feed off the smoke and music and amber bottles, the growling guys in sinister boots—hell, the growling women in sinister boots—and to stay focused, to prevail, to shut out everything except this one moment at a pool table. It may not be the same as having a throttle in my hand, as having wind in my hair as I take a turn moving at heart-pumping speeds, but it's damn close.

Pierson writes that motorcycles "can red-flag fear, call it out from its dark hiding place. They let us shadow-box with it, then give it the old cathartic heave-ho." That's what it's like on Mondays at the bar. That's the appeal of danger, and the appeal, to me, of pool. It calls out my fear, then kicks its butt. Sometimes, though, I get kicked back.

Mexico

NOT LONG AFTER I pick up a pool cue for the first time, I decide to take a vacation, my first in some time. This one will be different from my previous "nutritious" holiday excursions: no earnest sightseeing, no museum tours accompanied by headphones that provide soothing, patrician voices to explain the paintings of Paul Klee or the origins of a Ming Dynasty vase. No hiking or backpacks taller than I am or learning how to get in touch with my inner yogi through meditation, herbal teas, and vinyasa poses. The point of going to a remote bit of the Mexican coast along Baja California is to lie in the sun, gambol in the surf, paddle about kidney-shaped pools, and have beautiful tanned boys bring me umbrella drinks while I read books and talk to no one. My mission is successful. I do all of these things.

I eat well in the evenings, drinking good wine and eating grilled fish and crunchy, tasty breads; I indulge in a massage; I take a long boat ride; I stare at the horizon every night and watch painfully gorgeous sunsets. I walk barefoot on cool marble and finger painted trinkets in overpriced, inauthentic bazaars geared to people like me.

It's just what I need, just what everyone needs at least once in their life.

And then I get restless.

One night, near my hotel, I come upon an innocent-looking cantina. It's close enough to where I'm staying that I assume it's safe and caters to a mix of visitors and locals. What draws me inside is that when I peek through the door I see a pool table, with no one playing on it. It sits, abandoned and forlorn, in a dusty, dimly lit room the color of a Kraft caramel.

I walk inside. The place is nearly empty, except for three people: a squat, laconic bartender; a weathered, sandy-haired guy sitting at the bar nursing a *cerveza* and a glass of something amber and cloudy; and a slight, scrawny-chested Mexican kid with an acne-scarred face who looks like maybe he works at a nearby hotel and has just ended his shift.

All three of them stare brazenly at me when I walk in. I order a beer, then take it over to the pool table, which is covered with the standard green cloth. It's pockmarked and knotty, clearly past its prime. I select a cue from a large can in the corner. There are several cues, all of them junky and warped, sticking up like mop handles in a bucket. The guy slumped at the bar with his drinks is watching me, his expression sour. He has the boozy, wet eyes and bloated face of a professional drunk. He could be thirty-five or sixty-five—it's hard to say. He seems American to me, like a man who came here on a business trip years ago and never left, simply went on a bender that has continued for a decade. The kid and the bartender speak in low Spanish, laughing quietly.

I rack the balls and attempt to break with one of the crappy cues. The table is small and slightly tilted. The balls barely move.

This is ridiculous. It's as if the balls on this table have been glued together. I re-rack and try a second time, with similar results. More laughter from the bar. It's directed at me, and it's pissing me off.

Ignoring the anvil chorus at the bar, I hit the cue ball into the remaining mess, not wanting to re-rack yet again, and am able to get a slight spread on the table. The bartender turns on some music, some sort of Latin pop—salsa with a techno beat. I try sinking the green 6-ball in the corner. It's an easy shot, and yet the ball wobbles strangely down the table and doesn't go anywhere near the pocket. I'm not nervous. My stroke seems fine. What's wrong here?

I take a slug of my beer and try another shot, an undramatic cut into the side, with almost identical results. The little group at the bar continues to watch me unabashedly. The American guy still looks angry and unfocused; the two locals look increasingly amused.

I, however, am not. I hit another ball and it misses the pocket. I pick up the 10-ball, place it directly in front of a pocket, line up my shot, follow through, and still the ball won't go in. Something is definitely wrong. Something is cockeyed with the table. It has to be some kind of fix, some kind of joke, like those birthday candles that can never be blown out. I drink furiously from my beer bottle. The guys at the bar are having a field day, laughing at my expense. The bartender finally comes over, the skinny kid following him. The sunburned American lush doesn't move from his seat.

The bartender, chortling, speaks to me in Spanish. He beckons to the cue I'm holding. "Here, here" he says. I hand it to him and watch as he moves a ball close to the rail. He aims and shoots, trying to hit it down the length of the table into the far corner pocket. At the last moment, the ball bounces away as if an invisible rubber shield protects the pocket. I am greatly relieved; his missing the shot makes me feel like slightly less of a jackass. His young comrade bursts into laughter, pointing at him, then at me, teasing us both in Spanish. The bartender sets up another shot, and this time he nails it. He gives the cue to the kid, who proceeds to sink the first shot he takes, an easy, loping 7 into the side pocket. It's similar to some of the shots I've been taking—and missing. Again, I have the strong feeling that something is wrong with the table, that perhaps it is so warped that only someone who knows its vagaries can play on it.

"You play?" the kid asks me.

"Yeah, I play," I say, grabbing the cue back.

"Wooo-eee!" the bartender catcalls. The kid backs up in mock-terror. "Be nice," he says, and wags a finger at me. The American drunk mutters something, his eyes slits, his tall glass almost drained.

The two young men speak to each other in Spanish and go back to the bar, leaving me to stomp to the table, take another easy, no-nonsense shot, and watch as the object ball curves insanely away from the pocket at the last minute, as if it's being pulled by a string.

It doesn't occur to me, as I glower and drink my beer and slam the balls around, that I am alone in an unpopular cantina in Mexico, with three men I don't know, who are speaking a language I don't know. And surrounded by a lot of alcohol.

It's an unbelievably stupid situation to put myself in. I look up and see that it's now dark outside. No one else has come by. The three men at the bar are no longer talking, and they certainly aren't smiling. They look at me from under heavy eyes.

I begin to sweat. I can feel the men watching me. My beer is empty. I put the cue back in the basket and begin to scrape the balls together.

I leave a fifty-peso note on the bar as I'm leaving. The door is closed. It hadn't been when I arrived. The men begin to talk in low voices again. I feel their gaze on my body but don't look back, just fling open the door and thrust myself into the hot, humid night. I hurry down the street and pause to get my bearings. No one is following me. I can see my hotel in the distance and a path leading toward it. My heartbeat slows and I walk back to where I'm staying, wondering if my sudden fear is the result of too many sensationalized crime stories, or from some sort of survival instinct. Probably a little of both.

I make it to my room, which now seems startlingly lavish com-pared with where I've just been. I lock the door, close the curtains, pour some bottled water into a glass, flick on the TV, and flop on the bed, safe, relaxed, relieved.

Not half an hour later the phone rings, which startles me out of my daze. I answer, and a man speaks to me in Spanish. I assume it's a wrong number, a confused guest perhaps, and say as much, politely, before hanging up. A few minutes later the phone rings again. I answer, and it's the same voice again, only this time it seems familiar. He speaks to me in Spanish, laughing throatily. I hang up quickly, my mouth dry. It has to be one of the men from the bar. No, that's crazy. I hadn't given them my name; how could they have tracked me down?

The phone rings a third time. Bolt-upright and panicked, I pick up the receiver tremulously. Same voice, same laughter. This time I hear Latin techno-pop in the background. It has to be the bar. "Stop calling me! I'm calling the police!" I scream and slam down the phone.

Frantic, I double-check the locks on my doors and windows. Then I call downstairs and ask to speak with a manager. A man with an unctuous voice comes on the line. I explain to him that I am being harassed, that someone is calling my room, that I am worried it's someone who saw me at the bar with the weird pool table and followed me.

My voice is calm, but the man does not seem to take me seriously. "We are very safe here," he says.

"Yes, I know, but I'm worried, because this person has called three times in ten minutes."

When I checked into the hotel—which is beautiful and airy and modern, the color of a sunset—there had been some raised eyebrows when it was revealed that I was not there with a husband or a boyfriend, nor on business. That I was alone.

The manager says to me now, "Hey, you never know. Maybe he's nice. Maybe you'd have a good time."

I am quiet, stunned into silence. My going to a bar and shooting pool by myself says to him that I've asked for this, that I am getting what's coming to me. He doesn't voice this sentiment, of course, but I am feeling it coming from the other end of the phone. And then all cultural sensitivity flies out the window. I am enraged. I remind him, in rather loud and vivid terms, what will happen to him if something happens to me. By the end of our brief conversation he apologizes and says he will send up someone from security to have a look around, that he'll have him check later, too, and that I shouldn't worry.

I am mildly reassured. My worry isn't so much about my safety anymore, but about what I've just done, the situation I've put myself in. Yes, I am an enthusiastic pool player who saw a table and, rather logically, went over to play on it. But am I really doing something else? Do I want to create the story of the ragged cantina, of the tough-looking banditos, of the fiery, raven-haired pool player temptress who briefly glows in their presence? I am a woman with an enormous amount of good sense and intelligence, and yet I walked into that cantina alone. Why did I stay? I finished my beer, for God's sake. I tried to conquer that ridiculous, practical joke of a table, and now some idiot is calling my room for kicks.

I am far away and alone, and not because I'm in Mexico.

The Church of the Good Hustle

MY EXPERIENCE IN MEXICO does not turn me off to pool. When I return, I feel like a child who's had her hand slapped after ignoring a parent's warnings and reaching for something sharp. So I simply rein myself in a little, until I've played the game longer. I don't need to seek out pool adventures in foreign countries, since I can find enough pool drama right here in New York City, even—and especially—within my own team.

Despite the sense of foreboding that surrounds the players who provide this drama—players like Trevor and Roger, with their dark pasts, strange career paths, and unpredictable mood swings—I get used to league life: late Monday nights, sporadic practice at pool halls around the city in my spare time, frustration, exhilaration. I've been shooting pool for almost two years now. Mexico soon feels like an experience from another lifetime.

I'm also no longer showing up at pool school. Part of this change in routine is due to my continued desire not to see Wally, who still teaches there. But part of it is due to my feeling that I simply don't need pool school anymore. I've gained confidence; I'm more comfortable playing in front of other people. In short, I'm getting cocky.

My first pool team, the one I played on with Wally, went to the APA playoffs once. I suppose the first murmurs of cockiness began there: I was the only one to win my match that night (I'd been put up against the opposing team's weakest player). Everyone else on the team went down in flames. I have not come close to a playoff game since then, but that doesn't mean that my pool isn't improving—and attracting some notice.

An aging, failed actor I see all the time at The Wrong Side, a block-shaped fellow they call Bald Jack, his pate as slick and white as the cue ball in front of him, who has to walk slowly because of some health problems he won't discuss, turns from his bar stool one night as I'm scooting by and, grabbing my arm gently, says, "Heather, you're getting better."

I've exchanged maybe a few words with him over the course of a year—I wasn't aware he even knew my name. I stop, surprised and a bit charmed, then press him, making sure he isn't trying to pull some sort of pickup.

"You hold yourself completely different now," he says. "I see you in here every week, and you're so intense, you get so frustrated when you miss a shot, and so you miss more. You never looked confident before. But you just seem so much more relaxed now. I noticed it a coupla weeks ago. In your shoulders, your face. You keep it up." He points his finger at me. "You keep practicing. If you can stand 'em, and I know it's hard"—he smiles and we both look over at Paul G., who's dancing nervously on the balls of his feet like a scrawny boxer, and then at Trevor, who sits glowering in a corner as usual, arms folded defiantly across his chest, and Roger, who's doing an impersonation of some celebrity and is laughing hysterically at himself, even though no one else is—"if you can stand 'em, you learn from 'em and you practice. You'll keep getting better. I can tell." I nod at

Jack, thank him, say "okay," and continue to the other end of the bar, where I order a beer and wait for Maura, the bartender, to get to me, not able to stop my smile.

Even more delicious for me than the performance review from Bald Jack is the time I'm accused of hustling. The accusation is made somewhat under the breath, rather than confrontationally, but still, it's lobbed out there, in front of my teammates, and it thrills me, in part because it's so preposterous.

Books have been written, studies conducted, and movies made about the seedy, iconic American character known as the hustler. There's an allure, an electricity, a reverence associated with the term, despite—or perhaps because of—its dark, ominous, endlessly varying connotations. The first exchange in the movie *The Hustler* provides a pointed introduction to the word's place in the cynical American vernacular of the down-and-out. The film begins with Eddie Felson's friend and first financial backer, Charlie (played by Myron McCormick), gazing at the almost empty pool room in the nameless town the two men are passing through. "Quiet," he remarks. Eddie replies, "Yeah, like a church. The church of the good hustle."

My hustle, it turns out, is that I don't have one: I'm petite, I'm polite, and I have a tendency to lose the first game of my match because of performance anxiety. Thus, I'm usually written off early, with my opponent often not realizing—until it's too late—that I will become more comfortable—and shoot better—as the games progress. During one such match in a small, briny-smelling bar near the Hudson River, I bungle the first game, but by game three I have made an extraordinary length-of-the-table bank shot and am slicing balls into the side pockets with the precision of a surgeon. It's an unusually high-level performance for me, but the opposing team's captain is not convinced. "Nice shot, *two*," he snarls after my bank shot goes in the pocket. His teammate (my opponent) stands helplessly as I set up my next shot. "Another good one, *two*," the captain says after I cut in my next ball and leave myself in perfect position to sink another ball. "What is this?" he hisses to another teammate. "She's a two? This is a two shooting here? Gimme the damn score sheet." I continue my prance around the table while his finger slides down the score sheet and he looks up my rank. He doesn't say a word for the rest of the match, which I win. My teammates chortle and shake their heads throughout my display. They're familiar with my routine—and also with the notion of a game clicking for no apparent reason. They recognize the capriciousness, the unpredictability of a pool match—and the mistake of someone ignoring this facet of the game, the mistake of thinking the small, polite girl with the weak first game won't come alive.

When the match is over, I shake my opponent's hand. I shrug and smile my good-natured, I-don't-know-what-happened smile. I really don't know what happened; I simply had a great feel for the table that night. In my mind, it's my opponent's fault for underestimating me, for thinking I'm not formidable.

While my pretend "hustle" is completely unreliable (sometimes my losing that first game is a strong indicator that I will lose the second and third games as well), that does not mean that there aren't players in the league who aspire to bring hustling to an art form—and sometimes succeed. These charming wannabe Eddie Felsons glide through the bars of lower Manhattan with pleasant smiles and peaceful faces, like priests in cassocks, relaxing their opponents' defenses so that they can take them by surprise, jabbing with knives no one knows they have hidden under their robes.

HECTOR SILVA STALKS the bar like the anointed cool kid in high school, his eyes searching to see who's noticing him, his gait self-consciously swaggering, his fleeting smirk practiced, his dark hair, streaked with gold from a bottle, tightly coiffed after what must be a long period of time in front of a mirror in a tiny apartment somewhere. That Hector is just shy of forty makes this spectacle funny and rather pathetic, though he doesn't seem to think so.

Hector tops out at about five-four and I doubt he weighs more than one hundred and twenty pounds. He's narrow and knobby-kneed but carries himself as if he's barrel-chested and burly, unbuttoning most of the buttons on his shirt to reveal smooth, caffe-latte skin and bad taste in jewelry. He douses himself with cologne and wears stacked boots to give him a little more height. His head is big and round and seems to float above his body like a helium balloon, bobbing in time to his endless running conversation. Hector's large brown eyes remind me of whis-key. They peer out from under his much-talked-about "do," making him look almost baleful.

Hector rolls his R's and hams up his Latin loverboy routine, but he takes himself—and pool—very seriously. People tend to laugh at Hector, not with him, but it would be a mistake to think him harmless, because he is one of the more devious pool players I've encountered—patient and cunning and, unlike me, a bit of a hustler.

Hector likes having women around him, he'll tell you that straight off, but he doesn't particularly like playing against them in pool. He hates losing, but he hates losing to a woman even more. Perhaps this is why he makes it a point to sexualize every pool-playing encounter he has with a woman, no matter her age or occupation or sexual preference. It's as if he thinks that whispering to her of his prowess in bed will make her weak in the knees and thus easier to beat. Or perhaps it will humiliate her, make her embarrassed, angry, defiant, ashamed, but with the same result: She'll be off her game. It could also be that Hector really wants to talk about his prowess in bed.

Without a shred of irony, Hector boasts, loudly and regularly, about the size of his member. If he is to be believed, it is so impressive that women have gasped in its presence, never to be the same.

"Oh, Christ, is Hector talking about his dick again? Because I had a late lunch today and I'd really like to keep it down." This from

Maura, the sexy, sneering bartender at The Wrong Side, who is drawing beers for several customers on a busy night and is in no mood for Hector. She casts a withering glance in his direction. He grins and gives her an "I can't help myself" shrug. Then he slinks to my side of the bar. He's been trying to chat me up the past few weeks and I've been trying to avoid him, but tonight I'm cornered.

"You going to play tonight?"

"I don't know. I guess. If Paul G. puts me up."

"Paul, man, he's got some problems, you know. Your team needs a new captain."

"Yeah, I know."

"Roger, he's really your captain, you know? You should tell Paul G. to step down and just make it Roger. You know, officially like."

"Yup. I agree." I take a sip of my beer. Hector looks at me intently.

"So you look very nice, as usual. I notice that you wear perfume." He raises his eyebrows provocatively.

"I do sometimes."

"Well, I'm complimenting you. You smell nice."

"Thank you."

Now he lowers his eyelids and gazes at me in a manner that I guess is supposed to make me swoon. He hoists up one heavy-booted foot and puts it on a nearby chair, giving me the full-on rock-star treatment.

"So, you know, we should play pool sometime. Or just go out. I show you a good time." He raises his eyebrows again and actually casts his glance downward, at his "package." I am incredulous and pretend I haven't heard him.

"How old are you?" he asks abruptly.

I tell him my age (thirty-three), and he seems for once truly shocked. "Wow, I would not have guessed that. You look very young."

"I am young, Hector."

"I know, I know. You know what I mean. Are you married?"

"No, I'm not."

"That's a surprise to me. I will say this: You act different from your age."

"What do you mean?"

"You comport yourself like a married woman."

"What? What the hell does that mean?"

"Well, you know, I could show you a good time, but you sit there, so polite."

"So any woman who doesn't drop dead over you must be married, I take it?"

"Please. The married ones, they come to me, too." He says this with a smarmy grin and another raise of the eyebrows. I look at him standing there, leaning on one knee like a pint-size Marlboro Man, with his streaked hair and exposed chest and musky cologne, and wonder how he even came into being. Could this routine really be working for him?

"I'm sure they do, Hector."

He removes his foot from the chair, gives me a tight-lipped smile and a little bow, and says, "I will leave you. But you think about it."

I'm not sure what I'm supposed to be thinking about. I attempt a dead-eyed prosecutor's stare, but he's gone, bobbing toward the bar, looking for someone younger perhaps, or older, or married, or divorced, or recently released from a convent.

I relay the encounter to Liz later, full of my own vivid asides. She remains quiet until I'm through, and then, lowering her dark eyes and looking at me with as much seriousness as she can muster, she says, "Hector used the word 'comport'?"

HECTOR'S HUSTLE—trying to get women to go home with him—is not, in fact, his real hustle; he uses his constant pursuit of women to distract people from his real con, which is sandbagging at pool.

The sandbagger is a type that pops up regularly in pool leagues, and it's one that can't be ignored. Sandbagging is when a league player intentionally plays below his ability, stacking his game with innings and safeties (also called "nonperformance shots") as a way of keeping his rank down, because if he keeps his rank down, he has to win fewer games to prevail in a match. Thus he can actually rack up more wins by not playing his best. Pool is, after all, a game of millimeters, and if you have excellent speed control and a good eye and can manipulate those precious millimeters to your advantage, well, you're golden. Like any hustle, the idea is to do it so stealthily that your opponent—and especially the other team's captain—doesn't know it.

I can—and much to my chagrin, often do—lose several games in a row in a match, but if those games are long and drawn out, with many innings (my matches have gone as long as two and a half hours and have topped out at thirty-three innings) and with many defensive shots, I'm not going to go *down* in rank even if I ultimately lose the match. The APA's thinking is that if I'm able to put up that much of a fight against someone ranked higher than me, then I obviously have some skill, just not enough to beat my opponent.

The sandbagger tries to replicate artificially what I do naturally. He drags out matches against someone he knows he can beat so that he doesn't go *up* in rank. If he keeps easily beating 5's and 6's, he'll go up, no question. But if he turns in a score sheet that makes it seem as if he barely eked out a win against his opponents, then he gets the W and his rank stays the same: He won't go up. This means he'll stay, say, a 4, and will continue to have to win only a few games to prevail against these guys—and against lower-ranked players like me.

Sandbagging is illegal in the APA league. Roger can always spot those who do it. Despite his jovial, back-slapping demeanor, he is very aware of who is trustworthy and who isn't. He knows how everyone in our division plays and he can tell when someone is missing a shot on purpose. He says, for example, that Hector is a master sandbagger, and that he encourages and teaches his teammates to do the same. I believe him. Hector's a 3—the same rank as me—which is just short of a miracle, since he should probably be a 5. He takes an inordinate amount of time when it's his turn at the table, plays a safety on just about every shot, rarely shoots to make a ball until the very end of a game, acts disappointed when he "misses," then manages to bring it all home in the deciding game. What do you know, Hector won after all, just pulled it out of his hat. But unless it can be proved, there's nothing anyone can do about it.

It takes a lot of time, practice, and patience to become an expert sandbagger, but this isn't usually a problem, since most avid pool players have few interests outside pool. Most choose one pool bar and make it their home, and in some cases that's not even a metaphor. For people like Trevor and Paul G. and Hector, their pool bar is the place where they eat, blow off steam, get drunk, take phone calls, watch TV, make plans for the future, hide from their pasts. If they lose this place—as Trevor does when the owner of The Wrong Side finally cuts him off, and then eventually throws him out and tells him never to come back—it can be as devastating as having a spouse walk out, taking the kids, the dog, and the car.

There are more Trevors and Hectors and Paul G.'s in pool bars than there are Rogers or Lizzes, which might lead one to conclude that there is an us-against-them vibe in urban pool establishments, that when someone like me walks in from the street, a *New Yorker* magazine tucked in my bag, I won't be welcome. Not true. If you can shoot—or even if you can't shoot better than your blind great-aunt but truly love the game—then you can take a seat alongside any pool table in any New York pool establishment and not have a problem. With the exception of a few errant crazies like Gary, people from different backgrounds mix better in a pool bar than in any other place I've ever encountered.

The few die-hard, go-to-hell types I've met through my league, like Trevor, tend to direct their anger toward the world outside the bar, not within it. They know it's possible, even likely, that people can belong to both worlds. They accept newcomers in a way that the world doesn't always accept them, subconsciously righting a wrong, I suppose. When Trevor's anger at and envy of Roger boils over into vitriolic phone messages, it is, at that point, far away from the world of pool. Trevor's boundaries—the ones that most pool players keep intact—have dissolved.

I suppose one of the reasons for a pool bar's ready acceptance of outsiders is that a pool table is so pure in its function as a reflector of ability. Either you make the shot or you don't. Or either you make the shot pretty or you make it ugly. Perhaps you're good enough to hustle, or perhaps you're so inconsistent that sometimes you just lose it and snap a cue in half. Maybe you can play after drinking six beers; maybe you crumble after one.

And maybe, like me—and many before me—you arrive timid and awestruck and awkward, missing more shots than you make, applying boneheaded logic to tricky situations and paying for it, and then slowly, over time, and after obvious practice and struggle, you improve in front of people who you think aren't noticing but who never miss *anything*, not even the tiniest, subtlest difference. And when they tell you you're doing well, it isn't a hustle.

12

English as a Second Language

THE SUMMER NIGHT is thick and hot, and I'm done playing, ready to go home, but Roger persuades me to have one more beer with him. Despite Bald Jack's encouraging pronouncement a few weeks ago that I'm "getting better," and the accompanying rise in my confidence that follows, I lose my match tonight. Roger wins his and, as usual, is feeling garrulous, so I sit with him for another beer, my sundress sticking to me even though I'm directly under the fan. It's been a low-key night for a change. No outbursts from Trevor, and a minimum of petulance from Paul G. Gary couldn't make it—he's under the gun on a freelance deadline—and Liz leaves early to do laundry.

So Roger and I sit, sticky and languid, while he rattles on about the aging, cantankerous senior partner in his office. Then, abruptly changing the subject, he turns to me and says, "Let's go to Brooklyn."

I'm surprised—and touched—by the overture. It means that not only is my game improving, but my status on the team is rising, too. My presence, week after week, has become expected. I'm on the inside now, I think, looking at Roger's relaxed, pleasant face. His offer makes me feel accepted. And something else, too. My pulse quickens as the precise meaning of this suggestion starts to seep through. I know if I allow myself any more time to think about it, the night will be over before it begins.

"Okay," I say.

Since I came to the bar straight from work, I have several handbags of varying sizes with me, stuffed with screenplays and short, pithy script summaries and early copies of book manuscripts and memos from the L.A. office about how we need to stay away from "soft, character-driven pieces" and focus more on "potential franchises" and "properties that can attract A-list talent. Think: a contemporary *The English Patient*. And: Who is the next John Grisham? Find him," plus my red pool case, which Roger grabs as we head out. I herd my stuff into the cab he hails. Roger slouches in the seat and says, "I can't believe I'm doing this." I give the cab driver the address of a bar a block from my apartment. I hate the place, a cheerful, noisy pub that seems to play nothing but Van Morrison and shoves its bonhomie in your face, all benches and picnic tables and faux-Irish bartenders and people wearing "vintage" baseball caps. But I don't know where else to go. Roger is moody and I am serene as the cab rumbles over the Manhattan Bridge.

When the taxi comes to a halt, Roger pays the driver and we get out and go inside the pub. It isn't terribly crowded, which is unusual. Roger sits demurely at the bar and orders a seltzer, embarrassed, I think, at being drunk. I order one as well. Then the tension eases and we run through the usual laundry list of topics, talking, as we've done many times before, about where we grew up, went to school, our romantic lives, why Roger never votes. It's easy and relaxing, as always.

But it isn't long before we reach the Long Silence part of the conversation. We sit quietly, pretending to be engrossed in our fizzy water. The mood has shifted.

"So is this, like, your hangout?" Roger finally ventures.

"No, not really. It's just convenient."

He sips his seltzer. He doesn't look like he's enjoying it.

"I'm so embarrassed," he says.

"Why?"

"I'm just trying to sober up here. Ask me something else."

I try to think of something, but before I can, Roger says, "Shelly and I are sort of separated." He hangs his head.

This is new. "What does that mean? Has she moved out?"

"It means I'm sleeping on the couch."

"Well, that happens sometimes. Maybe it's just a bad patch."

"No, I mean, she's really had it with me. She wants me to look for a place to stay while she sorts things out, or whatever, and she's letting me stay on the couch until I find somewhere to crash. God, I feel like Trevor." Roger shakes his head. He laughs, but ruefully. I remain quiet, nursing my seltzer. I'm not sure why we need to go to a bar for each of us to have a seltzer, but going straight to my place seems a little reckless, and not something Roger and I would do. He has a need to talk, and I have a need to figure out just what the hell is going on and what I'm feeling.

"I've kind of fucked up." He sighs. "Shelly's really a homebody, you know. She hates to go out, hates to leave the neighborhood. She goes to bed at like nine thirty every night."

"Maybe she's depressed." Roger's eyes widen and he pulls back a little, startled.

"*Hmmm*, maybe. She is sort of a depressive, now that I think about it. She takes things hard. You know, gets upset. Like when her co-worker OD'd. And when her cousin went nuts and had to go to the psych ward."

"Well, those aren't small things, Roger."

"I know, but she kind of reacts the same way when she can't get a cab." I smile, but he's being serious.

"So what happened?"

"*Ahhh.*" He waves his hand in front of his face, as if at some imaginary billow of smoke, which seems to remind him that he doesn't have a cigarette in his hand. This is before New York's smoking ban, so he fishes one out of his pocket and lights up. The process seems to take a long time. He finally exhales a satisfying plume.

"Like I said, I screwed up. I keep going out and partying, staying out later and later. Last week I got home one night at like five a.m. I'd been playing pool and then just stayed out, and when I came in I guess I passed out on the couch. She got up at like seven thirty to get ready for work and found me sprawled on the couch with one foot on the floor and my arm dangling down in some crazy position. My hand was asleep. I was missing a shoe. From the nice pair that she gave me. I don't know where it is; I still haven't found it. I think I may have lost it outside. She'd been all worried about me, thought something terrible had happened, which is understandable, but Christ, I've got a cell phone. I guess I must've had it turned off." Roger takes another drag, less thick and more contemplative than the previous one.

"She calls me *Leaving Las Vegas* now, you know, as a nickname. Have you ever seen that movie, with Nicolas Cage?"

I tell him I have. I remind him that the main character drinks himself to death. Roger smiles and lifts up his glass of seltzer, as if he's making a toast. "Yeah, I know, I know, I'm trying to change. Shelly hates pool, you know, hates that I play pool, hates my team. She was asking questions about you. I guess I mentioned you, said you read a lot of books, too." I remember Shelly's book club. I find the notion of my being discussed in the Roger-Shelly household flattering and alarming. I hope Shelly doesn't have any *Fatal Attraction* tendencies.

"I wish I could give all my money away," Roger says suddenly.

Roger makes statements like this sometimes, out of the blue, when he's somewhere deep inside his head. I shift on my stool. The music in the bar—some Eric Clapton song—feels unbearably loud to me.

"I'd like to start my own law firm, make a ton of money, then just do nothing but pro bono work, or give all the money to Amnesty International. I'd like to go back to Bangkok"—he'd visited Thailand a couple of months ago—"and help out people who had their lives ruined by poverty and crime." He's as impassioned as I've ever seen him. "That plan wouldn't include Shelly, of course. She'd think everyone we met was hiding a hand grenade."

"I think that's really noble, Roger, I really do, and I'm not trying to be patronizing, but why don't you start by trying to fix your own life, as cliché as that may sound."

"Yeah, yeah, I know. But the thing is, even though I like to party, I don't *have* to. I can go a long time without drinking a drop and I don't crave it or anything." My face must reveal my skepticism because he adds, "And I'm not an idiot, I know that's what everyone says. But with me it's true."

I nod. It isn't worth arguing about at 2:00 in the morning in a bar that should be on a college campus somewhere. I'm growing sleepy.

"You wanna go?" he says, tentative, grinning.

"Sure." I watch as he stands up from his stool and places some money on the bar. For our two seltzers. It's sort of comical. Then he turns and I clutch his arm.

"Wait. You have to kiss me first. Here in the bar. Before we go." His face flushes; he looks surprised but also delighted. He grabs me and plants a wet, tipsy kiss on my lips. It's sloppy, laced with a tinge of aggression. I resist the urge to wipe my mouth. Instead, I begin the ridiculous, painstaking process of collecting my things. I stand up and say, "Where's my cue?"

Roger's gaze travels to the floor, as does mine. It isn't there. He starts to laugh, his big piano-key teeth filling up his face.

"I left it in the cab," he says.

"Very funny."

He keeps laughing. "No, seriously"—he's in hysterics now—"I left it in the cab."

I freeze. My next reaction is as swift as it is shocking: I begin to cry. I feel my eyes fill and hear myself croak, "I can't believe this. Are you serious? You *lost my cue*?" My voice is thick, heartbroken.

Roger sobers immediately, his cocky smile gone, his eyes huge.

"Oh my God, you're crying. Holy—" He puts his hand over his face and stifles a chortle. "Wait, are you really crying? Holy shit. You are. Oh, God. I am so sorry, I'll get it back. Please, just stop crying."

"You can't get it back, it's in a cab," I wail. "Someone's probably playing pool with it by now." I cannot believe I'm behaving this way, and I cannot understand why I feel as if I've been stabbed. I remember buying the cue at Blatt Billiards the summer before. I've only recently begun to feel as if I've earned the right to own it. The stick has given me both credibility and originality. And I don't even notice when it's gone, rolling around in the back of a cab somewhere like a forgotten umbrella. Now Roger looks sincerely chagrined. He promises to try to track it down or else buy me a new one. I, in the role of the hysterical child, say I don't want a new one, I want *that* one. He looks helpless.

Then, as quickly as it starts, I put a stop to it. In the space of a few seconds I straighten, wipe my eyes, and put it out of my mind. "It's fine," I say. I even manage a smile. What else can I do? Except the obvious. We leave the bar and go to my apartment.

The dynamic is certainly not a new one in the annals of coupling: one person's need serves as another's empowerment.

I don't "bring men home." It's simply not what I do. Not because of any moral position or prudishness, and certainly not because of a lack of desire or hunger. I suppose it's due to the intense amount of energy it takes for me to reveal myself, to undress (figuratively), to let go. I need to make a connection first, and that takes a while.

But I had cried in the bar, something I never do in front of people. Roger had been kicked out of his home, then he'd lost my cue—my first cue—and I had cried, horrified at my own despair. There didn't seem to be a whole lot left to reveal. We'd done enough.

And so tonight, newly stripped of my usual veneer, I think quickly, move purposefully, act boldly, then retreat, curled up and quiet and watchful. It's how I'm learning to behave when I play pool, and it's the first time it's ever spilled into something else.

There's fumbling at the door, soft laughter, the single-file tread up the brownstone's creaking stairway, which lists to one side, making visitors feel as if they might topple over at any moment. We don't turn on a single light, but the apartment's old wooden shutters are open, the windows tall, unadorned, letting in light from the street below, the lush night visible, expansive, a city out there somewhere. I drop my multiple handbags on the floor and step over them, into Roger's arms. Roger keeps hugging me, tightly, and I let him. I never close my eyes. He looks at me in what seems like amazement, studies me intently, as if he's never seen anything like me before. In truth, I think it's his own need he's marveling at. He looks and looks, and then clutches me again, breathing softly. We make our way to my bedroom and roll around on my bed, giggling in the dark, and in the end the encounter doesn't really fulfill its initial sweaty promise, just sort of rolls quietly to shore, like a small wave that's part of another's wake. But I feel different when it's over. I feel vast, immense. Roger, I suspect, feels momentarily soothed, and also confused.

Is it playing pool that's changed me, I wonder? Or was I changing already, and it was this internal transformation that led me to pool? Since I've immersed myself in the game and in the world that comes with it, I've not been myself: I've stuck with it, even though I haven't excelled. My emotional connection to the game has prevailed, has kept me tethered this time, unlike with baseball, where my need to do well led me off the diamond and into an art classroom. This feels like a revelation. It also feels terribly unsophisticated, and very pure. I lie on the bed next to Roger and look back: Becoming enraged at a guy who orders a pizza while we're playing a match; having my heart broken by a lanky, pool-playing cowboy who wants to find "the one"; taking in the quiet beauty of a perfect shot; feeling the excitement as I try to execute a perfect shot of my own, then feeling the dismay as I fall short by a hair; losing, winning, then losing again but still returning, despite disappointment, embarrassment, exposure; being touched by a complicated, maybe even broken soul like Roger's—all of this has drawn me in further rather than caused me to flee. And I realize it's because the whole experience has made me feel less alone. I wish Roger could feel the same way.

We lie in comfortable silence for a while, then he says he better go, and I smile and agree. He says he'll try to find my cue—he is emphatic about this—and I shake my head. I don't need that one anymore.

I'm not sure if he notices.

"OKAY, WHAT HAPPENED?"

This from Natalie, a colleague who takes one look at me when I arrive—noticeably late—at the office and wastes no time getting to the point.

"What do you mean?" I ask, mock-innocently.

"Oh, come on. Look at you, walking in here all bad-ass, tossing your hair, looking sleepy. You had some fun last night." She grins wickedly. "Who was he?"

I remember the first night I spent with a boy, in college, long after all of my friends had had the experience of rolling out of bed and into a campus diner for an afternoon breakfast, toting the cute, rumpled, comp. lit major they'd met the week before at a party and who'd been in their room ever since. It was early in my senior year, and the boy in question, a sexy, assertive finance type from a college nearby, and who was destined for Wall Street and a life of weekend golf and live-in nannies, was visiting me for the weekend. I'd felt shy, saucy, giddy, liberated, strange ambling down the street with him that afternoon, looking for a place that served breakfast until 3:00 p.m. I no longer felt like a walking personality, a rapid-fire wit with no physical presence. I was in the world, a vital participant, for once my body as alive as my mind. We dated for a semester, then he dumped me on my birthday, said he wanted to "spend more time with his friends before graduating" or some crap. I took it hard—it was my birthday, for God's sake—but I never viewed our abbreviated romance as a mistake, no matter how insensitive his timing, because he shook something loose from me. I think it was desire. It's the same feeling that shakes loose when I play pool, the same feeling that emerges in a bar in Brooklyn with Roger next to me and my pool cue nowhere to be found.

At first I won't reveal any details of my tryst to Natalie. But when she finally accuses me of walking around like I'm wearing a leather cat suit and says she "can't take it anymore," I relent and tell her a little: that I brought someone home last night, that he's a friend, that I don't know what's going to happen.

"Well, if I may say, you look fucking great." She swings out of my office, clomping off in her high-heeled boots, her compliment completely sincere.

I know what she's noticing. It isn't as simple or as crass as my "getting some," it's about my desiring an experience and allowing it to happen, and the potency that comes with that. It's also about someone desiring me—and my encouraging him to do so, to act on that desire, and for once not pushing him away. There's an empowering women's magazine article in there somewhere, I have no doubt. But rather than writing the opening paragraph in my mind, like I sometimes find myself doing, this time I just wallow in the experience, letting myself feel shy, saucy, giddy, liberated, strange.

THAT SAME DAY, not twelve hours after leaving my apartment, Roger calls me at work. He's been on the phone with the Taxi & Limousine Commission, he says, and no one has turned in a pool cue. I'm newly embarrassed about my teary display in the bar and rather surprised that he's called. At one point Natalie walks by, mimes putting a phone to her ear, and mouths, "Is it him?" I smile mischievously and wave her off. I was not expecting to hear from Roger for quite a while, had even wondered if maybe he'd skip out on our pool team the following week.

No, that's not quite true. I know he won't disappear, but I also don't expect him to walk out on Shelly and into my arms. Well, Shelly's already asked him to leave, so he wouldn't be walking out on anyone. But I know he wants to stay with her and patch things up. He needs someone to take care of. Despite Roger's charm, his sincerity, his noble ambitions, despite his good nature and generosity, his agile mind and, yes, his often gorgeous pool playing, Roger, it's clear to me now, is hanging by a thread. His emotional core is, like most people's, much more tangled and fraught than he lets on. Roger is a deeply sad person, and I'm not sure if our encounter is an attempt to reach out, to try to save himself, or, more likely, if it's what I fear: that he's finally given up; that he feels he has nothing to lose. Either way, it's best for me to tread carefully now.

Which lasts for all of four minutes.

Roger wants to buy me a new pool cue. I demur, but he persists until we make plans for Saturday.

We meet at a billiards-and-games store on West 26th Street. It's grotesquely hot outside, and Roger is inexplicably wearing long pants. We're the only customers. I beeline to the rows of cues in the back, sleek sticks lined up like weapons, and find the McDermotts, my brand of choice. They're beautiful and expensive. I consult a bored salesperson who's about my age and built like a highway barrel. As I fondle the cues, she shifts her weight from side to side, tucking lank hair behind her ears and occasionally examining her nails, which are square and unpolished. Roger is off in another part of the store shooting on a pool table, acting as if he's interested in buying it.

I select a cue with an emerald-green grip; for some reason, the gaudy color appeals to me. It has a leather wrapping so its owner will never need a glove. It's straight and glossy and stylish. It also costs twice as much as the one now being used by some cab driver in Queens, but I can tell it's worth it. Even the bored salesperson nods approvingly, shocked that I'm able to pick this one out myself.

I bring it up to the cashier. "Well that's Irish," she says, staring rudely at the green grip. She rings it up and tells me I can get a free McDermott case and cleaning supplies—"a fifty-dollar value"—if I fill out a McDermott questionnaire. I do, while Roger pretends that he can't find his wallet, informing me with faux horror that he has no money on him, cracking himself up. The cashier ignores him until he finally produces his Visa card. Soon we're walking into the scorching sunlight and heading downtown to SoHo Billiards to try out my new purchase. The billiards store has given me a cheap skinny case to carry the cue in until my new one arrives. I'm so thrilled I feel guilty. My old cue is forgotten.

After

"CAN YOU EXPLAIN what's going on?"

I've just picked up the phone at my office. The caller does not identify himself, but I know it's Roger.

"This fucking election thing. I just got back from the Caribbean with Shelly. And as you know, I never watch the news or surf the Net. Everyone in the office is talking about the campaign and the debates and how dumb one of them is and what a smart-ass, know-it-all the other one is, and I have no idea what the fuck is going on."

Roger is not about preamble. He starts conversations in the middle and works backward.

"So Election Day's coming up soon, that much I know," he continues. An impatient silence follows.

It's early in the fall of 2000 and both presidential campaigns are in full War Room mode. Pool league is not exactly a hotbed of political fervor, so other than an occasional short-lived rant by me, we never discuss current events at The Wrong Side, unless they happen to involve pool, sex, drugs, or someone's drunken antics. Roger doesn't even vote ("It's fucking stupid. Politics is corrupt. No leader is going to change anything.") but he likes to talk about issues, and I get the feeling he's starting to enjoy listening, too.

It's been about a month since our one-night affair, and we seem to be doing okay. In the aftermath of our evening together, I think about Wally and about my resolution never to get involved with another pool player. But it's obvious that Roger is different, and that I'm different. At least this is what I tell myself. Roger is much more mature than Wally, and I'm wiser about how to handle the relationship. I'm becoming more fluent in pool and in the world the game inhabits. I'm allowing myself to feel transformed by the experience rather than imprisoned by it. Roger and I will find our way through the awkwardness, I'm certain. Lightning will not strike twice.

"You wanna meet after work?" he asks. "We can play some pool or get a drink and you can tell me what's going on in politics and I can tell you why everybody's an idiot. Except me, of course."

"Okay," I say. "Where were you thinking?"

WE PICK A SLIGHTLY upscale bar in the East Village, not far from The Wrong Side. We settle on meeting for drinks instead of playing pool, so Roger says, "Let's go to a place that has the word *lounge* in its name." He already has a Stealth Bomber going when I get there.

"I'm in looove," he says after I sit down and ask him how he is.

This is curious. "Oh, yeah?" I raise an eyebrow. I've just ordered a Coke.

"Well, with Shelly." He looks slightly embarrassed. "We're still together. The Caribbean trip seems to have helped. She's giving me another chance."

"I'm glad, Roger." I feel insincere saying that. I should be glad. But in truth, I feel nothing, except maybe a little afraid. For him, not for me.

Roger looks tired, which is not how someone is supposed to look after he comes back from a tropical island.

"I'm sure I'll fuck things up," he says.

"Don't say that, Roger."

"Did I tell you Shelly's nickname for me?"

"Yes."

"*Leaving Las Vegas*," he says, ignoring me. I remain quiet. "Have you ever seen that movie?"

"You mean the one where Nicolas Cage plays a man who decides to commit suicide by drinking himself to death in Las Vegas? Yes, I've seen it. We've discussed this before. He won an Oscar for that role."

"Never let it be said that I don't aim high." Roger raises his glass.

"Roger, that's not funny. Are you trying to drink yourself to death?"

"No, of course not. Shelly's just got a dark sense of humor. I like that in a woman, you know." He grins. I sip my Coke; he sips his Stealth Bomber.

"So are we here to talk about the presidential election?" I ask.

"Nah, I don't give a fuck about that anymore. Nothing surprises me these days. It's just that everyone in my office was talking about it, had some sort of loud opinion on it. I felt like an idiot, just totally out of the loop." He taps his foot vigorously, so that his whole leg shakes. I'm not used to Roger being fidgety. He pulls a pack of cigarettes out of his breast pocket and lights one.

"I'm going straight home after this," he announces, trying to reassure himself. "Last night I stayed in, went to bed at eleven o'clock."

I nod.

"Man, I wish I could move to Russia, or Croatia, or somewhere in Europe." I assume he's referring to his elaborate "pro bono lawyer of mystery" scheme. "I bet you've been to Europe." He blows smoke out of the side of his mouth.

"Yes, I have. I haven't been there in a while though."

"It can be pretty romantic, huh?"

"Sure." I smile.

Roger chuckles. "I can see you in Europe, walking down the street with some French dude."

I look down. I'm beginning to feel sad.

"I love Paris," he continues. "The architecture especially. And Prague. Man, Prague is great. Even Shelly liked Prague."

We sip our drinks some more, and Roger smokes and rambles nervously about European travel until we've both emptied our glasses. He pays the bill and we leave the bar and walk for a bit, then stop at a traffic light and stand on the street corner. He's going across town; I'm heading to Brooklyn.

"Well, an early night for me," he says again. "You okay getting home?"

"Yeah," I say. "It's early, remember?"

He nods, his eyes flicking worriedly at the passing cars. "I sure hope I don't end up like Trevor. Shit, wouldn't that be ironic?"

"That's not going to happen, Rog. You won't let it." He looks uneasy.

"You gonna be there next week, for pool?" he asks.

"Of course. Why wouldn't I?"

He looks at the ground. "I just wanted to make sure. I still really like seeing you every week, even if . . ." His voice trails off. I gaze at his troubled face.

"Well, I'll call you this weekend maybe," he says casually. He puffs on another cigarette and gazes just above my head. "And I'll see you next week."

"Okay." I shift my bag to the other shoulder. "Are *you* okay getting home?"

"Well, I'll find out," he says. Alarm must have registered on my face. "Just kidding." Out of nowhere, I think I might cry. He pecks me lightly on the lips. "See you next week."

"Yeah, see you," I say. I watch as Roger walks slowly across 4th Street in a new pair of designer shoes, his hands shoved deep in his pockets, his head down.

Carry a Big Stick

I **TRY TO BANISH** my sadness over Roger, and my concern for him, to the far corners of my mind. I can't let what has engulfed him engulf me. The summer is over, except for the occasional humid night, and the briskness of fall is sparking through the city like a lit fuse, energizing the sidewalks again.

The new pool season has started, too. The fall season is always the one that seems to hold the most promise for me, but this one gets off to a weird and frustrating start. I lose my first two matches, a regular occurrence since being told I'm playing better. Perhaps it's resistance, a last stand, a way of insisting to myself that these exciting but often dark and unhappy environs really don't have such a pull on me.

Roger has been behaving erratically, showing up late or else leaving in the middle of one of our games only to return a couple hours later looking haggard and cussing a blue streak. His conversations with me are clipped and impatient. He seems angry, but also acts as if I'm pursuing him and he wants me to back off. His behavior makes no sense. So I ignore it.

I don't bring my new cue—the one Roger bought for me—those first couple of weeks because I'm having the tip reshaped and because I'm still getting used to the feel of it. But by week three, I'm ready for the unveiling. I show up with the new cue but do not reveal that it's a gift from Roger. (We keep that part a secret to avoid gossip, though I'm not sure how much longer the secret will hold.) Everyone gawks when I slide the cue out.

"Sweet!" This from Paul G., who's jittery and coked up as usual but in a good mood. He bounces over, his eyes narrow and glittering. He asks if he can hold the cue. Ricky, another teammate, walks in then and says, "Sweet cue." It's the ultimate compliment—to make a sweet shot, to hit the sweet spot on the ball, to own a piece of equipment that's simply "sweet." It's a pivotal moment; my spirits finally lift. I don't win that night, but my match lasts an agonizing two hours as I torture my opponent with safety shots and make him earn his victory. Something has shifted in my game, there's no doubt. I can feel it. My nerves settle more quickly, I don't get as upset when I lose. I'm doing it. Bald Jack is right after all. I'm becoming a pool player.

AFTER THOSE FIRST FEW LOSSES, I start to win, thrillingly. My new cue case has arrived in the mail by this time, a long black cylinder that resembles a bazooka and has a special pocket for chalk.

I have a real case and a real cue. I shoot in places with names like Pool Beg and Bull's Head and Barfly, smoky bars with bad jukeboxes and crowds that are a mixture of posturing toughs and guys wearing Dockers, cell phones clamped to their belts in little black cases that look like beetles. And although Roger and I ignore the lingering sexual tension between us, I remain buoyed by the experience, intoxicated with this new persona: *I play pool. I bring smart, cool, pool-playing men home from bars.*

I start wearing black leather boots with a high, stacked heel; favor a shimmery black tank top with long fringe that sways above the table when I shoot; and slip into snug, newly purchased jeans after work, jeans that cause my friend Ben to ask, wide-eyed, when he first sees them pasted onto my body, "Are those Helmut Langs?" (They're from the Gap, but so what? I wear them as if they cost $900.) Trevor tells me one night that I have the sexiest arms he's ever seen. Ricky, with his splendid, ungainly nose and tangle of blond hair and his outré punk attire, the hippest guy on our team, says to me on another occasion, after watching me shoot, as if it's just dawning on him, "You know something? Your ass is hot. I'm not kidding. You've got a hot ass. And I mean that with total respect." He bows graciously, then heads for the street to call one of his many unemployed actor-rocker friends, all of whom somehow manage to afford the newest high-tech cell phones.

As the city moves deeper into fall, I get bumped up a rank, to a 3, and by the end of the season, I trounce a woman a full three rankings higher than me. We're in a creepy place called Plug Uglies on 3rd Avenue, a smelly, narrow bar with a miniature bowling lane that runs alongside the pool area, annoying the hell out of everyone. My opponent has brought her quivering little pug puppy, which her boyfriend holds in his lap while she wonders how I can possibly be beating her, a 6, for chrissake. But I'm in what pool players call "dead stroke"—a state that is rare and wonderful, at least for the bar-league denizen.

Dead stroke is when you become completely consumed by the mechanical act of shooting a ball with a stick, to the exclusion of all else. The rest of the world fades into oblivion. The cue works as if it's another body part, one you can command like a leg or an arm, and you shoot brilliantly—indeed, flawlessly. You have effortless control over everything—your emotions, your speed, your dexterity, your confidence, your focus. Nothing can touch you. If you want your object ball to roll into a corner pocket, leaving the cue ball in a place where you can shoot the next ball into the side pocket, it happens, exactly as you envision it. And it happens again with the next shot, and again with the one after that. I can't miss that night at Plug Uglies. I sink bank shots, make crazy cuts. It isn't me. But then, maybe it is.

I'm dazed and flushed when the match ends. My opponent shakes my hand silently, then walks briskly to her dog, taking him into her arms. She needs comfort. I, in contrast, walk into a thicket of flailing, ecstatic high-fives from my teammates, who whoop and howl and yell "Goddamn!" Gene grabs my hand and says, "My God, you look beautiful," his eyes wide, taking in my face in wonderment. Roger is not a part of this burst of exuberance. He's at the bar. Where else?

A couple minutes later, a grizzled, elderly guy from the other side of the bar approaches. I hadn't noticed him before. He's a cross between Al Sharpton and somebody's vagrant great-uncle. His suit is shabby and his belly pushes forward, straining his shirt. He has steel-wool sideburns flecked with white.

"I just wanted to shake your hand, young lady," he says. "That was some fine playing. I was watching you. Fine playing. Have I seen you out in Bay Ridge?"

I shake his hand and thank him, my face hot and excited, and say no, it wasn't me he saw. "Are you sure? You sure you don't play out in Bay Ridge? I thought I recognized you."

I am, it turns out, a legend in Bay Ridge.

The idea that I can be mistaken for someone—anyone—who plays "real" pool makes me dizzy with delight, and in Bay Ridge no less, where I'm certain all the toughest, bad-ass, pool-playing motherfuckers congregate, remark on each other's sweet cues, and slide crumpled bills across tables, the women talking in voices as rough as gravel.

I FINISH THE SEASON with a winning record—my first—and we have a few weeks off. But when we resume in the early winter after the hiatus between seasons, everything feels different. Something has soured. Although I practiced a bit during our break, I lose my first match and feel glum. It's not even close. My shots are all over the place, my break wimpy. I'm puzzled and alarmed and feel that no one is supporting me, like the magic cue has let me down. It happens again the following week, and again. How can this be?

The captains of my team—Paul G. and now Roger, too, who's been "promoted" to co-captain—decide not to play me as much after I start losing again. Roger and I are barely on speaking terms by this point. Our night together has proved to be an enormous mistake, though neither of us saw it as that at the time. Despite the wisdom I've gained shooting pool over the past year, I'm still surprised at the way events have played out with Roger. I have no idea where he's living these days. (Neither, it turns out, does he.) The friction between us, along with the reduced table time, makes me angry and distracted, and unlike the long-lashed, sultry woman with the emerald cue who plays with exuberance and a little awe, the one often confused with a well-known shark out in Bay Ridge, this new player is losing her cool. I complain about the way I'm being treated, about the way women are treated in general, about the lack of appreciation for my stellar attendance record and my work ethic. I borrow from baseball again, but not from Johnny Bench, who would've kept his turmoil to himself. No, this time I borrow from the great petulant routines of Pedro Martinez, Gary Sheffield, Ricky Henderson, and Ken Griffey Jr. And I lose and lose and lose and lose and lose. Everyone on the team seems to be losing, even when they aren't.

THE DEEP FREEZE BETWEEN Roger and me continues, although his anger finally seems to have been extinguished. What's left is a sense of helplessness. We talk even less now, a direct result of his drinking more. A sad, fearful silence takes over.

The silence feels familiar, causes a tightening in my stomach that I haven't experienced in a while. There was a man once, a brash, exciting man with snapping blue eyes and a deep, scratchy voice who nearly sucked the life out of me when I lived in Baltimore. He's a journalist, with a tough, reckless face that crackles with intelligence and self-pity. I'm in my twenties and have uprooted my life in New York to go to graduate school in Baltimore, leaving him behind, except that I can't. The man is what the therapeutic culture calls "emotionally unavailable," a phrase as ubiquitous in New York as Kate Spade bags and waitresses hoping for their big acting break.

When I first meet Roger, there's something so open about his face and his loose, bouncy body, his green-brown eyes so welcoming and genuine, that he seems like a foreigner to me, like someone learning the language of a new country, not yet knowing the tongue's troubling nuances. And in the early winter, when events take that dark, unexpected turn, a curve that's coming even before Roger and I spend our night together, and his eyes start to cloud, there's a familiarity to his expression that for once does not draw me further in, but instead makes me step back.

In Baltimore, I try to get the man to look, to see me, to smile his true smile, not the cynical grimace that passes for one, but his jaw sets and his heart closes, even though big, luscious words tumble out of his mouth, keeping me blindly hopeful, racing home to wait for his calls from New York. This is painful, of course, and that seems to suit me just fine.

I survive on his table scraps for a while, until I realize that I am, quite literally, shrinking. It's not that I stop eating. I don't starve myself or make myself throw up or develop weird rituals when it comes to chewing or arranging meals on my plate—I've never done that—but I eat mechanically, consuming food without joy, simply as a means to exist, while my stomach churns and my mind races with never-ending thoughts of the man. And so I drop weight, out of sheer misery. My jeans begin to fall off of me. When I look in the mirror I see a gaunt, scrawny woman with overly defined ribs staring back. I hate the image. It's unhealthy, weak, powerless.

So, wrenchingly, over a period of several months, I sever ties with the man, drink milkshakes, join a gym, cry alone at night, don't pick up the phone when he calls. It finally occurs to me that perhaps my attraction to him is as much due to my own "emotional unavailability" as his. He's by no means the first man I've been involved with to inhabit these dark, closed-off qualities so comfortably, but the experience with him is the most difficult to endure, the hardest to crawl out of. I vow never to repeat it, and I don't.

The man from my twenties revels in his anger, feeds off of it. The energy it takes to sustain it helps him carve out a successful career and ruins all of his relationships. Roger, on the other hand, discards his anger, his raw deal. He ignores its potential power over him and instead buries himself in pool and Shelly and other people's hard-luck stories. But he's losing the battle. When I notice his eyes change that fall and winter, when his smile becomes a grimace that's all too familiar, I know the end is near. I continue to lose my matches.

AS THE AIR TURNS COLD, Roger sits at the bar and offends people, squanders his games, eyes barely able to focus, his chiseled cartoon features slack, his body and his face soft and dumpy and defeated. Paul G. loses his job and spends most of his time in Vermont now, skiing and God knows what else. We never figure out just how he's financing this extended vacation, but Liz and I speculate about some of Paul G.'s extracurricular activities—the ones we can't help but notice when he comes out of the bathroom twitching like a live wire. We consider the possibility that these habits are taking him in a darker direction these days, one that's enabling him to earn a rather questionable living. Ricky never shows up anymore, and we wonder if he's experimenting with heroin. We suspect that one of his actor friends is using it, a guy named Jorge who used to come watch Ricky play but stopped showing up at about the same time he started looking sweaty, gray, and nervous, telling stories about how he never sleeps anymore unless he's having "a good day." Once again, Gary punches a guy one night and gets thrown out of yet another bar. Gene, the teammate so flummoxed by my vocabulary, spends week after week mute and hangdog, staring balefully at all of the beers and sporty drinks people consume around him while, as a man on the wagon, he's forced to nurse his ginger ales, which look pale and meek in their pint glasses.

Meanwhile, the inimitable Tony—Big Tony, my nemesis (although I'm the only one who sees it this way)—the pool veteran with giant blow-dried hair and the proud owner of a Toyota Land Cruiser, returns to the APA pool scene and, having renewed his prescriptions from a long-ago "job-related injury," cheerfully offers Vicodin or Ativan to anyone not feeling loose, his own face slack, eyelids low and menacing. He continues to be one of the best shots in the league, playing out of whatever bar can stand him for a season. And he starts the engine of his Land Cruiser by standing on the sidewalk and pressing a button on his key ring, a feat he never gets tired of demonstrating.

Finally, relief: I win my last match of the season, against a spindly, pathetic guy with glasses who's probably played pool three times in his life. I leave the bar, still a little sour, hoping my rapid rise and spectacular fall will not be repeated next season.

It won't.

I get a call from Liz, who tremulously lets me know I've been replaced. The decision was made a while ago, she tells me. If Liz hadn't called, I would've shown up for the first match of the new season to find Gene's girlfriend chalking up in my place, some stacked, gooey blonde who used to play for another team—and one of the few people who played worse than I had last season.

I'm incredulous. I've been fired?

I am unable to say anything other than a soft, "Huh?" so Liz presses on nervously.

"I heard them talking about it in hushed tones, Roger and everyone, and I just didn't want to get involved. It was too crazy and absurd. Truthfully, I thought it would never happen, that they were just drunk. Then I find out they've really made their decision but don't plan on saying anything. They'll tell you when you show up. That just seemed so wrong to me."

Yes, it was wrong. All wrong.

"I'm really sorry," Liz says. She sounds genuinely distraught. "Are you still there?"

Until this moment, I have not thought about how the last several months may have appeared through Liz's eyes: my showing up with a new cue but not telling her where it came from or what happened to the old one; my saucy, exaggerated behavior followed by Roger's increasingly dark moods; our team's gradual change from a jovial group of misfits to the grumbling, sniping, bitter tangle we'd become, with me complaining loudly about it week after week, hands on hips. Then the eerie, domino-like collapse: Trevor disappears; Paul stops talking about copier products; Gary starts throwing punches; Roger watches through slitted eyes, slumped at the bar; Big Tony serves as comic relief instead of the annoying spectacle he usually is. Had Liz seen my ouster coming? How long has she known, or had an inkling? All over the city people are losing their jobs, yet I have no doubt I'm the only person who's been let go from her pool team. God, she must think I'm an asshole.

"Roger didn't want to deal with you anymore," Liz tells me after I ask her why this happened. "That's a direct quote." Our night in Brooklyn is as distant as the lights of New Jersey, as sad and lonely as the train out to Bay Ridge.

"Christ, what happened with you guys?" Liz says. "Was there an incident?" Her confusion seems sincere.

I don't confide in Liz about my once-burgeoning friendship with Roger or our sleeping together. I had wanted to keep that part of my pool life to myself, not only out of discretion, but so I could savor it. Now I want to keep it private out of shame. I tell her I have to go. I don't want her to hear me cry. What a horrible task she's been burdened with, taking it upon herself to deliver this news so I can avoid a more public embarrassment at the beginning of next season. Did she fight for me, I wonder? Or, despite our friendship, is she relieved to have me gone? My stomach twists. I hang up the phone, stunned and humiliated.

I've managed to lose two pool teams. Worse, I've lost them because of entanglements with men. This is mortifying to me, unfathomable. Television characters do this sort of thing, not me. I'm too old for this, aren't I? I feel unbearably young and stupid. I don't tell anyone that I've been cut loose, that once again I will not be playing pool on Monday nights. Liz is the only one who knows the truth. At work, if Natalie, my colleague, makes one of her sassy inquiries about my love life, I change the subject.

I begin to think about hustling, about sandbaggers, about whether I've been conned. Had I been hustled by Wally? Was he really from West Virginia, or will I soon find out that he's the son of a dentist from Shaker Heights? Had my friendship with Roger been real, or had that been merely a ruse to get me into bed? I torture myself with these doubts and flog myself for my poor judgment. But when I contemplate whether I've been hustled, I'm forced to ask myself, usually late at night while trying to fall asleep, the hour at which our bleakest and most honest thoughts enter our heads, who really has been hustling whom here? Have I been hustling myself all along? Have I, in fact, been doing this unconsciously since I first started playing pool on a team, because I like imagining myself as a different person? When I first become entranced by pool, the stimulation is intellectual, the allure is the quiet. But when I join the pool league, it becomes about performance, about noise. Shooting pool in a bar, I realize, makes me feel desirable. It comes as a complete shock to me to learn that I hadn't felt I was. The ultimate sandbag.

MONTHS LATER I CONCLUDE that my getting sacked is a gift. It spares me the pain of watching Roger's decline up close and of feeling somehow responsible for it, and it saves me from having to leave the team on my own, which would have taken more time and would've been far more painful, I think. But when it first happens, when Liz gives me the word, I feel as if I've been knocked down, as if I've been silenced, unfairly judged, deprived of making my own stand.

And so I do something impulsive and self-pitying and all too familiar. I give up pool entirely, just quit, without much fanfare.

I'm not "showing them"—there's no fire to my quitting. It's defeat, pure and simple. I'm weary. The adrenaline rush from my matches is gone—it narrowed to a trickle when I started to lose. And the sexual confidence I gained from my affair with Roger has been turned on its head. I'm embarrassed now rather than liberated by my sultry theatrics.

As with all departures, along with the guilt and uncertainty and anger comes relief. It washes over me, comforting and cleansing. I allow myself to feel—temporarily—as if I've fixed something. *What else can I fix?* I wonder. And so, newly emboldened by my contrived story that leaving pool is not a defeat after all but a victory, I turn my sights back to the one area of my life where I'm always on top, always in control: my work. I'm sick of the delayed gratification of working for a film company, sick of the whims and tantrums of my mercurial boss. It's what pushed me to start playing pool in the first place. *What the hell*, I think—*why not quit that, too?* And so I do.

But this move is different from my shoving my pool cue to the back of my closet. I plan carefully. Ever meticulous and focused when it comes to this particular front, I line up another job, a highly paid editorial position at a new Internet venture—this is in the latter part of 2000, when a smattering of flush, boldly funded websites and "new media" enterprises still cling stubbornly to life, having not yet entered their free falls. I inform my film colleagues and Larry, who responds by having one of his hatchet men call me to say that he's "very hurt." No counteroffer is made, no acknowledgment that I'm leaving to try something completely different and not jumping ship to work for the competition. Larry "has been good to me" and thus feels "betrayed."

That, I decide, will have to be Larry's problem. I have betrayals of my own to deal with.

LIZ BEGINS THE NEW pool season without me and, respectful of my feelings, does not discuss the reconfigured team or how it's faring. I start my new job. It's late winter now, the air spiky with cold, the streets gray and grimy and downcast, speckled with dropped scarves and wet, unmatched gloves.

If I catch myself thinking of Roger or of my inelegant ouster from Paul G.'s team, I immediately push the thoughts aside since the pain and embarrassment still feel fresh. I'm too busy to contemplate what happened there; indeed, I'm too busy to keep up with the changes that have occurred in my "other life," my *real* life—a new, demanding job, a subsequent desire for a new place to live—and it's also about this time, perhaps not coincidentally, that my eyes start to bother me. They sting and tear up when I put my contact lenses in, the lids and rims tender. Then my right eye turns a rather vivid red and eventually I can no longer wear my contacts at all, even for short periods.

I wish my "clouded vision" were a more subtle metaphor, one not so reminiscent of Greek tragedy, but yes, it appears that I am *not seeing clearly*, my eyes irritated and uncomfortable, and finally, after a month, I go to an ophthalmologist and learn I've contracted a weird but not terribly uncommon eye virus called EKC—epidemic kerato-conjunctivitis, or "shipyard conjunctivitis"—a nasty form of pinkeye that threatens the cornea. The doctor tells me I probably picked it up on the subway the way some people do the flu. It's easily treated with ophthalmic steroids that I administer myself for two weeks, little white droplets that remind me of half-and-half, soothing my eyes as soon as they touch them.

AFTER A FEW WEEKS, all traces of the virus vanish, then it returns, then it's cured a second time, then it's discovered that I've become allergic to my contact lenses, and I have to go see an optometrist and try several different brands until he finally finds an ultrathin pair of lenses I can wear. By this time it's spring. I've settled in at my job, working for another hard-charging, bullying, razor-sharp boss.

And I've moved. After three years in my charming, creaking, brownstone apartment, with my landlords living below me and one neighbor above, our mail shoved through the same slot in the ancient front door, I decide I want to live somewhere more spacious, with less of the forced intimacy of brownstone living. And I want this new domicile to be mine. It takes some time, but I apply my improved salary toward paying off credit cards and adding to my nest egg, and I am eventually able to make a downpayment on a co-op apartment in a nearby, slightly more downscale neighborhood in Brooklyn (the real-estate agent describes it as "earthy"). My new apartment has arched doorways, wood floors, and a big window in the kitchen that looks out onto a patchwork of scruffy backyards attached to brightly colored buildings—red, burnt orange, flinty gray—the sky filling in the space between the roofs, which sit at different heights like suspended pistons. I keep the window bare—no blinds or curtains or

hanging ornaments—so that the view greets me every morning unadorned.

One day the phone in my office rings, and when I pick up, a tinny
voice says, "Hi Heather, I've got Larry for you." I don't even have
time to be stunned. I hear the connection being made, then a far-off
"Go ahead, Larry." He's in the car. "Hey, baby, how's the new job?
Tell me about it."

In the two years that I work for him, Larry never—not once—
addresses me by anything but my name. Although he can be brusque,
he's courtly with young women, especially if he doesn't know them
well, sparing them his direct invective, helping them into their coats
and holding open doors out of longtime habit, even if he's simultaneously eviscerating a maître d' or cutting into an agent. Larry is old-
school in a lot of ways—a showman and a shrewd dealmaker rather
than a sleek executive spouting management jargon. He often addresses
colleagues and adversaries with terms of blunt affection or ribald
nicknames. It's a sign of intimacy and respect. This is the first time
I've ever been "Hey baby'd" by Larry. But I'm not offended. I'm
amused and, I confess, even a little touched.

There's something so warm and reassuring about his insistent
voice, about experiencing once again his jumping into a conversation as if he never left it, about feeling his unbridled confidence and
supreme powers of denial, that I find myself grinning and exclaiming,
"Larry! It's so great to hear from you. The job is fantastic. But how are
you?" We chat for a bit—"Tell me more," he says, and means it—and
I explain what the company is trying to do, which is to sell books and
other literary content online as if it were an independent bookstore
rather than a Barnes & Noble behemoth, and then Larry says, "Well,
you're gonna be great, and you know I wish you the best. Who knows,
maybe we can do something together someday." It's Larry's way of
apologizing, and of saying we're okay, and, frankly, of making sure he
doesn't miss out on a business opportunity. All of the sentiments are

quite sincere—and all of them completely Larry. We hang up (well, he clicks off and jumps to another call) and I sit at my desk, smiling, trying not to rub my eyes. I don't tell Larry about the strange virus. There's no need, because I can see again. Really see.

And so one Saturday I go over to Brownstone Billiards on Flatbush Avenue, only a block from my new apartment in Brooklyn, my pool case retrieved from my closet and slung over my shoulder as if it's never hung anywhere else. It's been an achingly long time since I've played pool, still licking my wounds and feeling burned, but I'm allowing myself to think, for the first time in quite a while, that it's time to come back, to hear the sound of the balls clicking across the cloth again, to get over myself, to find a new team. And I will find one—I'll meet a guy named Sam who slurps Guinness as if it's iced tea on a hot day, and prickly Alan, who's been playing pool forever; I'll meet Valerie, who I've seen before at pool bars and admired from afar, and will watch her swing her black hair and flaunt her nosering and do things her way; I'll play in the same division as Liz and have the opportunity to shoot against her new teammates and compare notes with her in a cab on the way home, just like old times. But first I need to recapture the spark that Roger extinguished, the flame that Trevor and Gary and Paul G. doused. I need to rekindle my desire for that rush of excitement, need to be once again in thrall to a new persona, the old one now nothing more than a memory hovering somewhere over a pool table in a Chelsea pool hall or an East Village pub. So I head down the road to Brownstone and try not to expect anything.

I used to practice there all the time before my "retirement." The place is dreary, full of pockmarked pool tables and warped bar cues. It smells, predictably, of stale cigarette smoke and mold. A lot of harmless older guys play there by themselves, without judgment. I slide my cue from its bazooka case, holding the two pieces in front of me. They look like parts of a toy, fig. A and fig. B, a toy with no purpose other than maybe to jab your kid brother in the eye. I put the shaft and the butt together and screw the joint tight, as I've done a hundred times. The stick feels sturdy now. This is the moment, I guess, when I'm supposed to turn the cue slowly in my hands and see the word *Wonderboy* burned into one side. Instead, I crouch over the table and knock some balls around, then begin stroking long shots, trying to remember how it's done. I hit the balls over and over, most refusing to go in, just missing the pocket or careening off the rail. I keep at it until finally a 4-ball wobbles down the length of the table, teeters on the edge, and plops into the corner pocket. My heart lifts. I look around and catch the eye of a skinny guy in an oversized football jersey a few tables away. He meets my gaze and barely nods. I hear him say under his breath, "Sweet."

Birds of a Feather

I'M WITHOUT A CUE the night I find my new team, my third since I stepped into this late-night world. I assume I'm on only a fact-finding mission when I walk gingerly into a bar near Crosby Street, a place I heard about from a guy on the subway. (I approached him when I noticed a cue case strapped to his shoulder.)

The bar is innocuous enough from the outside, but surprisingly cavernous once you walk through the tiny vestibule. It's absurdly dark, with a couple TVs blinking soundlessly from the corners. There are booths against one wall, people huddled in them, locked in intense conversations, and a maze of small, high tables and accompanying stools that you have to negotiate carefully as you make your way toward the back room—past the jukebox and the dart area—where three pool tables sit as if in a crop circle, two planted squarely next to each other, chalkboards with names scrawled on them hanging above the tables like family portraits, the third table arranged perpendicular to the twins, a table reserved for league play that seems, because of its unusual position, to be sitting on hallowed ground.

There are about ten to fifteen people crowded around the tables when I get to them. The scene is both painfully and reassuringly familiar: people standing around pool tables, drinking and laughing, falling into an occasional lull when a player attempts a tricky shot, stopping, sometimes mid-sentence or mid-drink, to watch.

I feel a lightheartedness in this bar, a buoyancy that left The Wrong Side and its denizens long ago. Despite my enforced absence from the game and the ugly reasons that absence came about, I don't feel like an interloper here. I'm merely another pool player, with my own story that I may or may not want to share with anyone. I can do or say what I want to. It's another aspect of playing pool that I miss, this freedom.

I hear a woman's loud voice call from the dart area, "Hey! That jackass just took over my table!" She's referring to the shaggy leader of a boisterous group of people that has just commandeered one of the pool tables without checking the sign-up board. The woman is making a stand, not caring whose game her voice interrupts. I have to smile. She is who she is.

The "I gotta be me!" ethos of a pool league comes as no surprise. Pool is a tolerant game. Historically, it has put up with a lot of characters, so it makes sense that it would attract a lot of characters.

Take Maxine, for example, who comes to my mind upon hearing the irate voice of the woman who feels her table has been swiped. Maxine is the rotund captain of a team that has played in my APA division on and off for several seasons. She's a loud, furious woman somewhere in her thirties, with a mop of purple dreadlocks and an enormous ass that makes her look as if she's wearing a futon. She has a cigarette habit that she kicked because of some serious health problems, but she's always struggling to stay on top of it. She'll yell, "I need a fucking cigarette!" with no warning, even if someone is in the middle of a delicate shot. *Especially* if someone is in the middle of a delicate shot. Maxine wants everyone to know what she's feeling the moment she's feeling it. And while she does not cheat overtly, she likes to push the envelope. Maxine uses her powerful lungs and her bullish attitude to tilt things her way when she can.

She has a particular disdain for the men on her team ("They're boys, they're not men. Look at them. *Jesus.*"), and she loves to pick fights with the opposing teams' captains over nothing. ("I'll take all the time I want on this shot, Mr. Man. You take care of your people, I'll take care of mine. You got that?")

Maxine lives in a far-flung borough and is always leaving to catch some unreliable train. Yet despite being incessantly pressed for time, she can never seem to get out the door in fewer than forty minutes. She'll assign the scorekeeping duties to one of her "boys" before she leaves, and the unlucky soldier will stare helplessly at the clipboard. She glares at him for a minute, then her big shoulders drop and her face registers defeat. She always looks at Liz or me during these moments, searching for a comrade in misery, someone she thinks might be as tired of being disappointed as she is.

Maxine gazes at her raggedy team one more time, knowing it's hopeless. To her, the whole world is hopeless. "You bring me my pen, you hear me, Carl?" she'll say to the confused, newly assigned score-keeper. "Don't lose that pen. You bring me that pen tomorrow. I mean it. *I want my pen.*" And then she's gone.

MAXINE IS ANGRY, but she isn't nuts. I'm not too sure about Honey, whose name has to be one of the more cruel jokes a parent ever played on a kid. Honey is a squat, raspy-voiced woman with staticky, bleached-blond hair. She wears a regular uniform of dark jeans, a dark baseball shirt, and a black leather jacket. A heavy backpack is usually slung over her shoulder. I can't tell her age: maybe thirty, maybe forty, maybe sixty-five for all I know. I hear her introduce her-self to someone ("Hey, honey, I'm Honey"), and I laugh, since there's nothing soft or luscious about this woman. She's hard-edged and wild-eyed, and she never shuts up.

Honey has a voice like a radiator, the kind you find in crappy New York apartments that clanks and spits and creaks and then rumbles like an old car engine for a while. Honey's motor never dies down, not even for a minute, as she wildly and shamelessly promotes herself and her exploits to any and all who will listen, though she doesn't really care if you're listening or not.

"Hey!" she yells to me one night, as if she's across the room (she's one seat away). Our teams are in a league match at some East Village watering hole. "What's her name?" she rasps to someone on the other side of her. Then: "Hey, Heather!"

I turn to Honey, her face smiling and contorted. "Yes?" What now? I wonder, girding myself.

"I like your shirt!" she bellows. I'm wearing a brightly patterned shirt of circles and diamonds in pink and red and purple, sort of early seventies and psychedelic, an unusual choice for me. It's formfitting and has three-quarter sleeves. "Thanks," I say to Honey.

"No, really. I love it. *I love that shirt.* It looks great. I noticed it right when I came in and so I just asked who you were because I like the shirt so much. I decorated my girlfriend's kitchen just like that. *Just like that!* I'm telling you, her kitchen looks just like your shirt. That's the first thing I thought of when I saw it." I try to imagine a pink and red and purple kitchen in New York. "I'm a decorator, you know, and I just redecorated her whole apartment. I made it all, like, totally George Jetson. But like I said, I love that shirt. It's all about the shirt."

"Well, I'm thrilled to know that I'm wearing your friend's kitchen," I say. "Next week I'll try to replicate her living room."

Honey roars—why, I don't know, because it isn't that funny—and so we talk about color palettes for a few minutes, and then she says, "Me? I'm wearing black until they come up with something darker." Then she shrieks with laughter.

I'm treated to Honey's pronouncements and stories and sing-alongs and opinions and self-promoting tales for the next hour or so. She runs her mouth without pausing for a breath, an express subway tunneling through the city. Honey, as I already learned, has a passion for decorating, though she isn't a real decorator, it's "just a hobby," but one of her rooms ended up in *Better Homes and Gardens* at some point during the past year, a fact that she brings up several times, and maybe, she muses, she should make interior decorating her career—I mean, she can't help it, she just has "the knack"—but really, she only dabbles in it, and, oh, she wrote a screenplay, too, which made it as far as getting a second look by some movie executive somewhere. She just had to write it, you know, to follow her dream, and she can't believe *anyone* even looked at it, let alone two "film people," but now nothing's happening, although that doesn't matter because she's done what she set out to do, and, yes, funny you should bring up sex (I haven't), because she's also a former dominatrix, now retired, but she recently organized the biggest fetish party on the East Coast, more than one thousand people showed up in New York City for it—a record!—and she's doing stand-up comedy, too, trying to get a callback at Caroline's, she was there today, as a matter of fact, having dropped off an audition tape last week—she'll show it to me if I want—and she's convinced she'll be making her comedy debut soon, she's so much better than those other jerks, I mean, what the hell did Caroline's want, anyway? Well, that's the business, it's fucked. But between the decorating and the pool playing and the fetish-group organizing and the stand-up comedy and the screenplays and dealing with all of her friends and their lives and their fashion mistakes, well, Honey is just goddamn busy all the time, and something's gonna have to give, because she just can't do it all, now, can she? Then Bruce Springsteen's "Thunder Road" comes on the jukebox, and suddenly Honey stops, mid-diatribe, and screams "Bruuuuuuce!" in a voice like corroded metal—people actually wince—and she promptly points out, and receives no objections, that there's "nothing like vintage Bruce." Then she and an equally blond and black-leathered companion, a petite woman whose face is a softer, more childlike interpretation of Honey's and who's materialized from out of nowhere, begin to sing along with Bruce, Honey's voice raking the chords of "Thunder Road," overpowering the warbling of her tiny companion.

I sit there, glassy-eyed, my ears ringing as she and her pal continue their Springsteen serenade. She doesn't speak to me again for the rest of the night, though I hear her screaming "Me and Bobby McGee" less than an hour later into the ear of a frightened man in loafers, who sits with his back against the wall, cornered, staring longingly at a fixed point near the men's room.

While I've shot pool several times with Maxine—long, drawn-out matches where she tries everything to unnerve or annoy me, even stunts as childish as claiming she can't remember how many games we've played—I've never had the privilege of going up against Honey in pool. I think it's an experience I can safely live without, though I know the game, at the very least, would not have been boring.

As I look around the new bar, the one I've wandered into near Crosby Street, I realize that all of this—the characters, the weirdos, the sandbaggers, the bad tempers, the even tempers, the advice about which shot to take, the admonishments to "just have fun," the pool—is about to start again. I'm ready.

I don't know who to talk to about finding the bar's team, so I just keep walking, as if looking for the restrooms. I catch the eye of a skinny guy slouched on a stool, blowing wisps of hair out of his eyes. "Say, is this pool league?" I inquire, feigning innocence. He nods.

"Are you on a team?"

"Yes, I'm on this one." He gestures to a high table strewn with beer bottles and pint glasses. "I'm new," he adds. His accent is not quite British but cheeky and European all the same.

I introduce myself and explain my mission. He says his name is Andrew, and he reemphasizes his newness and his complete lack of authority.

"You should talk to our captain, Sam."

"Which one's Sam?" I ask, trying to appear full of confidence and verve.

Andrew leans back and asks another guy, one with glasses and a dark beard, "Where's Sam?" and instead of pointing his finger, the guy, who I now notice has a visible, rather sinister black tooth poking out of his mouth, bellows, "Sam. Hey, Sam! *Get your ass over here.*"

Another bearded man materializes, also wearing glasses, in his mid-forties, balding, with pale, fleshy upper arms. He's dressed entirely in black, from the black leather vest he wears over a sleeveless black T-shirt to the dark Guinness he clutches in his hand. In the other he holds a cue. He raises his eyebrows, looks from the bellowing guy to me, then back again. His face is kind.

"Don't look at me," the black-toothed guy who summoned him says. "Somebody wants you." He jerks his thumb toward my general vicinity. Now all three men are staring at me. I tell them my name and say, "I play pool, I've played on a couple of APA teams, but I'm homeless at the moment." Sam smiles. I feel encouraged and barrel forward. "I've been on a break, but now I'm looking for a team, and I hear there are a couple here so I thought I'd ask if maybe you had an opening. You know, on the off chance." I let my voice trail off. My eyebrows lift in hope.

"So how long of a break?" Sam asks.

"Um, one season, I guess. So what's that, four months?"

Sam nods. I don't want them to know why I left my two previous teams. I don't think it will affect whether or not I get "hired"—I'm sure Sam and his cohorts have seen it all—but I don't want to start playing for a team with a scarlet A on my back, even if I'm the only one who knows it's there. So, sticking with some semblance of the truth, I volunteer, "I started a new job and had a schedule conflict. But that's been worked out."

"Where did you use to play?" Sam asks. I'm not expecting this sort of grilling. What if he knows Roger? Or Paul G.?

I tell him I played out of The Wrong Side for a while, and before that Lucky's, the name of Wally's bar. Then I stop talking. And wait. Sam rubs his beard.

"You know, we actually do need someone."

I'm shocked. I think I've blown it somehow and assume I'll be sent to yet another bar.

He continues rubbing his beard. "What's your rank?" I hold my breath for a second then say, "I'm a three."

I was a 2 for almost two years, but I went up to a 3 my final season with Paul G.'s team. And whether Sam needs a 3 is the looming question at hand.

"Can you give us a minute?" Sam says. I nod, mute. He and the loud guy with the scary tooth move away from me, and yet another guy is summoned, a crisp, clean-shaven man in a Gomer Pyle fishing hat who looks to be in his fifties. They huddle together like NATO leaders. Their bodies give away nothing.

"That looks like a big, important meeting," Andrew says. I'm still trying to place his accent.

"I guess they're deciding my fate."

"Well, I was sort of recruited, you know. I'm unemployed and all I seem to do these days is play pool in bars, so a friend of mine suggested this. I think they need a couple more players. You might be in luck. Then we can both be new." A mischievous smile spreads across his face. He's flirting.

Our discussion is cut short. The men return. Sam takes a big gulp of Guinness.

"So I think this is gonna work out. We need 3's and 4's. Where else have you played again? I've already forgotten."

I marvel at the fluidity of these teams—and the pool world in general, how you can float in and out of it and within a matter of minutes, your past is "already forgotten." It's one of the more inviting aspects of the game, though sometimes this same fluidity also leads to a lack of accountability. I can attach myself to a new team this easily, but then so can Paul G., who has a drug problem, and Roger, who's falling apart, and Trevor, who has "issues with authority," and Gary, who is wonderfully funny but will be throwing punches in no time.

I'm overanalyzing. I stop myself mid-worry, name my previous bars again, and nod vigorously at Sam to express my enthusiasm.

"Okay, then," he says. "So, do you wanna play?"

"Sure!" I chirp, sounding like a demented cheerleader.

"Well, great. Get your cue if you have one. This match will be over in a few minutes, after Bill gets his ass kicked."

I'm confused. "Wait, am I on the team?"

"Yeah."

"When you said, 'Do you wanna play?' did you mean, like, now? In a match? For this team?"

"Yeah, what'd you think I meant?"

I have not come tonight thinking I'll be playing a league match. Hell, I haven't even brought my cue, which, upon reflection, was colossally stupid of me. I don't know what to do, since I don't want to lose this team now that I've found it. I look around the dizzy, swirling bar. The Ramones are playing on the jukebox, young people are slamming balls around the tables, yelling and carrying on. A waifish cocktail waitress named Sue-Ling keeps popping by, asking everyone if they're okay. I watch the guy named Bill stare helplessly at his table. Then I blurt out what may possibly be the most ridiculous sentence ever uttered in a pool bar:

"I'm defrosting a chicken."

Why at this particular moment I feel the need for such brutal domestic honesty, I'll never know. Yes, I had bought at my local grocery store, as I often did, a shrink-wrapped, refrigerated package of skinless, boneless chicken breasts, shriveled and smushed together like used socks and pressed into a little foam tray that I promptly tossed into my freezer. I take them out and defrost them when the spirit moves me, dicing the chicken and throwing it into a pan with oil and garlic and various green vegetables, referring to the mixture as "stir-fry" to make it sound more exotic. And yes, I had, before leaving the house that day, moved the chicken from freezer to refrigerator in anticipation of this culinary event. But as I stand encircled by my new billiard compatriots, in a place where balls are *thwunked* and darts are thrown and shots are downed, this mundane part of my daily existence emerges, inexplicably, as something hugely important, something I have to blurt out like a confession. I'm back at Chelsea Billiards again, insecure about my game and looking for an escape hatch.

Sam and his bearded, bellowing sidekick, whom I now know as Jacques, and the older guy with the side-part with whom they consulted about my status (who is now sporting half-glasses and peering over them with schoolmarmish disapproval), and Andrew, the slurry, slouching South African (I finally placed the accent), with his mop of brown hair and that wry, flirtatious smile, are all gazing at me, silent, perhaps dumbstruck.

"I'm defrosting a chicken," I repeat. "I'm . . . I didn't know I'd be playing, and so I thought I'd make this chicken thing tonight, and—"

I'm defrosting a chicken. I'd said it again.

They're all chuckling now. I have, in fifteen seconds of poultry overshare, managed to saddle myself with an earnest, housewifely, hospital-corners mantle that it will take me months to shake off.

"Listen, I didn't plan ahead, and I live in Brooklyn, and I guess what I'm saying is I kinda have to get home. Is it okay if I start next week? I can play then for sure." It will take me that long to live down the embarrassment.

I get a thumbs-up from Sam, who, now that I've declared I'm leaving to prepare a bird, is examining his clipboard, trying to decide who to put up in my place. The following week I'll return and win my debut match against a pouty-lipped gamine named Carly.

Stir-fry aside, I'm back.

The Game Beautiful

THE SOUND OF a rack of balls being broken by a wooden stick is instantly recognizable. It's angry and thrilling and shocking. It announces you—and the kind of game you play—as if through a bullhorn.

"You're startling someone, taking momentum from him before he takes it from you," a longtime league player says to me not long after I join Sam's team. "It's like mugging a mugger." He makes this statement while observing his teammate turn a neat triangle of balls into a thunderous starburst—and then watches the opposing player's eyes widen ever so slightly.

If breaking a rack of fifteen pool balls is a way to turn the tables on a criminal, my break isn't working. Not only isn't it working, it's helping out my would-be assailants. I'm being mugged, robbed, burgled, and carjacked on a weekly basis. My break is the equivalent of throwing a monogrammed silk handkerchief onto the table. It's meek, soft, dainty. More than anything, it's embarrassing.

I've never had a lot of power in my arms, but the key to an effective break is in the rest of your body; your arms are really just there to hold the cue steady. The push from your legs, the thrust from your hips, this is what enables you to stroke powerfully, to send the cue ball barreling through the triangle of balls like a sledgehammer.

One Monday evening I'm shooting a practice game at my new bar with a minuscule woman from England who I know from the pool league. Her break is symphonic. It's also something of a sight gag, since she can't weigh more than ninety-five pounds, and yet sometimes she barrels into the rack so hard that she sends some of the balls flying off the table. Her name is Katya and at first glance she appears harmless, with a long, blank face, a low voice, and thin, straight, neatly parted hair.

It's my turn and I've just broken the rack. The balls fan lazily into a little bouquet in the center of the table, with the requisite four balls just barely touching the rails. None of them have gone into a pocket.

"Do you always break like that?" Katya asks politely.

"Yes." I sigh. "It's pathetic, isn't it?"

"Could I give you some pointers?" She speaks in a softly accented voice. I assent immediately. She quietly re-racks, her blouse riding up as she leans over the table to reach the more far-flung balls. She's pale. Her jeans are faded. She has thin lips and small, deep-brown eyes that I can't read. She looks at me, then at the table.

"Use your hips," she commands. I blink in astonishment. A sly smile plays on her lips. "You've got to use your hips," she says. "Trust me. It will change your life."

Katya stands at the head of the pool table and places one hand firmly on the rail. "Don't be afraid to grip it," she says. "You can hold on for dear life." Then she looks down.

"Watch my feet." She places her left foot in front of her right one, as if taking a step. She wiggles around, makes some minor adjustments, like a small bird settling on the branch of a tree, then bends her knees. She lines up her stick and aims it squarely at the cue ball.

"Don't watch the stick or the ball," she says. "Watch my hips." She pulls the stick back smoothly, her right hip following, and as she rams the cue into the white ball her right hip comes with it and pushes forward—pushes *her* forward—so that her right shoulder, her back, her whole body, really, seems to be guiding the stick. I keep my eyes on her and hear the cue ball crack the other balls. It's loud. The balls go everywhere.

"See?" Katya says. I nod. "Try to copy that if you can."

My new break is inelegant to say the least. In fact, it borders on cartoonish, but it is getting the job done. Just as Katya demonstrated, I now hold on to the rail with my bridge hand when I break, my fingers curling over it, and lean back, my weight pulling on me. Then I bend my knees slightly, keeping my legs about hip-width apart, one foot a few inches in front of the other. I continue to grip the rail as if to keep myself from falling backward. I look like a quotation mark. After a few practice strokes, I pull myself forward as I'm stroking through. It's that strong pull across the rail, my hips moving forward, that gives me the much-needed extra power to make the balls crack and spin.

A strong break feels fantastic. The thwack vibrates through your body and is, if you'll forgive the heavy-handed symbolism, utterly satisfying. No wonder so many people want to smoke a cigarette afterward. After my break I usually end up bent over the table, almost lying on it, like a hastily thrown beach towel. I look ridiculous, but the balls are in a much better position these days than they were when I started out. I'm not sure how this new break "announces" me. I prefer to think of it as something quirky and artistic rather than the awkward overcompensation of a small, slender-armed woman. Katya's break doesn't look like mine. Her break is like the crack of a whip; you'll miss it if you blink. She says that once I get more used to this new hip-swiveling method, I won't have to clamp my hand on the rail and act as if I'm pulling myself over a fence, that it will become more "natural." All I know is that the balls are finally going in and occasionally I even feel . . . satisfied.

Encounters with people like Katya—and the impromptu lessons that come from them—are more regular now. As with many sports, there is a long history of mentoring in pool. If you're open to it, almost every player can serve as a teacher or guide. For example, Sam, my new captain, tries to help me with my defensive game since my offensive game is so spotty. He introduces me to the subtle joys of "playing safe," which seems to me an apt metaphor after my previous two pool team debacles.

"Why'd you make that ball?"

I've just sunk the 7-ball in the corner. Sam and I are at a poolroom in the East 20s, practicing before our team's match, which is in an hour and a half. I sense this is some sort of trick question. "Well, it was a pretty easy shot."

"Yeah, but now what? You don't have another shot after this one. What're you gonna do next?" Sam folds his arms across his chest and gazes at me, a slight smile visible beneath his beard. I remain silent.

"If you'd left that ball in the corner, without sinking it, just blocked the pocket with it, you wouldn't be faced with this decision, and you would've left nothing for your opponent. Now you're risking moving things around in his favor." I nod. "I know it's fun to make balls, but if you learn when to hold back, you'll be much better off. Especially when you're playing someone really good. Like me." Sam grins.

Sam learned his defensive technique—a technique far more sophisticated than the basic defensive moves he's showing me—from Jacques, who was there the night I was officially added to the team's lineup and who has since moved to New Mexico. (Pool mentors come and go. You have to learn from them when you can.) Sam is also teaching me the nuances of English, or sidespin, a gold mine for any pool player who learns how to apply it properly.

This method of controlling the path of the pool ball became commonplace after a wily, colorful Frenchman, a man known only as Captain Mingaud, made, in the early 1800s, what is considered the defining change in billiard equipment, and thus, to the game itself: He attached a leather tip to his cue. The result was increased friction between the cue stick and the cue ball, which enabled the player to apply sidespin to his shots, a technique that came to be known as "applying English."

Mingaud, who served time in a French prison (he supposedly asked that his sentence be extended so that he could spend more time working on his sidespin), dazzled spectators with his use of extreme spin, which was also referred to as "side," "twist," and "screw." Mingaud could send the balls all over the table in stunning patterns that he flawlessly manipulated and improved. By the 1870s, "English" became the commonly used term for achieving these feats; it worked its way into the vernacular when British players began employing the technique in their games in America. Still, the irony remains: It appears that a Frenchman invented English.

My attempts to apply English are faltering at best, but as Sam tells me, "If you choose the right shots in the right order and play safe when you have to, you really shouldn't have to use English. It's just something to learn for when you improve, so you can try fun stuff, like this." Sam leans over the table, strokes the cue stick so that it hits the right side of the cue ball, low, sending it toward the 4-ball, which then curves beautifully into a pocket.

SAM USED TO WORK in the "technology field" and had to wear a suit and tie, which he hated. At some point, his job became a casualty of media-conglomerate cost-cutting, and he simply didn't get another one. He no longer has a career—or a marriage. Both are merely memories of a different time in his life. It's a familiar story, sadly, and I've never pressed him for details. I feel as if I already know them. Sam has dark brown eyes that often look sad, even haunted. There's a sense of the "wrong turn" about him, of incomprehension at how he got to where he is. But unlike Trevor, who flashed and spat and fought and lusted, Sam seems to have accepted defeat and decided to make do with what he has. For example, he is an expert carpenter, which occupies some of his time when he's not at his pool bar. He makes all kinds of quirky wooden baubles—pocket markers for the pool table in the shape of coffins and skulls and other black-arts symbols; carved, painted containers to hold quarters (enough for multiple games of pool). They are cunning and delicate and mysterious. Not unlike Sam himself.

Sam is handy at larger projects as well. He goes out to Alan's place regularly to help him fix or upgrade parts of his house—gutters, bathroom tiles—but mostly they shoot pool. It's restorative for both of them. Alan, the guy on our team with the funny Gomer Pyle fishing hat, has a pool table in his house in the suburbs and practices on it every day. He's a retired businessman and has been playing in the APA league for more than fifteen years. He reads a lot about pool, watches tapes, makes diagrams for himself. He has much wisdom to impart. He and Sam work on their games by playing straight pool.

BETWEEN 1912 AND 1960, straight pool was the only pool game played in tournaments in the U.S., and it continued as the game played in the world championships until 1974. Today in New York City, if you go to an all-night poolroom late, say around midnight—a place like Broadway Billiards on 21st Street—you can see guys playing straight pool, silent matches that stretch on until the first rays of the sun peek through the sky. Straight pool is considered "old-school" in the best sense of the phrase. Rather than thinking of it as an old-fashioned game, pool players with any sense of history—which means most pool players—think of straight pool as something pure, simple, true.

The goal of the game is to be the first person to score the designated number of points. For example, in a *Twilight Zone* episode from 1961 called "A Game of Pool," Jonathan Winters and Jack Klugman shoot a literal life-or-death game of straight pool. They are playing to three hundred points, so the first one to earn that number wins. Straight pool is a simple ball-and-pocket game, meaning the players can shoot any ball at any time; they are not assigned stripes or solids based on what goes in on the break. They can even go for the 8-ball when they have an opening—it does not have to be the final ball to be put away. But each player must call the ball he's aiming for, and if it's a combination shot, he must state which balls will be hit and in what order. If he hits another ball instead, any balls sunk as a result are put back on the table.

The secondary goal of straight pool is to earn the necessary points while taking as few turns at the table as possible. This can be achieved only by making long, uninterrupted runs—thus preventing one's opponent from playing. (A "run" is a series of consecutive points earned during a single turn at the pool table.) Willie Mosconi, considered by many to be the greatest pool champion of all time, set the all-time high run record in straight pool in 1954 with 526. It was in an exhibition match, not a professional tournament, which makes it no less jaw-dropping.

Mike Shamos's 1994 book *Pool: History, Strategies, and Legends* provides an excellent explanation of the finer points of straight pool. For example, the opening shot of straight pool is known as the "safety break," and it is quite different from the thundering eight- and nine-ball breaks one sees during professional pool events on ESPN. When a straight-pool player begins the game, he or she has to make the cue ball hit only one of the fifteen object balls and then cause at least two others to hit the rails. Most players aim for a ball at the corner of the triangle, using a delicate but razor-sharp stroke.

Playing good pool is all about position, and in no game is position more important than in straight pool, since the key is to keep the run going for as long as possible. Confidence is crucial here. A player facing a shot in straight pool should feel that he has a high probability of sinking the ball—and continuing his run. If he doesn't, if he is even remotely unsure, then he will most likely decide to play safe, or execute a safety. Unlike in eight- or nine-ball, straight pool has the rather courtly rule of making players announce their safeties before playing them. The player must then hit an object ball and either sink another object ball as a result or cause the cue ball or an object ball to hit a rail. If a legal safety is made, no penalty is imposed, but any ball pocketed during the execution of a safety is put back on the table, and the player's turn is over. Since there is no limit to the number of safeties a player can make, the player's opponent must patiently and cunningly bide his time and wait for the player to make a mistake, to leave him that one tiny opening that will enable him to take over the table and try for a long run himself. A straight-pool match can—and usually does—go on for hours. Sam and Alan have the time, and if they don't, they make time.

That Alan and Sam are carrying on a grand tradition—and passing some of that tradition on to me in the form of advice about my game—is wonderful, and only occasionally draining. My fresh start with their team allows me to relax and consider aspects of pool that I haven't yet, namely, its vast and colorful history.

I always assumed that the game was English, invented by bewigged, frock-coated English aristocrats. W. G. Clifford, author of *Billiards Through the Centuries* (a book that is, inexplicably, only thirty-eight pages long, despite its imposing title), certainly supports my hackneyed thesis. Could billiards be anything but English? his slim volume asks.

Clifford is supremely biased toward England being the mother of billiards, though he doesn't have what I would call ironclad proof; he simply lists important, reliable personages who, like him, believe that billiards could have emerged only in England: Sir Philip Sidney, the author of *Arcadia*, held this belief (this would be around 1580), and John Arbuthnot (1667–1735), the Scottish mathematician, royal physician, and wit, considered billiards entirely English. Ben Jonson and Samuel Johnson—these men are not known liars, and they, too, according to Clifford, were convinced that billiards was a game purely English in origin.

But even after assembling his lists and testimonials, Clifford, a true lover of the game, reluctantly concedes that it's just as likely that billiards originated in France, and that it was first played there on a triangular table that was introduced at the Château du Blois while Henry III (1207–1272) was visiting.

Furthering the case for France in his pithy, meticulous book *Modern Billiards*, which was first published in 1880 (more than fifty years before Clifford's), publisher and historian Hugh Collender is even more specific, positing that it was Henri de Vigne, a carpenter and cabinetmaker in France, who came up with the game—and the table on which it's played—for the amusement of King Louis XI, who reigned from 1461 to 1483. (An inventory of items purchased by the King lists "billiard balls and billiard table for pleasure and amusement." His table was reportedly set on a bed of stone with a cloth covering. Balls were driven into a hole in the center.) Two of the French king's successors were billiards players as well: a little over a century and a half later, King Louis XIV, and then, six decades after that, Louis XVI, who played along with his memorable wife, Marie Antoinette. Indeed, the queen owned an exquisite cue made out of a single piece of ivory, a possession so treasured that she kept it in a special locked cabinet—and wore the key to that cabinet around her neck.

Frustratingly, Collender's volume also points out that billiards could just as likely have been introduced centuries before these dates—possibly in France, but in England, too, for that matter, when the Knights Templar returned from their first or second Crusade, though historians since Collender call this notion ludicrous. He even proffers that billiards may have started out as the game of marbles, or even as golf, or perhaps that billiards *evolved into* golf.

My favorite story involving billiards's early beginnings is of course the darkest one: In 1576, Mary, Queen of Scots, while a state prisoner in Scotland, was reportedly enraged at being denied access to her billiard table, a beloved possession she had brought with her from France. While trapped inside the cold walls of Fotheringay Castle on the orders of her first cousin, Elizabeth I, she complained of the cruelty, of the inhumanity, of depriving her of this singular pleasure.

I have read this account of Mary's complaints in enough serious volumes and loony websites to think the story is not apocryphal. It delights me. Not her misery (though I can, in my own way, relate) but her passion. The idea that this woman—the daughter of King James V—was hooked on the very same game that has lured me to smoky bars and lonely cantinas and dank pool rooms thrills me—not because it's somehow validating, but because it just seems so absurd. I always preferred Elizabeth. I think I may have sold Mary short.

I don't believe Mary longed for her billiard table out of defiance or petulance or arrogance. I suspect that she was simply a wreck, knowing that her wily, ambitious young cousin was going to outsmart her. So she longed for the game and for the smooth, sturdy table on which it's played, as a palliative, an oasis of stillness and quiet in her churning, increasingly dangerous world.

They tortured her, of course. They never brought her the table. She died without ever playing another game. Don't ever underestimate the power and cruelty of a Virgin Queen. But either as an insult or as a tribute, after her execution, her body was wrapped in the cloth from the table.

Throwing billiard scholars another curve, there's the line "Let's to billiards" that Cleopatra says to Charmian in Act II, Scene V, of William Shakespeare's *Antony and Cleopatra*. Charmian declines, claiming, "My arm is sore; best play with Mardian." Mardian is a eunuch. Cleopatra suggests fishing instead.

For years, because of Shakespeare's play, people assumed that billiards was being played by pharaohs in Egypt. Why else would the playwright have written the game into his drama about the ancient Egyptian queen?

Despite Cleopatra's passion for billiards in Shakespeare's play, the reference is anachronistic. Shakespeare was having fun with the audience. Billiards did not exist in ancient Egypt. Likewise, reports that Socrates played the game are also false, as is the fantastic claim that Saint Augustine saw a billiard table while traveling in Africa. Historians such as Collender have debunked similar intelligences, including the story that Cathire More, an Irish king in the second century A.D., bequeathed to his nephew a collection of billiard equipment that included brass balls and cues. This turned out to be nothing more than a translator's error.

Antony and Cleopatra was written most likely in 1606 or 1607 and was registered for publication in 1608, and it's certainly true that billiards and its ancestors were around before that. But pool's history, while long and vivid, is also rather murky and mysterious. Collender puts it best, I think: "Billiards was practically without beginning. As with untold other excellences, so with that."

Every country seems to enjoy taking credit for creating billiards, not just England and France: Persia, India, China, and Russia have all waved their flags at one point or another, but no one knows for sure who actually came up with the game. The assumption has always been that the word *billiard* comes from the French word *bille*, which means ball, or else, as Mike Shamos notes in his *New Illustrated Encyclopedia of Billiards*, from the word *bilart*, which is a type of stick. Most billiards scholars agree that mentions of the game were not widespread until the twelfth century, and that in its embryonic form it was played—like croquet—on a lawn.

The first mention of billiards as an *indoor* game was in 1470. (When it rained, the billiard bed, made of stone, would be moved inside.) Henry VIII (1509–1547) played something called *shovilla bourde* (shuffleboard) in which "one rolls a ball or two on the 'shovilla bourde' just to see what happens"—a bit of trivia I learned from an article in *The American Poolplayer*. The game was a precursor to billiards, most likely; croquet falls into this category as well. These games, or variations of them, were scaled down in size over the years, moved from the lawn to the table, and eventually brought inside the house. It is no wonder that the cloth covering the billiard table has always been green: It is simulating grass, which is the "cloth" on which all of these games started. Clifford writes, "Billiards, as 'the game beautiful,' owes everything to the captivating green cloth, [which] enchants the eye."

In their earliest incarnations, the cues used in billiards were called *maces*. Rather than ending in a narrow, round tip like the ones used today, the early sticks had wide, flat, somewhat trapezoidal pieces attached to the end instead, reminiscent of a scoop or a shallow shovel. Thus, the mace shoved the balls along the table rather than struck them.

But this could be problematic if a ball was nestled next to a rail. In these instances, the player was allowed to turn the mace around and use the other end of it to propel the ball. The handle on the opposite end of the mace was known in France as the *queue*. This is, of course, where the word *cue* comes from. The cue—the instrument that succeeded the mace—was invented in the late 1600s.

But the "crowning glory" of the billiard table, at least according to Clifford, was its brilliant cloth, which used to be made of a coarse, thick wool, similar to a horse blanket, that gripped the ball as if it had fingers. Today's wool cloth is "superfine," so the ball no longer hops and rumbles down the table like a caboose but instead rolls smoothly and silently like a modern engine. When billiard cloth is too smooth, players refer to the pool table as a "fast table." Likewise, players grouse that a table covered in thick, pockmarked, or nubby cloth is "slow."

AS WITH THE GAME'S early origins, there are various hypotheses about when and how "the noble game of billiards," as it was originally called, crossed the Atlantic and found its way to America. One notion is that the Spanish explorer Hernando de Soto introduced it while slashing his way through Florida. Another, more embraceable, scenario is that the English brought it with them to Virginia in the early 1600s. And a third, no less interesting or likely explanation, is that the French Huguenots began playing it in South Carolina in the 1690s. Nothing substantiates any of these tales, but, like most rumors, they have lingered long after they should've been put to rest.

The best bet is that the game was introduced in the "New World" around 1700—possibly even earlier—once self-sufficient colonies were established. Making billiard tables was a flourishing business in England; thus, it wasn't long before newly transplanted cabinetmakers in the colonies began applying their skills to the billiard-table trade as well. At that time, the tables were seven feet by fourteen feet and had eight legs, six pockets, and cushions stuffed with, of all things, hair.

George Washington was known to have had a bit of a billiards obsession; entries in his diaries during the French and Indian War tell of his wins and losses in Pennsylvania and Ohio—and the money that changed hands as a result. (His largest winning was estimated at $1.75.) Abe Lincoln is said to have been mad for the game as well. And the dome at Monticello, Thomas Jefferson's home, was reportedly designed as a billiards room, but because a law was passed in Virginia in 1781 taxing billiard tables, even those in private homes, the domed room never housed a table.

But by the early twentieth century, billiards no longer had to hide—from taxes or from the law. It was a game for gentlemen and for hardworking men. Indeed, the game had become so widespread and popular, whether from the English or the French or the Spanish, that it spawned its own set of player cards: In the early 1900s, billiard cards were like baseball cards—informative, colorful, and omnipresent, glorifying the famous pool and billiard champions of the time.

So what, exactly, is the difference between the pool I play and the billiards of Mary, Queen of Scots? To begin with, billiards is a carom sport only, one that involves a player using a cue stick to send balls to different spots on the table by using the rails, or *cushions*, as they're called, and the other object balls. Billiards is played with three balls: two white and one red, with one of the whites designated as a cue ball. (Sometimes it's played with a white, a yellow, and a red ball to make it easier to distinguish among the balls.) There are variations to the game, such as three-cushion billiards, which requires that the cue ball make at least three distinct cushion contacts before hitting the second object ball for the first time.

The early version of indoor billiards did not include table pockets. A billiard table, or carom table, is a rectangular table covered in cloth, *without* pockets. Table pockets were not added until the late 1700s. This later version of the game, pocket billiards, the one we consider the true precursor to pool, was played on a six-pocket table as it is now, but with the three object balls—two white, one red—instead of fifteen balls of different colors. Players could score either by "making a billiard" upon two object balls (otherwise known as a carom shot; a carom describes contact between the cue ball and two other balls; it's the contact with the *second* ball that actually completes the carom), by pocketing the red ball, or by pocketing one's cue ball after contact with an object ball (this is the reverse of what happens today; now the idea is to sink an *object ball* after contact with the cue ball).

The terms *pool* and *pocket billiards* are almost always used interchangeably, even though technically they are not synonymous. Pocket billiards simply describes the kind of table on which the game is played; it notes the addition of pockets to a billiard table, which changes the point of the game. The game of pool, however, does not refer to the playing surface or pockets or to some obscure billiard rule but, rather, to a different essence entirely. The word *pool* comes from the French word *poule,* which means "a collective stake or ante." In other words, pool refers to *betting,* to players wagering on the outcome of games by "pooling their bets" (something else I learned from Mike Shamos's encyclopedia). This is one of the reasons pool has always connoted something slightly more sinister than billiards. Simply put, originally pool was pocket billiards with money behind it. But the seediness that people often associate with the game came about later, and for no other reason than proximity.

Initially, pool was played in betting establishments that were known, not surprisingly, as *poolrooms* (these rooms were different from public billiard halls, which were called billiard *parlors* until the late nineteenth century). Poolrooms actually had nothing to do with billiards. They were places where men could bet on horse races. The people who ran these rooms installed billiard tables simply as way to divert their customers, who had to wait around to find out the out-comes of the various races on which they were placing money. Thus the mean, low life of the horse-betting hall was directly connected to billiards, at least as far as the self-righteous public was concerned. If the room owners had installed Ping-Pong tables or miniature golf instead, perhaps Paul Newman would've starred in *The Paddler* or *The Color of Birdies.*

As a result of pool's link to wagering on horses, the crusty members of the billiard industry of the late nineteenth and early twentieth centuries loathed being associated with the game of pool, with its gamblers and con men and bookies and shifty horse people. They felt the true essence of the aristocratic game was sullied by dirty money. So a turn-of-the-century PR machine went into action, with industry big shots taking out ads in local papers to try to disassociate billiards from pool, battling, in fact, to eliminate the name *pool* altogether. Industry lobbyists preferred the term *pocket billiards*, claiming (incorrectly) that it was the proper, *accurate* term, not just a more palatable one. In 1911, "Continuous Pool," also known as *straight pool*, which was the game played in official pool championships, was publicly changed to Pocket Billiards. But it didn't stop there. New York State actually passed a statute that forbade any billiard establishment from using the word *pool* in its name or on any signs on its premises.

Eventually, this evangelical fervor died down and poolroom owners once again started using the name *pool* to refer to the game. Soon the name eclipsed pocket billiards altogether and pool became the standard term used for playing a game with fifteen multihued balls and six pockets; *billiards*, as a stand-alone term, referred now to the carom game only, the one without pockets. There are more than two hundred versions of the game of pool today, intriguing variations that employ different numbers and combinations of balls and have quirky rules about the kinds of shots you can take, the number of players you're allowed, even the number of pockets you can use. Straight pool, eight-ball, and nine-ball are merely three of the most common forms of the game.

AFTER FINALLY SORTING OUT maces and cues, English and twist, billiards and straight pool, just to confuse matters for the novice pool enthusiast, there's the glorious game known as snooker, the same game I observed through the windows of Chelsea Billiards in the fall of 1998, and a different animal altogether. It's an eccentric, complicated game that can be maddening or thrilling, depending on your passion. (I find it mind-boggling, but perhaps it's my American thickheadedness.)

Snooker is English in origin, played on a large English billiards table, meaning one with pockets that's usually six feet by twelve feet in size, with twenty-two balls. The set of balls comprises fifteen reds, six "colours" (British spelling intentional), and a white cue ball. The key to snooker is that each of the balls has a numerical value. The reds, which at the beginning of the game are racked in a neat triangle at the head of the table, are worth one point. The other colors—yellow, green, brown, blue, pink (yes, pink), and black—have numerical values that range from two to seven and have designated spots on the table. At the end of the game, the player with the most points (not the most balls sunk) wins. Also interesting to note: Snooker is the only billiards game in which you earn points for defensive moves. In fact, "snookering" your opponent, or leaving the cue ball in a position where he or she cannot hit a red ball (or, if all the reds have been sunk, the appropriately valued colored ball) is a huge part of snooker strategy.

Snooker, too, has its own quirky history. The game is said to have been invented around 1875 by bored British army officers stationed in India who combined elements from various billiards games they knew from their respective hometowns into a new hybrid. As the legend goes, a British colonel in a regiment stationed in Jubblepore, India, while playing the strange game one day, realized, much to his annoyance, that he didn't have a shot after his opponent missed his shot. Furious, he called the man a "snooker," which, as Mike Shamos relays in his encyclopedia, was "a term of derision applied to first-year cadets at the Royal Military Academy in Woolich." And thus a new game was born.

ACCORDING TO THE *Sports Participation in America Report*, which was released in 2006 by the Sporting Goods Manufacturers Association, "Approximately 35.1 million people in the U.S. played pool and/or billiards in 2005." Considering how long—and in how many different forms—pool has been around, this astoundingly high number of enthusiasts is not surprising. And as with baseball and other sports that inspire passionate devotion, most serious pool and billiard players feel some sort of connection to the game's multilayered history.

Sociologist and pool historian Ned Polsky writes in his famous 1967 essay collection *Hustlers, Beats, and Others* that even down-and-out pool hustlers have a strong "awareness of, involvement with, and reverence for" their predecessors and the accomplishments of those predecessors, much stronger than the regard that other kinds of "deviants" have for their historical counterparts. Even teenage pool hustlers, he adds, are, more often than not, full of respect for their forefathers and foremothers and have a reservoir of pool lore at their fingertips.

What most players want, of course, whether teenagers or old-timers, city dwellers or suburban homeowners, hustlers or straight-arrows, patrons of barrooms or poolrooms, is to be part of a grand tradition—and maybe even to make a little history of their own. I am now a member of this eclectic group as well.

Sore Loser

IT'S A CLEAR, sparkling Monday evening and we're playing at a bar in the far West Village. The walk to it, through narrow brick streets, past tall, immaculate townhouses that look set-designed, beautiful people out and about, some walking tiny dogs, is glorious. The air is delicious and sweet. Sunlight glances off the Hudson River as the sun sets, flushing the sidewalks pink. It doesn't feel as if I'm on my way to a dark little pool bar, but that's where I'm headed. I arrive, buoyant and eager, at Biff's, a microscopic bar where, it seems, even the pool table is drawn to scale, a good half-foot shorter than the three-and-a-half-foot-by-seven-foot bar tables on which we usually play. The table is legal but annoying. It looks doll-like to me, as if a Happy Meal version of my team will start playing on it soon.

Biff's outer room is narrow, with exposed brick and a somewhat upscale beer selection. The clientele, unlike in most of the bars we play at, is "alternative"—educated, artsy, gay. The place is small enough that the bartender can keep track of everyone, and he says when I walk by later in the evening, as if we're old pals, "You want another Sierra Nevada?"—a bottle of which I'd ordered when I first arrived.

Pool at Biff's is played in a tiny back room, the table covered in black cloth, giving it a Gothic look and making the place feel like a cave. In contrast, there's a pleasant patio in the back, with a couple of tables. It rains for a little while, leaving the patio glistening and fresh, a good spot to escape cigarette smoke, though it doesn't prevent Sam from lighting up a cigar while he's standing out there drinking a Sam Adams. In one corner of the pool room, a bizarre video game sits fatly against the wall. It flashes a series of images of big-breasted, scantily clad women, pouting their bee-stung lips and touching themselves provocatively. I wonder how this is going over with the militant feminists in camouflage shorts and cutoff tank tops huddled around shot glasses on the patio. But tonight isn't about Simone de Beauvoir, it's about Valerie feeling much more comfortable losing a game than Fred, who doesn't like it when *anyone* on his team loses, least of all him.

I met Valerie the previous week, and it's putting it mildly to say that she has presence. She's long-limbed, just shy of six feet in her heels, and slurps down beers as if they're water. She has silky black hair that jets straight down her back. She swings it off her shoulders like black rope, then a curtain opens and you see her lovely, blazing face and movie-star smile.

Valerie wears vivid blue-violet eye shadow—lots of it, two different shades, brushed exotically out to the sides—with dark blue eyeliner and accompanying dark mascara. She is Elizabeth Taylor with a nosering.

Valerie likes to paint on thick, luscious lipstick, too, deep berry shades that stand out on her pale face like ripe fruit. A row of silver-hoop earrings stair-steps up her ears. Metal looks good on her. Her teeth are an especially brilliant white and she flashes them often, out of excitement, ribaldry, and sometimes anger. The latter occasions inevitably erupt when Fred insists on coaching her.

That Monday at Biff's, Valerie is playing well, even though she looks gargantuan alongside the tiny table in the tiny room. I imagine the table is a challenge for someone tall; for me the adjustment is not that great. The table can't seem to contain her energy. Valerie tends to hit hard, often putting too much into the ball so that she overshoots, the cue ball caroming off rails when much of the time what she really needs most is for the table to remain still. Her aim is good and her confidence high, but the object balls, once hit by her zigzagging cue ball, routinely scatter across the table after she shoots so that she has no idea where they will end up. In other words, she's not playing for position. She's aware of this but doesn't seem to care, and she's extremely feisty about unsolicited coaching from tiny, neurotic men.

Fred—who's the only person on the team besides me who doesn't smoke—looks about twelve years old, with his bowl haircut and across-the-forehead bangs framing little round wire-rimmed glasses. He's shorter than I am, which is a real accomplishment; I'd put him at five feet even. Fred loves keeping score—a task usually considered onerous, one that everybody dreads. I think it's because he likes holding the clipboard, which gives him an air of authority, although it also makes him look like a camp counselor.

Valerie is holding her own against her opponent, a skinny, slouching, gel-haired hipster who looks as if he should be hosting a program on MTV, but he's winning, in part because he's familiar with this small table, and Valerie is, as usual, banging the shit out of everything.

Fred keeps interrupting Valerie as she's about to shoot: "Do you want to talk about it?" She ignores him, so he says it again. "Do you want to talk about it, Val?" This is what the coaches always ask, they use this exact phrasing—not because they want to "talk about" anything, but because they want to tell you what to do, which can sometimes save you from a blunder that will haunt you the rest of the game, but it can also rub you the wrong way, which is what it always does with Valerie. She heaves a loud, exasperated sigh and ignores Fred, but he won't stop pestering her. He keeps suggesting they "talk about it" at almost every turn, and she digs her heels in, won't even look over at him. Late in the deciding game, she finally finds herself in a situation that seems to stump her. She stands back and cocks a hip, staring hard at the table. It's a tough shot—hitting the bright red 3-ball the length of the table to knock another ball into the corner pocket. If she succeeds with the combo, she'll be able to sink the 3 next and then make the 8. It's rather ingenious but complicated. Valerie likes to take the hard road, though. She prefers the challenge. Right on cue, Fred interrupts, wondering if she'd like to talk about it. Valerie gives him the finger and says calmly, "I'm going to kill you." Fred stays quiet this time.

Valerie makes her shot the way she wants, and while it doesn't turn out how she'd hoped, it's not disastrous either. Her combination didn't work, but she seems to have flummoxed her opponent with where she left the cue ball. As Mr. MTV studies the table, Valerie turns abruptly to Fred, her long hair whipping around as if she's going through a car wash—I think I actually heard it snap—and hisses, "*Don't do that.* I knew what I wanted to try. If I make a mistake, it's my mistake. Now fuck off." It's not that Valerie likes to lose, she just doesn't like being told how to win.

One time Valerie shows up late to a match, looking slightly dejected. It's raining, the torrential variety, and I comment on it, as one does. She sighs. "I know. *I bought an umbrella.*" She says this with what seems an excessive amount of intensity. "I've never owned an umbrella," she explains. "I'm not joking. Never. *I like the rain.*" I take this in and smile.

"I walk in it all the time," she continues. "I mean, who cares, right? It's just rain. I like it." I think about it and yes, I do recall Valerie arriving wet and unfettered on several occasions. But today's rain has finally gotten the better of her. There's simply too much of it, coming down too hard. It has defeated her. So she bought the damn umbrella and now she feels as if she's betrayed herself. I don't know how to comfort her, other than to nod sympathetically. And I really am sympathetic. She seems to be in pain.

Valerie's body reminds me of a panda's, soft and curvy and secretly powerful. Her belly is often visible, hanging over her jeans, under a tank top. She walks coolly, her gaze fixed, her back straight but her hips swinging from side to side, daring you to comment. Her boots make intimidating clomps. She's confident in her body and in her game. Sometimes I ask Valerie how her match went, if I've been off shooting at another table or getting a drink at the bar or fussing in the ladies' room or, if we're at Biff's, staring at slutty video games, and she'll sip her beer, take a drag off her cigarette, and say, "Oh, I lost," like it's nothing, not even worth a shrug, and I am always surprised. I always assume she's won.

VALERIE IS SUCH A gracious loser because she never really seems to view her pool matches as potential losses in the first place. Her confidence is so high—and her disdain for people who try to compete aggressively with her so pure—that a loss to her is never more than an "off night." I've never encountered another pool player with this quality. Even Sam and Alan will show frustration or a weakening of resolve on occasion, and each has his own rituals to combat these feelings.

My own history with pool losses is rockier. When I finally leave the cocoon of Chelsea Billiards's pool school and play for my first team, Wally's team, out of a loud, raucous bar on Third Avenue, I am so terrified of playing that just finishing a game without wetting my pants seems an accomplishment. But once I get my first win—it's against a woman named Rebecca who plays out of Barfly, another Third Avenue watering hole, where the pool table is set at a strange angle in the back of the bar, so that for certain shots you have to use a "shortie," or short stick, to shoot; otherwise, the butt of your regular cue will ram into an unfortunately placed pillar—once I beat Rebecca and begin to *desire* winning, begin to yearn to play better, to play well, to play excellently, to play perfectly . . . well, my patience with losing deteriorates pretty quickly.

Anyone who plays any kind of sport, whether solitary or as part of team, knows this spiral well. For pool players I believe it is especially piquant, perhaps because, as I observe again and again, losing seems to be such a part of the pool-player personality: the combative, self-pitying underdog, the unemployed boozer with an ax to grind, the tiny, bespectacled engineer with something to prove, the charming young lawyer, drinking himself to death in front of my eyes. I don't fit into any of these categories, and yet I, too, seem to metamorphose into someone else once I've had a taste of winning on that green cloth.

The journalist David McCumber writes in his terrific book about pool hustling, *Playing off the Rail*, that playing and observing the game on the road for so long gave him the opportunity to think about the psychological nuances of losing. He learned up close and personal just how losing felt, which he describes as "being hit in the nuts with a hot steam iron." But then he adds that at the same time, knowing how to lose is a valuable quality, because it seems to him that "only in that frame of reference could the sweetness of winning be fully appreciated."

McCumber's point is a strong one, and one that eludes me for quite some time. For a while my losing demeanor just plain sucks. After that first win at Barfly, I start practicing more at Chelsea Billiards, wanting another W next to my name on the clipboard. One evening after work, down in the smoky basement, playing a pickup game with some girl who's come to the pool hall with her giggling friends, I miss an extremely easy, straight-on center-ball shot, a common occurrence for beginners, and I proceed to throw and splinter a cue, John McEnroe-style. It's a cue that belongs to the pool hall—I don't own one yet—and while it isn't a very good piece of equipment, it's unconscionable of me to treat it like my own personal golf club. I toss it angrily to the side, where it cracks against the edge of the regulation-size table and falls to the floor. A shocked silence follows. I'm part of that silence, stunned and embarrassed by my own petulance, and at the same time still steamed about missing the shot. My opponent looks frightened, like maybe I need to be on Thorazine. I pick up the cue, which is still in one piece, thank God, and examine it. There's a very obvious crack in its joint, with a sliver of wood jutting out as if the cue has been struck by a small bolt of lightning. I look around sheepishly. People have returned to their games. I shuffle to the wall, put the cue back into one of the cue holders, and quickly select another, hoping no one's noticed. I return to a now-abandoned table, the balls in the same spread as when I left them but my opponent nowhere to be found. Shamefaced, I quietly work on sinking the remaining balls.

Of course this is exactly the kind of behavior that can get you into serious trouble in a real game of pool, not only because of the bad sportsmanship and the breaking of a rule (you can't throw equipment around or your game is forfeited) but because it gives your opponent a distinct psychological advantage. No one's ever cowed by this kind of behavior. They're buoyed by it, energized because your weakness is exposed. What the hell had I been thinking, hurling a pool cue?

FOR MANY PLAYERS, the wins and losses at pool cut deep, define them. Perhaps this is because pool night is the one night of the week in which people who don't often have control in their daily lives can finally have a taste of it. When that control—or the illusion of it—is shattered, the losses often turn ugly.

That's because losing at pool is ugly. The game is beautiful, and the kind of loss where you really blow it, really mess up a shot that should've been easy, mars that beauty like a black splotch on a delicate watercolor. Maybe this is why the players—myself included—often react so strongly to a bad night at the table, because they are staring at ruin, and sometimes it hits a little too close to home.

Sam, the fuzzy-bearded captain of my team, becomes enraged if, during a match, someone says, "Good shot," and the shot in question is a standard, run-of-the-mill, easy shot. It drives him over the edge, sometimes resulting in an embarrassing display of loud-voiced theatrics. To him, a comment like this is patronizing; it is, I suppose, like complimenting Dale Earnhardt Jr. on a nice left turn at a traffic light.

Sam is particularly sensitive to such encouragement when he's down. He doesn't like to be soothed or reassured. He likes to play angry. "I play better when I'm pissed," he's told me more than once. "I hate friendly games."

The people I've met through pool are often drifting in and out of employment, Sam included. Half of the people on my team are unemployed. And the ones who do hold jobs, with the exception of Alan, seem to experience a high level of frustration in them. Maybe this is why the wins and losses begin to take on so much meaning. Or maybe it's just the alcohol.

I sometimes wonder, as I look around my bar at the assemblage of people sprawled on stools, loping back and forth to the restrooms, leaning against the wall where the chalkboard hangs, names written creakily, half-legibly—Gina, Ryan, Marty, J.P.—if there isn't an element of enjoyment, of relish, even, in being down on your luck, in being the guy on whom people have given up, the scrapper, the I'll-show-you-all fellow. The pool players who spend all of their time in bars and poolrooms, the ones I've encountered regularly, who now seem to me to be just part of the scenery, their faces and mannerisms and cue strokes as familiar as my own shoes, often ham up the role of underdog, or rogue, or loveable loser, or guy you don't mess with. They mutter and laugh ruefully about being broke, drunk, unemployed, or some combination of all three as if it's a badge of honor. Then, the kicker, the surprise, the antidote to everything: They kick your ass on the table, with complete control. Often with grace. Of course, if they don't, if they lose, it can get hairy, especially when the wrong mix of personalities is involved.

I DECIDE, not long after joining Sam's team, to use Alan as a role model when it comes to my "carriage" during a match. Alan exemplifies all that is good and gracious about the game. He is the antithesis of the guy out to prove something. His shoulders are free of chips.

Although technically I met Alan that first night in the bar, when I walked in from the subway searching for a team, then departed clownishly to prepare my recently defrosted chicken, it takes me a while, many Mondays, to get to know Alan, and by this I mean barely scratching the surface, for he's not an easy man to know, despite his propensity for telling long, drawn-out stories.

Alan is fifty-seven, which makes him the elder statesman of the team, and one of the older guys in the league. He looks much younger. I'm shocked when I find out his eldest child—a son—is my age. If they made a movie of Alan's life, I'd probably cast Tom Hanks as the lead, the nice, clean-cut guy with a secret darkness inside him. Alan seems to have walked out of a 1950s movie. He looks like an astronaut. He has thick, straight brown hair, side-parted and kept closely cut. His face is handsome, remarkably unlined, his jaw still firm and square. His expression is inquisitive, never tense. I find it hard to believe that anyone can be this relaxed. I think the questioning look is something he developed years ago to hide any inner pain or darkness that might lurk. His eyes are dark brown, alert, as if he's waiting for something to happen. The eyebrows that frame them are thick and wiry, each one extending in a prominent half-circle. There's something earnest about Alan, though he himself often comes across as prickly. Ask Alan a question, and he'll reply, deadpan, his eyes boring into you, "What, are you writing a book?" Or sometimes he'll simply put his hands on his hips and say, "I don't think that's any of your business." It takes me a while to locate the mischief behind these retorts.

Alan also likes to tell self-deprecating jokes that poke fun at his "boring personality," at his lack of sex appeal. "You have no interest in this story, do you? I don't blame you. Neither does my wife. Hell, she has no interest in *me*." Alan and Lily have been married for more than thirty years.

When he shoots pool, Alan wears half-glasses, a quirk I love. He peers over them or through them, depending on the shot. They hang from a cord around his neck when he's not shooting, giving him the air of an old-fashioned librarian. He commutes to our pool matches from a suburb north of New York, usually by train, but occasionally he drives, arriving in the biggest, ugliest Fleetwood I've ever seen (the Pimpmobile, as he calls it), which seems to take up about seventeen city blocks when he parks it, angling it into the space as if it's a boat he's trying to attach to a trailer. Alan takes pool—and its rules—very seriously, because he has such respect and feeling for the game. "My passion is pool," he says to me once, in a voice that to anyone else would sound free of passion.

Alan has been in the league more than fifteen years, and his record is exemplary. He's a 6—one rank below the best—and completely calm when he's playing, cool-eyed as he studies the spread of balls. The confidence he exudes as he circles the table is a pleasure to watch. At times, it inspires awe in even the hardest of hard cases. I've seen Alan break and run a table, and I've seen him come back from a 0–3 deficit and win the next five games to take the match. And when this happens, he never gets cocky or overbearing. He walks up to his opponent and forcefully, respectfully extends his hand. "Good game," he says, making eye contact. This is usually followed by a modest shaking of his head and maybe even a "You almost had me there," even if he's just trounced the guy. When he makes a brilliant shot—which is often—he shakes off my compliments. "I'm not doing anything. The guy's giving me the game."

When Alan shoots, sometimes (and I've seen this with other excellent players as well) he bends over the table, his body in the shape of a perfect A, legs spread wide, knees locked, his body completely taut. To someone who doesn't know pool it probably looks odd, even silly, as if he's in some sort of military-inspired exercise class, but it works.

Despite the qualities that put Alan a cut above most guys who are tangling in these bars, classy, noble qualities that I feel are obvious, losing does something to people. It momentarily blinds them to the obvious. The women and men who revel in their hard-luck stories— until they find that they can't overturn them for a few hours as they'd planned—are a constant danger in the league. When another player, or a circumstance, gets the better of them, they lose sight of what's good about the game—and a guy like Alan who plays it—and they reveal the part of themselves, the part of all of us, really, that no one wants to see, the part that most people manage to keep buried somewhere, far from sunlight. It's ugly and upsetting to watch it unfold, which is what happens on this particular Monday, when Valerie is ignoring Fred and I'm sipping Sierra Nevadas and the patio is wet with rain, and cheap, bosomy women flicker across a video screen in the corner while a punk from Biff's, who looks like an inebriated reality-TV host, decides to let loose his petulant, angry-at-the-world, disenfranchised adolescent soul in a match against Alan.

Alan's opponent, Reggie, a tall, sinewy guy in his twenties, with puffy brown hair that caps a long face, giving him the appearance of a handsome Q-tip, is ranked a 4. He's a good player—sure of himself, even a little swaggering. He wears a frayed button-down shirt over a T-shirt, letting it hang open casually. The sleeves are scrunched up his arms, which are covered with wiry, dark hair. He sings along with some of the songs on the jukebox and swigs from a beer bottle every now and then, appearing to the world just a regular joe. Since Alan is a 6, he'll have to win five games to win the match, whereas Reggie will have to win only three.

Alan likes to chew gum when he plays, and tonight is no different. I can hear him chewing, quick and rhythmic, like a kid. He keeps his chalk in his pocket, never on the table. As for the cubes that sit on the table, the ones provided by the bar, Alan moves them around so that they are never near him when he's making a shot, an idiosyncrasy he and I share. (We both find the little squares a distraction when they're in our line of sight.) Alan shakes his head if he has to make a difficult shot, or if he makes a rare mistake, but other than that slight, occasional movement, his face is a perfect mask, controlled by an invisible switch he turns on and off. He moves purposefully and politely and never raises his voice or takes his eyes off the table. If a gnat lands on the cloth, he notices it.

The match begins and the two men trade games back and forth. Alan takes the first game, but Reggie is no slouch. He holds his own and, sure enough, comes back to win the next one. Alan remains unruffled. He dominates for the first half of game three, but Reggie stages an impressive comeback. The two men start playing more defensively. Alan executes several wicked safeties, but Reggie always manages to squeeze out of them and hit an object ball so that he doesn't give Alan ball in hand. It's a long game, but Alan finally finds himself on the 8, where we all knew he'd end up. It's a makeable shot in one of the corner pockets, but shockingly, after sinking the 8, Alan sends the cue ball into the opposite corner, something none of us saw coming, and scratches, losing the game. This means that Reggie is now "on the hill"—that is, if he wins this next game, he will have won three altogether and thus take the whole match.

Alan stays cool, shakes his head at his blunder, but racks the balls confidently. Reggie has been drinking beer throughout the match, and with an unexpected victory handed to him, he's getting cocky. He laughs too loudly at the jokes and ribbing from his teammates, doesn't look at Alan, tosses the chalk in the air and catches it, wanders around, waiting for Alan to finish racking and step back.

Reggie breaks strongly; the balls scatter and one goes in. And off they go.

Alan bears down in this game, since it's do or die, and this, along with Reggie's cockiness, is working in his favor. Reggie seems to realize that he may have overstepped himself and so he starts to rein himself in. His mischievous grin disappears and his brow furrows. I can feel the concentration of both men. We all feel it, and we fall silent. The safety dance begins again.

Each man is trying to lock up the other. Their shots are small and tight and steely. A predatory jolt has been injected into the game. Alan chews his gum furiously, moves the chalk around the table compulsively, fingers his own chalk in his pocket, says nothing. Reggie grunts and groans and mutters and stretches his body to its full height after bending to make a tiny shot against the rail so that Alan's 1-ball is blocked.

I would've thought Reggie would be the one to blink first, but to my surprise it's Alan, who, in a daring move to break out some of his solids, scratches on his shot. Reggie gets ball in hand. He's finally going to get a chance to run it out. He calls a time-out, standing off to the side as his teammates consult. Alan shakes his head and stands next to Fred, disgusted with himself. Sam is nowhere to be seen, but that doesn't mean he isn't watching. I am constantly surprised when Sam emerges from the men's room or from another pool table or from a conversation around a jukebox knowing exactly what the last shot made was, and by whom, and what his player should do next.

Finally, Reggie's designated coach sidles over and begins talking to him in a low voice, his hand pantomiming what he thinks he should do. Reggie nods, makes a few mumbled comments of his own, then dismisses his coach and approaches the table. He places the cue ball in front of the 12, which is near the center of the table. He moves it closer, then farther back, adjusting it by millimeters until it's where he wants it. He stands up, then bends down to position himself, draws back his stick, and his forearm touches the cue ball, which moves a hair to the right. It's all Fred and his clipboard need.

"Ball in hand! That's ball in hand! He touched the cue ball!"

Alan, who's been watching as well, nods and walks over to pluck the cue ball from the table. Reggie's face crinkles in confusion.

"Wait, what? What are you doing?"

"It's ball in hand. You touched the cue ball before you shot, and it moved. That's a foul." Alan's hand hovers over the cue ball. He doesn't want to pick it up before they've agreed that it's ball in hand, or he could end up being the one fouled.

"You're kidding me, right?"

"It's in the rulebook!" Fred screams. He leaps off his stool and flips frantically through the dog-eared copy of the APA rulebook he keeps with him at all times. Fred is the Al Gore of our pool league.

Reggie's teammates come alive. The slouching hipster with too much hair product who played Valerie earlier starts loudly complaining: "Oh, come on. You can't be serious."

Sam materializes, as he always does, and says, "But that's the rule."

The team from Biff's is not arguing about whether it's a real rule or not, nor are they contesting the fact that Reggie moved the cue ball. They just don't think the rule should apply. It's too nitpicky, too nerdy. Fred is now showing the captain of the other team his rulebook, his stubby index finger sliding over the text on the precise page. Reggie, whose eyes have gone wild and who's been standing with his arms open wide while his captain consults with Sam and Fred, goes berserk.

"Are you fucking kidding me?" he bellows. He turns to Alan, who by this time has taken the cue ball and put it on the table in front of one of his solid-colored balls.

"I don't believe this. There's no way you're gonna call this. Are you *kidding* me?" Reggie's face flushes red, his eyes bulge, and sweat beads pop up on his forehead and upper lip. I think he might start foaming at the mouth.

"What's a matter?" he spits. "Did you think I might beat you? Huh? Is that it? I might beat you and you can't take it?"

Alan stands stoically, the mask on tight.

Reggie is waving his arms now and pacing like an irate tomcat. He stops and jabs his finger in Alan's face.

"You are a small man!" he roars. "You are a small, small man. You hear me?"

"That's verbal abuse!" Fred shrieks, and begins madly flipping through his rulebook again to find the page that prohibits a player from verbally abusing or insulting his opponent.

"You don't think you can beat me," Reggie continues. "You thought I might win, *so you called this bullshit rule*. You are a small man, but I don't care. I'll beat you anyway. Take your damn ball in hand, you little, little man."

I stand next to a barstool, frozen, my eyes wide with horror, my throat dry, my stomach in knots. *What is this? Why isn't Alan defending himself?* He doesn't so much as twitch.

This drunken oaf, this punk with beady eyes and Q-tip hair who's probably thirty years Alan's junior, has the audacity to call him a small man? Alan is one of the biggest men I know, that any of us know. And still he refuses to sink to this guy's level. Even with Reggie bellowing and spitting in his face like an enraged bull, he won't engage. It drives Reggie's fury to new heights. Sam is now chest to chest with the other team's captain, their faces angry and close as they argue. The air is hot and the room seems to have grown darker. MTV Boy and Fred are hurling accusations and threats back and forth. Then the door creaks open at the far end of the bar and Valerie waltzes in, having left a while ago to get cigarettes.

"What the hell's going on?" she says, bewildered but cheery. "I leave for one minute and miss all the action."

I can't join in her jocularity. I can't even fill her in. I feel sick and my hands are shaking. I can't stand seeing Alan in this position. Anyone but Alan.

"I'll tell you later," I say. Valerie sees my grave, stricken face and stays quiet.

Reggie is still pacing and growling like a caged animal. One of his teammates tries to calm him down. Alan still hasn't moved or said a word.

Finally, Reggie's captain comes over, puts his hand on his shoulder, and tells him to let it go. He touched the cue ball, they all saw it, and that's a foul. It may seem ridiculous and mean-spirited, but a rule's a rule and they have to abide by it, but they will tell Tyrone, the league administrator, what happened, and he can decide if the game should be played over. In the meantime, just calm down and finish the game. Reggie won't meet his captain's gaze; he looks over the guy's shoulder at a fixed point on the wall and nods, his jaw tight.

Alan looks to Sam and finally speaks. "We starting now? My shot?" Sam nods and folds his arms, grabbing his elbows. Reggie leans against the wall and says nothing. Alan puts the cue ball on the table right where he wants it, runs out his remaining balls, and pockets the 8 for a win. It's now tied at 2–2. Alan still needs three more to win. Reggie needs one.

He gets it the next game.

After Alan breaks and sinks a few, he hits one of Reggie's object balls before hitting his own. "Ball in hand," Alan says, and hands Reggie the cue ball. Reggie doesn't call a coach. He just takes the ball from Alan and places it on the table. He finishes out the game, right down to the 8. The two men pack up their cues and retreat, but not before Alan extends his hand, expressionless. Reggie shakes it briefly. Although I know it's the classy thing to do, I hate that Alan has shown Reggie any respect, any dignity. The handshake makes me sick.

I go up to Alan and ask if he's okay, and he shrugs. "Hey, he moved the cue ball, that's how it goes." He's acting as if nothing out of the ordinary has happened. I don't want to embarrass him further. Of course he wouldn't want to talk about it or complain or reveal any emotion. I touch his back, then go to the restroom, and on my way back out I watch as Reggie approaches Alan with his hand outstretched and a hangdog expression on his face.

"Hey, no hard feelings, man. You played a good game, and I was outta line. I'm sorry I lost my cool a little bit."

A little bit?

Alan shakes his hand. He says something I can't hear and the two talk, both of them smiling. I suspect that this is how Alan would have wanted this scene to end, that he's probably relieved. I think he may have even complimented Reggie on his game, which brings bile to my throat, but the way Alan sees the situation, Reggie did play well. He's a 4 who beat a 6 fair and square. Alan needs to end on a grace note, and damn if Reggie doesn't provide it. The schmuck.

I don't think I could ever be that gracious. But maybe that's the difference between a small player and a great one.

It's a Level Thing

WE'RE AT THE BAR late on a Sunday afternoon, about a month after the tense match at Biff's. Sam has called a team practice, something he does on occasion, and, inspired, he walks over to one of the pool tables and demonstrates what he claims is the way many women stand when they shoot pool—legs and feet pressed together, knees bent as a means of lowering themselves to a more appropriate height, as if they're scrunching down to talk to a small child. Sam looks silly, and he quickly—and presciently—adds that none of the women on his team do anything so dainty. From across the bar, Stella, a fiery redhead with a booming voice, calls out, "What did you say?" and stomps over to Sam's table, her hair swinging across her shoulders as she advances. She stands inches from Sam's face and demands that he retract his "bullshit" characterization of women pool players. Sam backs away with both hands up. "I said none of the women I play with do this. I meant you and Nora and Heather. . . ." He assures Stella that we're wonderful exceptions, that we stand "just like men" when we shoot. Stella folds her arms and juts her chin, feeling triumphant but still a little defensive. Nora, Stella's friend, is a new player on my team, small like me but fierce when she plays. Nora concedes, to make Sam feel less attacked, that she believes men and women do shoot differently.

"For example, men love to bang the shit out of the balls on the break. It's like their version of 'And in this corner, weighing two hundred ten pounds . . .'" Stella hoots and nods vehemently, raising her hand to slap Nora a high-five.

It's interesting to me that the women players I've met in my pool league do not want to be told that they shoot "like women," and yet their behavior does not support their wanting to be thought of as shooting like men. They're determinedly sexy and insist on keeping themselves separate from the macho male posturing that goes on every week in bars and poolrooms across the city. They don't want to shoot like men *or* like women. They just want to shoot like pool players; they want to shoot like themselves. They make fun of male behavior on the tables—the chest-thumping and competitive grousing—and have no wish to emulate it, yet they are claws-out furious if they're told they "stand like a woman" when they shoot. It's curious, this desire to be sexy and sexless at the same time, to want to exist in a gray area that's gray not because it's a combination of black and white alternatives but because the area is so neutral. They use pool as an unadorned backdrop that allows them to be whatever they want, whether standing out or blending in, or maybe a little of both, depending on the night and their moods.

Anytime I've asked men how they feel when they lose at pool, invariably they make statements like, "It's like being kicked in the nuts." "It's like having someone whack you in the balls with a skillet." "It's like someone dumping a bucket of ice on your willie." Or my personal favorite, "It's like being caught on the beach in a tiny Speedo with no towel, after coming out of the ocean. And it's February."

To a man, they all associate losses at pool as literal losses of manhood. It's linked not to sex, but to *their* sex, to their "having a set" or not.

Women, however, don't appear to lose their sexual identity in this way when they don't play well. Rather, they seem to gain a stronger sense of it when they win.

One night, not long after I first take up pool, while on vacation in Las Vegas, I notice a women's team in a bar where a league tournament is being held, a team called The Odd Ducks, all of them in their forties and fifties, all wearing quirky, square-sleeved bowling shirts they'd had specially designed for the tournament, each woman sporting a helmet-shaped haircut and wearing glasses that look as if they were purchased at a local drugstore. When one of them wins, they all grab one another and bump hips and swivel and shimmy, completely free for one glorious moment before regaining their placid, no-nonsense composures. If one of them loses, they don't decry the loss of their uteruses or deem their breasts too small. They are outside of their bodies then, in their heads, faces drawn, upset that they've let people down, self-critical, apologetic, quiet.

WOMEN POOL PLAYERS HAVE their own professional association now—the WPBA (Women's Professional Billiards Association), which was formed in 1976—as well as contracts with ESPN to televise their matches, tense, exciting tournaments with high five- and even six-figure purses, and endorsements that have boosted their once-paltry annual earnings—in the case of a star like Jeanette Lee, to a level higher than that of many of the men.

But forming an association of their own did not correct most of the problems facing women pool players, at least not right away. Fran Crimi, the house pro at Corner Billiards in New York, a member of the WPBA's Classic Tour, and a BCA (Billiards Congress of America)

Master Instructor, puts it bluntly: When the women formed their own alliance in the 1970s, the billiard industry and the male players didn't take them seriously. "Only a few top players were taken seriously—the rest of us were considered a joke, the whole association was considered a joke."

Crimi, who is in her forties, intelligent, soft-spoken, and contemplative, admits that the condescension wasn't just because they were women but, she says with brutal honesty, because they didn't play well as a collective group. "A few stood out, like Jean Balukas, but they weren't enough to make up for the whole group. A lot of the reason the women didn't play that great is that they weren't expected to. It was the whole mentality: We're going against the grain, we're not supposed to be here. And it affected our performance, it affected how we viewed ourselves."

In the feminist fairy-tale version of this story, the women would have warmly banded together and, with the grit and grace of suffragettes, would have stood up to the male-dominated game. But it was far more complicated than that.

"There was a lot of conflict [among the women] in those days," Crimi recalls. All of the women felt the frustration of being someplace where they're not wanted, and so we fought a lot with each other, everyone was very competitive, there was always something at stake at every event."

They did finally agree on a proposal, which they submitted to the men's association, to hold the women's tournaments side by side with the men's. "The men," Crimi says dryly, "thought it was kind of cute." Women would be "sort of a sideshow." Cute or not, it worked—audiences got a big kick out of it. The women were a hit. At that time—the late seventies and early eighties—the total purse for a women's tournament could be as low as $500. The first-place finisher, if she was lucky, might make her expenses back. Purses today are in the $100,000 to $120,000 range. And for the recognizable stars, a single personal appearance at a private function can bring in several thousand dollars.

Typically, in the larger tournaments, such as the ones in Las Vegas, sixty-four men and sixty-four women compete, with the winner of each division awarded $15,000; the players who finish in the bottom twenty-five percent bring home $300. It's a hard way to make a living—for men and women. This is why some pros don't always show up for their matches, even if they have a good chance of winning. If they get into one of the big-money, after-hours games that invariably crop up at a tournament, they might decide they're better off sticking with that, since they can earn a lot more money if the game goes their way. The game played in these professional tournaments is nine-ball, though the nascent, one-hundred-fifty-member International Pool Tour (IPT), founded—and funded—by controversial entrepeneur and Natural Cures guru Kevin Trudeau, is giving professional players an eight-ball option, too—and significantly larger purses (sometimes to the tune of $1 million). Whether the IPT will have any longevity remains uncertain.

For women, the progress was there, but it was painfully slow. What really put women's pool on the map was when the women decided to officially join forces with the men in the 1990s. The two associations formed the PBTA—Professional Billiard Tour Association—which was to be a marketing arm for both associations. Each group had members on the board of directors, and Crimi was one of them.

Then, in 1993, the WPBA decided to break off from the group and, using the Ladies Professional Golf Association as a model, put together a credible package for sponsors that became the "Classic Tour" that chugs along to this day. A contract with ESPN soon followed.

Television coverage led to access to the players, some of whom had extremely dynamic, memorable personalities—and the burning ambition to go with those personalities. Jeanette Lee, a fiery young Korean-American player from New York City, who would come to be known as The Black Widow for her sleek, black, sexy clothing; her killer instinct; and her fierce facial expressions, was up-and-coming at this time. She was attractive, focused, and also shrewd, among the first to retain an agent and a manager.

When I talk to Crimi about all of this, while sipping coffee at Corner Billiards one morning in a room of empty pool tables, I toss out my theory about men and women and the different ways in which they approach the game. I mention how for me and many women I know in the APA league, it's all about playing well—playing excellently—not necessarily about winning.

She smiles and shakes her head. "That's a level thing," she says. "People at your level feel that way. . . . Maybe it's a little of a women's thing, but when you get to be a top-level player, you want to win." She leans forward for emphasis. "You want to win," she says again. "Playing well is not good enough. That's what the pro tour is—we're playing to win. And if we don't want to win, we don't belong out there."

Oh.

I feel a little foolish, since I immediately see Crimi's point, which doesn't wholly alter my theory, and it certainly doesn't alter my fascination with many of the women I've met on the amateur circuit, women I'm often too shy to befriend.

It's not as if confident women are an anomaly to me. I am one, I grew up surrounded by them, but these women—women like Valerie, Nora, Stella—astound me. I am cowed, awed, envious, admiring. I've been conditioned to excel in the classroom and the boardroom; to speak in long, forceful, articulate sentences; to hold my own in high-pressure jobs with demanding bosses. But this poise deflated like a punctured balloon when I walked into my first poolroom. Around the likes of Val and her crew, I witness a completely different kind of confidence. It's physical, graceful, animal, atavistic, sexual. They all have jobs, of course—Nora and Stella work in the financial services industry; Valerie recently landed a position in, of all fields, human resources, a delicious bit of irony that her superiors will never have the chance to appreciate. And so they button up in crisp suits during the day, and Valerie removes her nosering, but rather than obsessing about their work and their place in their respective companies, they shake off their frustrations as soon as they walk into a room with a pool table, channel any negative energy or anxieties they might have into their games. By not being cocooned inside the usual boring urban neuroses, they seem, like no other women I've encountered in New York, completely free. They don't give a damn about high-profile universities, hip neighborhoods, trendy restaurants, successful boyfriends. This doesn't mean they don't enjoy or take an interest in these aspects of life, but they aren't imprisoned by them—or by not having them.

My perception of this supposed freedom from the shackles of everyday urban existence is of course hopelessly naïve and romantic, but I don't care. I love watching them. They play great pool, throw a decent game of darts, smoke cigarettes like noir ingenues, and never seem to get hungry during a long evening of pool (I'm always famished, like a kid on a long car trip whining for a snack). They drink real beer (never lite), shrug off their pool losses like old bathrobes, wear leather jackets and thin scarves when it's ten degrees outside and never seem to get cold (Nora likes to shoot pool in a tank top, no matter what time of year it is). They strap on messenger bags and stuff their "work clothes" inside, snap open cell phones, wear dark lipstick, listen gamely to the boyfriends who worship them—tough, beautiful women who inspire me all the time, whether I'm looking at them through the lens of brainy-girl romanticism or not.

The men are a different story. More often than not they exude thwarted ambition; it's palpable. They're angry at what they haven't accomplished, and yet they remain dreamers. The women seem more realistic to me—even, at times, fatalistic. They assess the limits of their lives immediately and accurately. The men all want to "own a bar someday."

Although I have learned—and continue to learn—a great deal from the men I've met through pool, I remain wary of them. I've left two of them in the dust (or they've left me, depending on your interpretation). But the women I revere. For a long time I try to emulate them and am unsuccessful, until I realize the best way to do this is to find my own individual style. It's what they do. It's certainly what my friend Liz does. And she, unlike Wally and Roger, has been as loyal and stalwart and interesting a friend as anyone could ask for.

"RANDY'S A PRICK, and your teammates are assholes."

I make this pronouncement to Liz as I angrily stuff my cue into its case. She's patient, stands next to me, Secret Service–like, and allows me to vent. I've just lost, brutally, to Randy Pomeroy, a superb player who smirks and condescends to me the entire match, saying things like, "Oh, did you scratch there? So I get ball in hand, right?" just to twist the knife. In a throwback to my old ways, I let the scrawny, pencil-necked turd, in his little army-green shorts and Izod sport shirt, get under my skin, and it costs me. He beats me five straight. Now, for some unfathomable reason, I'm taking it out on Liz, who plays for the guy's team out of a long, cavelike bar near the financial district.

Randy, meanwhile, struts around the jukebox, recounting a particularly gorgeous bank shot he made during our match to a klatch of bar patrons, his face small and rabbity and gloating, bobbing in and out of the small crowd he's gathered. I should look away, but I can't. He has preposterous knees, knobby and pale. I realize with horror that they remind me of little cue balls.

"How can you stand these guys?" I explode, referring to the rest of the sorry bunch that make up Liz's current team. She seems startled by my venom, but she quickly regains her calm.

"Yeah, I know. Randy's a problem, no question. But the rest of them, well, they can be nice." She catches my skeptical glance. "No, really. Even Randy. Especially at the beginning of the night, before they start pounding beers. I know it's annoying, though. There was no excuse for his behavior tonight. The thing with the scratch? Unbelievable."

Liz's sympathy and good nature make me feel worse. God, I'm a heel.

We leave the bar, cue cases strapped to our shoulders, and grab a taxi. I grouse and grumble most of the way home but manage to cough up some bonhomie before I alight from our cab. The next day I send her an abashed, apologetic e-mail. And of course she tells me not to worry, it's "no big thing." Her grace never falters.

NOT LONG AFTER I first meet Liz, I notice that she has a flirtation going with Gary, the guy on Paul G.'s team with the hair-trigger temper and the itchy fists (mostly reserved for the opposing pool players) and a rough, deep voice that comes from many years of Camel cigarettes. She thinks I don't notice, as she's subtle about it, but Gary is not.

"She's gorgeous and she doesn't even know it," he says to me as we sit watching her play a match.

Liz and I never talk about it. Part of the silence, I suppose, is due to the fact that Gary is married. He cats around from time to time, when things aren't going well at home, at least that's what it seems like. Once in a while some young, pretty woman wearing lots of lipstick will show up at The Wrong Side looking for him. We'll be introduced, make polite, awkward conversation, and then we never see her again. Like the curvy woman with the short, brown ponytail and the long skirt who shows up one night. She comes in early, about 8:00. She and Gary disappear for a while, then come back. She seems so young to me, not more than twenty-three or twenty-four, and so obviously smitten with Gary, her eyes soft when she looks at him, her smile shy but impossible to keep off her face, like she can't help herself, she has no choice but to beam in his presence. Not long after an episode like this, Gary will invariably tell some hilarious story about visiting his in-laws up north, meaning his relationship with his wife is back on track. Liz laughs with the rest of us, and sometimes Gary even throws his arm around her, delighting in her delight at his stories. Liz is stoic when it comes to Gary, and appropriately wary, even proper, but she isn't a nun. I notice secretly clasped hands, furtive kisses on street corners, the occasional shy smile, though nothing beyond that, which makes me sad in a way, as I want Liz to have more, to have everything.

Although I'm used to lengthy, intimate monologues from my friends on the intricacies and dramas of their relationships—and have been the deliverer of such monologues myself on more than one occasion—this is terrain that Liz and I avoid. Such talks would complicate our simple, pure connection, so we stay away from it, except for the occasional offhand remark. So I never know how far the flirtation with Gary goes, only that they always go home separately and that, on the surface at least, Liz doesn't seem to mind.

Liz grew up in a little town in Missouri. She lived in L.A. for few years after college, then moved to New York and took a production job at a magazine. I learn after a while that we have more in common than pool, baseball, and the heartland. For example, we both seem to have an attraction to outsize personalities, although we respond to them quite differently. For me, no matter how charismatic the personality, I can't abide bullies. Indeed, I can't tolerate so much as the tiniest bit of bullying, even if it comes from someone who behaves most of the time like a decent human being. I've thought about this a lot, and it's no great leap to surmise that this particular sensitivity comes from my childhood. My brother was mercilessly picked on as a kid, making his youth singularly unhappy. I was younger and a girl, and thus had no power over the situation. I was both enraged and embarrassed by this. How could kids be so cruel? And how could my brother not stick up for himself?

It's hard to resist the easy psychology of this one: that my working for a series of powerful, charismatic media moguls who like to order people around and who pounce on weakness the second they smell it is no accident, that I seek out these highly charged environments so I will have the opportunity to stand up to these tyrants, men and women alike, avenging a wrong over which I still harbor subconscious guilt. This same pop psychology can, I suppose, be applied to my entanglements with pool players. I'm taking on a bully every time I stare across that sea of green cloth, whether it's my own game or somebody else's.

I once get into a screaming fight with my captain, Sam. I've been on the team for a while by this point, and we're playing the last match of the season out of a pleasant little bar tucked away on a quiet corner of the West Village. Sam allows a drunk friend of his to openly criticize Katya during a match. (Katya is the petite Englishwoman who taught me how to break, a puzzle no one else had been able to crack, and I feel indebted to and protective of her.) Sam seems to think his friend's boorish behavior is acceptable because he "always has such a good eye for the table." I tell Sam this isn't about his eye, it's about his mouth. Sam cites other players who've behaved far worse than his friend; I proceed to deliver a loud lecture on moral relativism, which does not inspire him. I then collect my things and stalk out of the bar, thinking violent thoughts about drunk pool critics and their reprehensible defenders.

Liz would never have done this. She would've remained quiet, then would have soothed the rattled Katya, maybe bought her a beer. I admire her for her equilibrium, but sometimes it drives me nuts.

For instance, she stays on Paul G.'s team long after I depart its ranks, long after the whole team has disintegrated, and I never understand why. There are nights, she says, when the whole team is slumped over the bar and she has to play her match on her own, no spectators, no support from her mates—keeping score herself, marking the clipboard between innings, hoping she won't have to call a time-out since there's no one around, or no one sober enough, to coach her.

One particularly dour evening, Roger comes over to the table and offers Liz a long, detailed piece of advice, mapping out a strategy that will help her win the match. "Um, that's great," Liz says. "But I'm solids, Roger. Not stripes."

He pauses for a full minute, staring at the table. "Really?"

"Really."

"Well, I don't know what the fuck you should do then. You're on your own." Then he walks away, laughing to himself and shaking his head. And still she stays, until Randy Pomeroy's team has an opening and she takes it without looking back.

NOT ALL OF THE women I meet are as generous as Liz, or as worthy of my adulation as Valerie. Melanie, the too-pretty woman with the icy voice who crushed me with her indifference when I was a wide-eyed newbie at Chelsea Billiards pool school, is not inspirational, nor does she seem all that "unshackled" to me. I realize, with the benefit of hindsight, that she's nothing more than a pill, a woman who, despite her soap-actress appearance, is hyper-ambitious and totally insecure, worried that any generosity on her part might come back to haunt her. Everyone is an opponent to her, even a woman who misses the cue ball her very first time at the table. Her strategy works: Although she may not be beloved, she makes it to the pros, and I suspect income-generating endorsements are not far behind.

Valerie and Nora will never be as skilled at pool as Melanie because they do not have her gnawing ambition, but they are also not burdened by the insecurities that come with a burning desire to conquer. And although they don't necessarily consider me one of them, they never exclude me, and they certainly do not hold back any help they might be able to offer.

I don't know Stella all that well, but one particularly miserable night, when I'm being clobbered by some oaf in a bar near Canal Street and getting one unsolicited piece of advice after the next from Alan and Sam, Stella, who doesn't play on my team, just comes to watch Nora once in a while, marches over to me and says, "Hey, listen, all a coach does is give you options. You don't have to take any of their advice if you don't want to." She puts her hands on her hips. "Don't try to please Alan and Sam. Play for you," she says, pointing her finger at my chest. Then she turns and marches back to her chair to finish her beer with Nora. All in a day's work. I think about her comment the next time I receive unwanted advice during a match and it calms me.

Another night I'm watching Valerie play, and she's following her usual script, which is to shoot too hard and ignore her coaches. There's a moment—just a moment—when I think I catch her looking a little bit glum. Sam eyes the unfortunate spread of balls on the table—a spread Valerie is entirely responsible for—and says, "Aw, don't worry, Val. We still love you."

Valerie looks over at Sam, who's grinning beneath his beard. She stares at him impassively for a few seconds then says, "Bite me."

I'M NOT SURE what it is about Valerie and Nora and Stella that so enthralls me. Perhaps I'm grasping for some sort of authenticity, or maybe I have some misguided romantic image of myself as a trash-talking sister with a heart of gold. Whatever the case, I'm clearly trying to mold my identity into something new.

People go to great lengths to confound their identity—the identity that they believe has been assigned to them by their parents, by their place of birth, by their age, by the jobs they've chosen, by the neighborhoods where they live, or by the people they've married. The powerless middle manager who takes up boxing. The bookish copyeditor who cultivates an obsession with rock climbing, or maybe the stock market. The housewife who becomes a religious convert. And, I suppose, the petite, self-styled urban sophisticate who develops a passion for pool. This is not to say that these appetites are manufactured, and certainly the zeal for the activities taken up to satiate them is real. But the burden of becoming someone else, the pressure to have an interesting, even exotic, "lifestyle" seems, at least today, to fall especially hard on women.

I came across a literary review once that addressed these very issues via two different books about female backpackers—young, heroic, culturally sensitive vagabonds who traverse the globe in hip, ethnic clothing. These women are "in thrall to their own self-conceptions," the reviewer, *Salon*'s Michelle Goldberg, writes.

Once I lift my eyes from the pool table and take in the *world* of the pool table, I begin to create a secret, separate persona of my own and am soon in thrall to it, much as these backpacking beauties are in thrall to their many-stamped passports. Being a hip-swiveling, stick-toting siren certainly isn't a bad way to spend a Monday night, but at some point I need to stop writing the damn story in my head and just live it—my life, not some lifestyle.

I'm never going to be like these women, but the beauty, I learn eventually, is that I don't have to be. I finally understand, after many months, that I can have my own low-key style, that I can get a slice of pizza if I'm hungry, can limit myself to one beer and not feel like a lightweight or a prude, can wear two sweaters and a Thinsulate-lined parka—even when it's above freezing—and that's okay. It's just my style. We all have one, even me, and once I realize that my under-the-radar presence is working to my advantage—that it is, in fact, encouraging my opponents to underestimate me and helping me to earn wins—I embrace it wholeheartedly. And so do my teammates. Without my even knowing it, I've been accepted, maybe not by divas like Melanie and her ilk, but certainly by everyone else.

I **NEVER GET THE** opportunity to play Melanie, despite her prominent place in my psyche and despite the fact that she is the only woman I've ever fantasized about trouncing. I do play a woman once who reminds me of her, a beautiful and expressionless Asian woman whose pulse never seems to rise above 50 when she shoots. She's ranked a 5 and I'm not expected to win, but something in her manner, a certain dismissiveness, the way she tosses back her sleek, shiny hair, strikes a nerve with me. It's so reminiscent of Melanie's backhand that day in Chelsea Billiards that I make the match about some score that I need to settle, and suffer as a result.

My opponent, who's not interested in my demons—or even in her own, it seems—plows right through me. She spots weakness the way an IRS agent spots a cheat, and she takes full advantage, her eyes moving coolly from me to the table, her lips pressed into a thin line when she shoots. Sam asks me at one point why I'm so agitated. "Lighten up," he says. "We're just here to have fun."

"I don't want to have fun, I want to win," I spit. This is not the A-student talking; it's the competitor—a player who wants to prevail, not to please. Even Valerie seems taken aback by my vehemence. Fran Crimi, the pool pro, would not be. She would be thrilled.

I play pretty well that night, all things considered, executing as many defensive shots as I can to try to protect myself, but my cold, beautiful opponent beats me five straight games. I need to learn to leave my baggage at home.

I don't storm out after it's over, or indulge in any other histrionics. I keep my turmoil to myself and stick around for the rest of the matches that night. Then I slip out and go home.

Once over the bridge and into Brooklyn, the cab driver whizzes past my block and has to screech to a halt on Flatbush Avenue. I step out of the taxi, annoyed, and readjust my cue case, which is falling off my shoulder. It's late, and no one seems to be out on the street. Then I spy a kid loping down the sidewalk, no more than seventeen or eighteen, in a T-shirt and baggy jeans, his baseball cap flipped backward, holding a slice of pizza. He slows down as he passes me. He's close enough that I see a line of fuzz above his upper lip. Shaving is not going to be part of his routine for a few more years. He ambles by with his slice and looks back at me, his lip fuzz spreading into a disbelieving grin. "Awww . . . no way," he says, chuckling and indicating my cue. He turns so that he's walking backward. "You any good?" he calls.

I smile thinly. "Not tonight. But sometimes."

He shakes his head and I hear another faint "No way" as he turns, brings the greasy pizza slice to his mouth, and heads off to parts unknown.

Sometimes I am quite good. Just not tonight. That's how it is. End of story.

Slumping Toward Bethlehem

YOUR SPELLS OF *excellent pool will always, sorry to say, be followed by periodic declines in performance.*"

Philip B. Capelle, longtime pool instructor, writer, and enthusiast writes this in his book *A Mind for Pool: How to Master the Mental Game*, which I buy in a moment of despair for one reason only: It contains a chapter on slumps. I'm in one, deep in one, and I don't know where to turn.

Although I don't know it at the time, my losing five straight games to the chilly, tight-lipped woman who reminds me of Melanie is the beginning of a cruel, startling decline in my play. It's more than my bringing "baggage" to a game. I become convinced that the cause of this decline is otherworldly, an invasion of darkness from an entirely different plane.

Being in a slump isn't just about losing; it's about thinking you can't win. The losses seem to stretch before you like a lonely highway with tumbleweeds blowing across it. There's a sense of inevitability about the emptiness. The highway will always look like this; progress resides so far away that it can't touch this route.

I have certainly slumped before. I slumped right off my previous team, thanks to Roger and Paul G. and their controlled substances and my not-so-controlled self-righteousness and misplaced passion. But that, I believed, was well behind me.

And I'm right. My first season with Sam and Alan's team is a glorious one. I win my first three matches in a row and end the season five and three. I'm ranked a solid 3, and even dare to look over the horizon and ponder becoming a 4. I'm having fun.

But something happens to me, and this time there are no mitigating outside factors, like a drunk lawyer with a guilty conscience or a cursed cue stick to blame it on.

When you're in a slump, you feel as if you have no control, as if something bigger than you is in charge, moving your object balls into aggravating, impossible places. The other guy, of course, gets all the "lucky" shots. You get all of the unlucky ones, the freak scratches, the inexplicable miscues. (As Alan is fond of saying about his pool game, "I'd rather be lucky than good any day.")

It's my third straight loss that tells me I'm not merely losing but am, in fact, in a major slump.

I'm playing a well-known league oddball named Crystal, who is ranked a 3, like me. I've observed her play a few times and don't find her terribly threatening. She's slow and unimaginative, but this kind of play gets her down to one ball on the table before I can come close to touching her. I sink nothing for what seems like hours. I still have six balls to pocket by the time Crystal is on the 8. So I chip away in my painstaking, hanging-by-a-thread manner, and it works. Using my balls to hide the cue ball, I play safe against Crystal until I'm able to edge myself into position to run a few. Wouldn't you know it, I come from behind and get on the 8, but it's a near-impossible cut shot. I agree to a coach from Sam.

I line up my shot, take my time, and, thanks to Sam's advice, shoot the cue ball perfectly—it slices the 8 and hits the rail, then zooms off toward the opposite rail, nowhere near any scratchable pockets. Meanwhile, the 8 travels in a perfect line to the corner pocket, right where I want it, sliding toward the lip and then . . . it just stops. It nestles gently on the edge of the pocket, part of it hanging over the black hole, and refuses to roll that final millimeter. The 8 sits there, staring at me smugly. I cannot believe what I'm seeing. It's a gorgeous shot; the game should've ended with it. Instead, Crystal takes care of it for me, flicks in the 8, and we're done with game one.

Crystal has a tight, scratchy voice and always looks as if she's jumping at her shadow. Her expression is mostly one of perpetual alarm, except for those few occasions when it's simply vacant. She's shaped like a gourd and teeters from side to side as she walks. When she shoots, she often draws her face into such a painful grimace of consternation that people occasionally ask if she's okay. Tiny blue eyes—hard little stones with no spark—poke into her skull. Her face is lined and puckered, like an overripe fruit, though I don't think she's much past forty.

That night Crystal is draped in an oversized shirt that looks like the smocks elementary-school kids wear in art class. She doesn't smile, but she opens her mouth sometimes when she's thinking, and I observe pointy, nicotine-stained teeth. She stares at the table, rooted to her spot, a mollusk briefly seeking shelter in the sand.

When Crystal is done contemplating, she presses her lips together and hoists her cue. I notice that her hands are narrow and delicate, as if they've been taken from some pampered little girl in the suburbs and sewn onto her thick arms. I'm losing to a thick-armed, suburban-fingered mollusk in an art smock.

I stand to the side and scowl while Crystal takes her shots. She beats me again, and then the match is over. I pack up my cue and leave in a silent rage.

PAST PERFORMANCE IS THE best indicator of future performance; the humiliating match with Crystal is predictive. I continue to lose. I can't seem to stop jumping up before I finish my shots; I think too much about which shot to take and make bad decisions; routinely, at the last second, I move my right hand before stroking though, the hand that holds the butt of my cue, thus altering my aim just enough to miss the pocket—the same amateur crap I've been doing for three years.

Liz, on the other hand, is in the zone. She's on her way to being named the most valuable player in our division. (She will end the season 10 and 1; her one loss will come in the playoffs, meaning she is undefeated during the regular season.) It's thrilling for her, and it's killing me.

Even the most rational, the most skeptical, become superstitious during a slump. I am not normally someone who looks for omens or consults my astrological chart or reads tarot cards, but I become convinced that Liz's winning and my losing are connected in some mystical way—the same way that, when I was a girl, I believed Johnny Bench's home runs were somehow connected to me. The more Liz wins, the more I lose, or so it seems to my slump-addled mind. I start to believe that I can't win a game until Liz loses one. Does this mean I am consciously hoping she loses? I'm not sure. She's my friend, my comrade, my Midwestern soul mate, the only other woman in my radius who yelps and screams when the Royals slugger Mike Sweeney steals home off of the (at that time) Yankee pitcher Andy Pettitte, and it makes me ill to think that I might, deep down, have desires as dark as wishing she'd lose. So I concentrate—hard—on being supportive. I will myself into thinking only positive thoughts about her game, saving the dark ones for my own.

And then the inevitable happens.

I am demoted. I go down to a 2. And Liz, she goes up to a 4.

No one announces it to me. I walk into the bar, a balmy spring breeze swirling among the buildings outside. I order a cranberry and seltzer. Eventually I get around to looking at the clipboard with the score sheets attached. And there it is, next to my name. A new number. My stomach becomes leaden. That I've lost enough games to be knocked down a rank is, while not exactly a surprise, still horrifying. I can't remember anyone—on any of the teams on which I've played— being demoted like this.

I comment on the new number, make some wisecrack, but I feel my face burn. I am absolutely crushed. It turns out everyone already knew, they just hadn't said anything to me yet. Out of kindness? Sympathy? Disgust? I don't know. Sam comes over at one point to tell me that I'll be playing soon, and I say sure, no problem, "especially with my new, easy-to-use rank." He laughs, relieved, I think, that he doesn't have to be the one to break the news to me.

I don't want to embarrass myself further by bursting into tears in front of my teammates, so I excuse myself and go to the ladies' room to take deep breaths. In truth, it's about time Tyrone, our league administrator, caught on: My record is abysmal. I lost the next two matches after the one against Crystal, making it five losses in a row, two of them clean sweeps in which I didn't win a single game in my match. (Since I lost the last three matches of the previous season, my slump has actually expanded to eight losses in a row, which Sam tells me to ignore.)

But I can't ignore it. Players' ranks are based on how they've fared over their last ten games. In my last three matches, I've played a total of thirteen games and lost twelve of them. I've won one out of my last thirteen. That's a 0.077 average. This is what gets guys sent to the minors, or released altogether. Tyrone has no choice but to demote me. To put this into even starker perspective, I'm winning less than eight percent of the time. Liz's winning percentage is in the nineties.

Thinking about it during one of my pretend bathroom breaks, I realize that my life and Liz's seem to be inversely proportionate. To review:

Liz is undefeated (10–0).
I've lost eight in a row (the end of last season/beginning of the current one).
Liz's team goes to the playoffs.
My team finishes in last place.
Liz goes up to a 4.
I go down to a 2.
The Kansas City Royals (Liz's team) are in first place.
The Cincinnati Reds are tied with the pathetic Milwaukee Brewers for last place.
Liz is yin to my yang, but not in the way I want.

On the same night that news of my lowered rank is delivered, Liz's new rank is unveiled. Although I try to hide it, I'm devastated. I feel ill. Liz leaves an excited message on my cell phone. Not only has her rank gone up, but she wins her first match as a 4, too, a nail-biter so tense and tricky that the patrons in the bar where she's playing fall silent and crowd around to watch the final two innings. The room filled with applause after her win, she says in her message. It's the scene I've always dreamed of for myself. I feel grotesque, the jealous Salieri to her bubbly, brilliant Mozart.

I wait a few days before returning her call and confessing that my rank has changed as well.

Liz is instantly sympathetic. She tells me that one of her teammates, Kenny—thick-bodied, New York born and raised, a devoted father and husband—lost his fourth straight match the previous week (in this case by scratching on the 8-ball) and immediately threw his cue across the room and stormed out of the bar in a childish fury.

In other words, I'm not alone. And I, at least, haven't hurled any equipment or made any abrupt, overly loud exits.

"I know it's been a tough, frustrating season so far," she says one night in response to my despair. "I remember what it's like to be in a slump, knocking on the door every week but somehow coming up short."

Yes, that describes it.

"But take it from me," she says. "There is a light at the end of the tunnel. You're too good to give up like that. Everyone's different, but I think the final hurdle to consistently closing the deal is absolutely psychological. At least it was for me. I'm not sure exactly how or why I went from taking an opponent's mistake and thinking, *Liz, for God's sake don't blow it* to *Now I'm going to make you pay*, but that's the difference for me now. You can get here, too, I promise. I'm living proof that losing streaks can become winning streaks." I don't remember her ever having an actual losing streak, but her words lift me all the same.

THE FLIP SIDE of a slump is, of course, a winning streak. This is my first slump, but I've yet to experience the joys of a true winning streak. When contemplating such streaks—which I do now that I am in the midst of enduring its opposite—I can't help but think of Foo, a longtime player in the league who holds the most memorable string of wins because of the way they stopped occurring.

Foo is part Filipino, part African-American, a warm, corpulent man with a spherical face capped by a spongy pillow of tight, dark curls. His features—eyes, nose, mouth, cheeks—disappear when his face crinkles into a smile. He's like a rotund sunflower, big and beaming and cheerful.

Watching Foo move about a poolroom is a treat. His body, by age forty-five, has ballooned into a fantastic shape, his stomach stretching out in front of him like a desk, short, plump arms hefting at his sides. His legs form a neat triangle, tapering to a little point from which his shoes stick out clownishly, endearingly, white socks often visible beneath his pants cuffs. Foo wears a glove when he plays, a black nylon-and-spandex job that fits over three fingers and a thumb. One night, at a pool bar in the West Village, Foo stands up, snaps the glove on, and says, "Look. The Polish moonwalk," and walks in a straight line across the room, face deadpan, stomach thrust forward—the joke, of course, that he isn't walking backward and sliding his feet à la Michael Jackson but instead is walking "normally." The pool players who have gathered around the pool table convulse with laughter and Foo beams, chortling at himself, wagging his gloved hand at the crowd.

Foo's agility at the table is legendary. The contrast of his big, fleshy, imposing body wielding such a silky, delicate, sure-handed stroke is both comical and beautiful. The player who does not take Foo seriously suffers miserably at his hands. I should know, since I am one of his victims. He beats me handily one night, then invites me to be his partner in a game of doubles. That's just how Foo is.

Foo "works in computers," though I'm never quite sure what he does with them. He's happily married, devoted to his pool game and to his longtime team. They, in turn, are utterly besotted with him.

On a piercingly cold night in December, Foo is enjoying the streak of his life. It's the end of the season, and his team is once again in first place in its division, in part because of Foo's consistently superior play. He's dominating his match again that night, picking off the wins one by one, shaking his head as he makes shot after shot. He's on his way to sweeping his opponent in four straight games, running the table like a pro, with five-, six-, even seven-ball runs. He's just finished a game by pocketing the 8-ball with what should have been an impossible bank shot. The shot earns applause from both teams, and Foo's face crinkles into his trademark, feature-engulfing smile. He stands still for a moment, gazing placidly at the feat he's just accomplished, then abruptly pitches forward onto the table. He bends at the waist, his legs straight, his body lying flat. Foo's teammates laugh at his antics as they always do. Pretending to faint after making a bank shot that transcends Euclidean geometry is just like him. But then one of them notices that his face is slack, that one cheek is crushed into rubbery folds under the weight of his enormous body, that he isn't moving or answering when his friends say his name. Someone calls 911; two teammates move Foo to the floor and whisper reassurances to his unconscious form. He's taken to the nearest hospital and is pronounced dead a few hours later.

Foo had diabetes, and his death is attributed to complications associated with the disease—stroke, coronary, no one is really sure what felled him—but it is quite an exit. People on the pool circuit are stunned and saddened by his death, but everyone remarks on the way he went out, his fabulous streak stretching into eternity.

THE FOLLOWING WEEK, we have another home match and I'm put up against a beautiful, serene guy named Troy, a 4, who is, as always seems to be my luck, "on" that night, like a three-way bulb, sinking everything, getting a perfect leave after every shot.

Troy has gorgeous, velvety skin, the color of rich earth, and amazing cheekbones that draw admiring stares from all the women who saunter by the pool tables on the way to and from the restrooms, and from a few of the men, too. He has a taut, coiled, compact frame that he somehow inhabits as if he's lounging in a hot tub, making his menace subtle, almost undetectable. He exudes a quiet confidence and keeps calling me baby, like, "Nice shootin', baby," or, "Your shot, baby," in a low, smooth voice that sounds like jazz.

With my new, lower rank, I have to win a mere two games to take the match, and Troy has to win four. I lose the lag (why should I win anything?), which means I have to rack and Troy gets to break. He proceeds to sink five balls after the one he pockets on the break. But I must have a little bit of fighting spirit left, because I manage to keep him from the 8-ball and chip away at my stripes until I have only one ball left on the table, plus the 8. Troy gets the opening he needs, though, and wins.

I play three strong practice games earlier in the evening, including a particularly delicious one where I beat Marty, an idiot who lecherously haunts the bar most Mondays. He once said to me, oozing sincerity, "You're adorable—petite, yet womanly." It's the *yet* that really irks me. I've been wanting to throttle him in a game of pool ever since. So I'm pretty warmed up by the time I face Troy. In game two, we're neck and neck the whole time. I have two opportunities to run out my last two balls and win. But I blow both opportunities, and Troy wins number two.

Now I start to get really depressed. In what is becoming a familiar internal refrain, I decide to quit the team—and pool altogether—after the season is over. What's the point of putting myself through this week after week? My dark thoughts begin to stray toward other parts of my psyche. I am now upset not just with the level of my pool playing but also with the state of my entire life. I start thinking about my job. As with most companies, the honeymoon period at the startup has come to an end. The new and exciting has become mundane and routine. Worse, we're not making any money, and there have been whispers about layoffs. Meanwhile, my dating life has been nonexistent, prompting relatives to ask me questions like, "So how's your apartment?" or "How's your iMac?" since inquiring about an inanimate entity is safer than asking about potential suitors, biological clocks, and whether HBO's *Sex and the City* is really an accurate depiction of life in New York.

It is this empty, lonely, unfulfilled state that drove me to this maddening game to begin with, caused me to stick around long after

I should have recognized my limitations and left. My apartment is fine, I tell them. It's my pool game—and thus everything else—that sucks. Unfortunately, I will have to finish the match with Troy before I can announce my retirement.

Troy starts out strong again in game three. He runs out all of his balls, which means all seven of mine are left on the table, splayed pathetically like a discarded bridal bouquet. It's a situation I used to revel in, being able to duck and weave using my own object balls as cover, but tonight the tableau leaves me feeling beleaguered. I mechanically begin the tactic of sinking one ball, then making a safety shot, sinking another, then safetying again. It's snail's-pace pool, but I have all those damn balls there, I figure I might as well use them to my advantage.

Finally, one of my safeties pans out and Troy, who remains as cool and smooth as an ice rink, cannot make a shot. The 8 is completely blocked. So I'm awarded ball in hand, and as I stand there holding the cue ball, gazing at the table, Sam calls a time-out and insists we "talk about it." I take his advice, and it works: Troy now has to make a long, difficult shot on the 8 to win. My 13-ball is in his line of fire, between the cue ball and the 8. He can just whiff by it if he's painstakingly careful, but one millimeter off and he's a goner.

Troy takes his time and makes the shot, but the 13 moves. It's almost imperceptible, but it does move and Troy's team doesn't contest it. Troy sinks the 8-ball with the shot, but it doesn't matter. It's the same as if he scratched on the 8, since he touched the 13-ball first.

And then it dawns on me. Apparently, despite my best intentions, I've won a game. I'm not even sure what to do with this information. All I have to do now is win one more, and I will actually get a W on the score sheet. My slump will be over.

I break the new rack, weakly, and don't sink anything. The table is still open. So Troy hunkers down and proceeds to run most of the table again. I stare in disbelief. Can't he miss one ball, just *once*?

Then it's my turn to shoot, and I find myself once again in the position of having more than half a dozen balls to pocket. So, as before, I decide to use them as safety objects. But this strategy is foiled when I accidentally sink a ball that I want to leave in front of the pocket. I realize too late that I've stroked too hard and too quickly. Since the ball has gone in the pocket, I'm forced to take another shot, which I miss, so we're back to Troy shooting again. Meanwhile, the pocket I wanted to block is now an inviting target.

I stand off to the side, which affords Sam the opportunity to storm over and yell at me about how I've executed all of the wrong safeties and have simply gotten lucky with the ones that have worked. He's really angry, snapping at me like a dog that's been poked with a stick. His normally kind, open face is pinched and fierce. I feel hurt, put-upon. Sam's disappointment and exasperation are making an ugly situation worse. I'm already hard enough on myself; I don't need any extra scolding.

But Troy doesn't wrap up the game like a Christmas present, as Sam and I expect him to. He misses a shot—causing him visible surprise—so I have another turn at the table. I make it all the way down to the 8-ball, but I can't sink it. Troy can, though, and it's now 3–1.

Sam stalks off to get a beer. No one is paying attention anymore. All of my other teammates have left; it's just Sam and me and the other team. I pick up the triangular rack and start to gather the balls. My head is swimming.

I've gone down to a 2. I've given up three games already; this is my last chance. My captain has just yelled at me like I'm fifteen years old and have dented the family car.

And I snap. I feel myself fill with anger. It's a case of "pool rage." This has never before happened to me during a match. The anger is unfocused at first; I don't know who I'm mad at—myself, Sam, Troy, the universe. My face buckles into a dark scowl; my eyes go dead. I don't say a word except to mutter a single "Fuck this" under my breath.

I slam the balls into the rack, fold my arms, and glare at the wall. Troy breaks, gets a nice spread but doesn't sink any balls, so the table remains open. Sam is off laughing with the other team, which strikes me as particularly cold and disloyal, even though we socialize with opposing teams all the time. This is *bullshit*, I think. And then: *I am not giving up pool again. No fucking way.* This defiance comes out of nowhere. And when it arrives, my anger narrows into a funnel. I can feel it seeping into my skin. I want to tear something to pieces. There's a pool table in front of me. I decide that will do. I grip my cue stick so tightly that my hand hurts. I stomp up to the table, look at it for a couple seconds, and then run it. I sink six balls in about two and a half minutes, not even stopping to chalk my cue. I am in an absolute cold fury. With every ball that goes in, I'm thinking, *Fuck you.* I make cut shots, sneak behind other balls, weasle into pockets. I can't seem to miss. Soon all I have left is the 4-ball and the 8. After they're dispatched, we'll be done. As Sam tells it later, Troy stopped, mid-beer, to watch me, and said to his teammates in disbelief, "I'm gonna lose this match."

And to everyone's astonishment—including mine—he does.

After both of us execute a series of patience-trying safety shots, I find my opening. I sink my 4, and the cue ball ends up on a perfect diagonal with the 8, one that will take the ball neatly into the side pocket. I feel my arm tremble as I line up, and I will it to stop. Then, after a few meditative breaths, my skin still tingling from the unexpected surge of rage from before, I shoot perfectly. The 8 glides in and that's that. In Liz's words, I've made Troy pay. My slump is over.

Troy shakes his head, comes over, and kisses me lightly on the cheek. He smiles and leaves the table without saying a word.

It takes a demotion in rank and my utter humiliation to get me to cough up a win. *Blunt not the heart, enrage it.* But channeling negative energy, to be effective, cannot be just a fluke. Something inside me has been awakened in the match against Troy, and I know I have to learn how to turn it on and off like a light switch. I remember a quote from Yogi Berra that Phil Capelle tacked on to the end of his chapter on slumps: "Slump? I ain't in no slump. I just ain't hitting."

It's then that I realize: I'm ready to ask for some help.

Authority
Always Wins

ON A DULL, cold Monday, the sky threadbare, my team's bar awash in discouragement and boredom, a combination that often sets in toward the end of a lackluster pool season, I'm approached by a slight fellow named Armand, a guy who's been playing pool for years. I peg him as being in his late fifties, which turns out to be wrong (I learn later he's in his mid-forties, but, like so many hard-drinking pool types I've come across, he's lived so hard that he's aged prematurely). He has salt-and-pepper hair, a matching mustache, and a heavy Latino accent. His walk, as he makes his way toward me, is stiff and a little chesty, as if he's simultaneously trying to cover up and boast about a recent, interestingly achieved injury.

It's been three weeks since my match with Troy. After a great surge of relief and optimism after my win (which was followed by another, less notable win—my opponent scratched on the 8 in the final game, which I had been on my way to losing), I seem to have lost my footing again. I assume—incorrectly—that the end of my slump will "solve" whatever has been wrong with my game, not realizing I should use this opportunity to refocus and unpack my approach to pool now that I no longer have the pall of superstition hovering over me. I'm starting to feel like I'm right back where I started when I meet Armand.

I'm in the middle of a frustrating match, one destined to be a notch in my barely interrupted slump, when Armand stands next to me and says kindly, "You shoot like a lady." (It's the worst possible insult, as far as I—and the other women on my team—am concerned; well, that and referring to the bridge as a "chick stick.") I glance at him briefly, without reaction, then continue my game. When the match is over he seeks me out again, saying, "You shoot good, but you don't use the cushions. I can teach you. I give you classes." At first I treat him politely but dismissively. But he persists, again offering to "give me classes." I ask Sam about him while Armand is watching another game, and he says, "Armand? Are you kidding? He's an amazing shot. He's been in the league as long as I have. He's taught me some of my best stuff. Not someone you want to bet against."

So the next time Armand comes around, I engage him in conversation. I soon find out that he used to teach at Chelsea Billiards. This gets my attention. Armand taught the Saturday classes and I attended the ones given on Monday, which is why we never met. But he knows Mark, my first teacher, and is impressed with my pool pedigree. I ask Armand if he's expensive, and he says, "You a friend of Sam's?" I say yes, that I've played on his team for three seasons now. "Then I do it for free. For a friend of Sam's, I teach for free."

He asks me if my trouble is the actual shooting, knowing how to do it, or if it's "in my head." I say it's in my head, and I proceed to describe, using modern psychobabble, how I "care too much about league matches," how I allow myself to get distracted, how I'm "seeking some sort of approval."

"You're a-scared of losing." He pronounces losing "loosing." I say no, it isn't that, it's more my own "perfectionism and drive" and my "monomaniacal desire to do well."

Armand nods. "You're a-scared of losing." I shake my head and attempt to offer another searing analysis of how I get "too lost inside my head," and Armand cuts in again and says, "Yes. I know. You're scared of losing." I'm finally quiet. I think about what he's said. Armand, who I've just patronized, is right. In a single sentence he's cut through it all, sliced through the bullshit.

I'm scared of losing.

Which is why I do, time and again.

I tell him I'll let him give me classes and make a note to get his number and e-mail address from Sam.

ANOTHER MONDAY. I lose, brutally, to a fellow native Ohioan named Oliver. The slump appears to have been reborn. Oliver is a wide, hulking brute and an excellent shot—he's recently gone up to a 4—but that doesn't make me feel any better; no one likes to get beaten four straight games, even if the odds stacked against you provide something of an excuse. I never once make Oliver sweat. I'm fighting for my life every game, getting angry with myself. It's nothing new, which only makes it more unpleasant.

Watching Oliver's shots hit the mark every time as mine sputter and fail, even when it seems like they shouldn't, reminds me of the movie *The Color of Money*, the 1986 sequel to *The Hustler* that's forever being rerun on late-night cable TV. "The balls roll funny for everybody, kiddo," Paul Newman as Eddie Felson tells Vincent, his hotheaded, reluctant pupil, played by Tom Cruise. Why does it seem like they roll funny only for me?

As I'm packing up my cue, thinking horrible thoughts about everyone in the bar, Armand sidles up to me. At first I don't recognize him. He's shaved his mustache and his hair is darker, a little bit of vanity squeezed from a bottle. I learn later that the mustache comes and goes, depending on Armand's mood, and the seasons, and the current tint of his hair. He is wearing pointy shoes made of shiny, caramel-colored leather. They make him look like a Spanish leprechaun.

I'm shocked at how boyish and unlined his face is up close. His eyes are tired, and I notice he's developing a visible cataract in one of them. I wonder if he knows, and if it affects his game.

I ask him about those lessons he promised me, and at first he looks confused, even irked. I prod him a little, reminding him of our conversation from the week before, my ladylike play and lack of cushion skill. His face spreads into a smile. Of course, now he remembers. He nods vigorously.

Yes, he can teach me, he says, but he continues to act rather odd, as if he's still having trouble placing me or recalling exactly what it is he promised. He says, with great seriousness, that I'll have to watch him carefully, and that when I do, I'll think I can't do it, I can't possibly replicate his amazing feats on the green cloth, but then— he pauses for emphasis—then I'll be completely surprised. At this he puts his hands to his face and makes his mouth an o shape to demonstrate surprise.

He tips an imaginary cap to me and ambles off. Twenty minutes later he's back. He feels the need to explain why he was in such a strange mood before. He recently finished a long match with an ornery, sore-losing opponent, a guy named Isaac who sports a sleek, black ponytail and a hoop earring that makes him look like a pirate. He plays for a bar in TriBeCa, and as I remember him, he is capable of being quite a jackass, and so I'm not surprised to learn he's been acting "unsportsmanlike."

Armand is ranked a 6, and he's excellent. I suspect he could be a 7 if he wanted, but then no one would play him. He claims (and receives no argument) that he taught Alan and Sam everything they know. He played billiards growing up in Chile and didn't learn pool until he came to the states twenty years ago. He adores three-cushion billiards. He lost himself in it growing up. His father died when he was only six months old. His mother, an iron-willed woman, ran her family in the manner of a drill sergeant. She remarried and had five more children—all boys, all devoted to baseball and beer, none with even the vaguest interest in billiards. Armand likes his brothers, but I get the feeling he isn't so fond of his stepfather. "Eh. He's alright, I guess." At least he allowed young Armand to play billiards.

Armand makes his living repairing pool tables at pool halls and bars across the city, in all five boroughs, as well as on Long Island and throughout New Jersey. He also sells tables and equipment, is an "independent dealer," which he'll tell you with a devilish smile and raised eyebrows. He never says how he gets hold of his goods, mostly old tables with good names—dilapidated Brunswicks, for example— that he'll take off of someone's hands and repair easily, then mark up for a huge profit if the right person comes along. He used to play big-money games out in Jersey, against "guys who announce they have to take a dump as soon as you're about to win." These scatological trick-sters would go off and spend ten to fifteen minutes in the bathroom while Armand was left pacing and cooling his heels, waiting to take his shot. "They're trying to fuck you up, to ruin your concentration." He shakes his head. Where is the honor in that?

Armand is done with money games, he says, except for the occa-sional $20 game that comes his way. He likes to play simply for the joy of it. Which brings us back to why he was so angry earlier.

Isaac, his opponent, is a 5, so it's a four-five race, meaning Isaac has to win four games to prevail and Armand, the superior player, would have to win five. The match goes all eight games, and Isaac is being obnoxious and difficult, insinuating more than once that Armand is sandbagging, or cheating, trying not to go up in rank by extending the match to as many innings as possible. But Armand is simply too good and too experienced to do that. He doesn't need to cheat. He loves pool too much and gets no pleasure from that sort of ruse, least of all in league play, which is pure recreation for him.

Armand turns so that he's looking me full in the face, his watery eyes earnest, sparking with anger. "What is this, I'm not bringing my game? I always bring my game. When you play me, I give you my game. I give you my heart. I play hard. Always. I give you my heart, my *heart*, every time. And it hurts sometimes, you know? My heart gets broke." At this he smiles.

Armand is infuriated by this insult from Isaac and so finally, in the last game, on the last shot, the one that would have given him the match, Armand does the unthinkable: He purposely misses the 8-ball. Just to piss off his opponent, not even caring about the win. "I was so mad," he tells me. Then he lowers his eyes and smiles mock-demurely. "It must be my Spanish center," he says, his hand on his chest.

Once he's explained his state of mind to me, Armand cools down and tries to describe, in his occasionally impenetrable English, how his teaching methods work. He'll demonstrate, I'll imitate. He says I'll absorb "seventy-five percent" of what he tells me. And my game will improve.

At first, he assures me, I'll watch him and think, *No way, I'll never be able to do that.* And then in a few weeks I'll shock myself and do it. He'll lend me tapes, which I should watch. He fumbles for a word in the middle of his monologue and says, "It's like . . . calligraphy. First you just make one line that goes like this"—he makes a simple motion with his hand in the air in front of us, on an invisible desk. "Then next week, you do another line, like this." He swooshes another line, in a different direction. "Your teacher says you're going to make an A. 'No-no,' you say. 'That's impossible, it's too hard. I can never do that.' Then the next week, you practice this line"—his hand air-draws another one. "Then, finally, you draw this." He draws an approximation of a calligraphic A in the air in front of us. "'Look! An A! I've made an A. I can't believe it!' And now you go try to draw a B. You see?"

Yes, I say. I see. "You're getting a foundation. Learning fundamentals and building on them."

Armand nods vigorously. "Yes. Exactly."

He also asks me (again) what I'm scared of. I describe my match that night, how I was finally close to beating Oliver and then clutched on an embarrassingly easy 8-ball shot, one I'd set up beautifully.

Armand understands. He asks me why I didn't call a coach. I'm silent.

In that situation, he says, when you're nervous, call your coach, just to chat. Your coach "is your aspirin, your Tylenol, your Advil, your weed, your *shit*," he says with emphasis. "You need him, so use him. Is okay."

He then adds that my fear, my constant clutching, is because of three letters. Do I know what they are?

I shake my head no.

"E-G-O." Ego. I smile.

Although Armand's further explanation is a bit garbled, the essence is that I absolutely should not, cannot, be conscious of my own performance. I need not to care so much about winning or losing, not to think about and measure myself or worry, "Oh, I missed that easy shot," because then it's about only me and not the game. Ego. You're your own worst enemy, in other words.

"Don't worry," Armand says. "I teach you."

ALTHOUGH I OFFER TO meet him anywhere he wants, my first lesson with Armand takes place practically in my backyard. He hops the subway from Greenwich Village, where he lives, to Brownstone Billiards, where I usually practice because it's so close to my apartment. When we meet he spends a good deal of time trying to smooth over his bungling of our first appointment, which he missed the day before. I'd shown up at Brownstone at our designated time and was shooting balls for an hour and a half before Corey, the sweet-tempered young guy who works the counter most weekends, calls my name over the loudspeaker, telling me I have a phone call. I feel extremely important and pool-authentic as I go to the phone, knowing that the few other scraggly players in residence are watching from their tables. I take the phone from Corey, who shrugs. There's a lot of static on the line, but the gist of it is that Armand is on a job in the Bronx, trying to move a pool table up several flights of stairs with "a bunch of idiots." He doesn't think he'll make it out to Brooklyn, unless I'm willing to wait another two hours. We decide to try again the next day.

The rescheduling of our tutorial is met with strenuous protestations from Alison. "All this effort for skeet shooting?" she says. Alison likes to pretend she "doesn't know from pool." When we talk on the phone, she asks me how the boccie is going, if I read the recent bridge scores in the paper, if I'm enjoying my water polo league. I play along, and eventually she drops the act. She seems concerned about my taking lessons from Armand—a man who doesn't seem to keep his appointments, a man I met in a bar and barely know—even though we'll be playing just a short walk from my apartment. "What if you end up in his sub-zero refrigerator?" she demands. "How will I contact you?" Alison likes to make sure I have everything in perspective. I assure her that I do.

Armand is waiting for me at the pool hall the next day, somewhat chagrined. I wave off his apologies. Everyone at Brownstone knows him when we walk in because he's serviced the pool tables there many times. ("They're shit," he whispers to me, and I have to concede that most of them are in a pretty pathetic condition that no amount of recovering is going to help.)

We choose a table in the back, and Armand tells me to start shooting.

"What? You mean just anything?"

"Just make some balls. I want to see your stroke."

So I start sending balls into the far corner pockets, missing a few out of nerves but then relaxing with the rhythm of it and making the rest.

"You don't hit hard enough" is Armand's first comment.

"Yeah, I know."

"I've never seen such a delicate stroke. Your form is good, but you have no power, no authority. You hold back. You have to hit with authority. The balls, when they go in, should make a sound, maybe even jump up. You showing them who's boss."

I nod.

"Let me," he says. Without appearing to exert any extra energy, he proceeds to slam in ten balls in a row. "Listen," he says. "Listen to that. You hear? That sound, *that sound*. You must make that sound. That's authority. That's what you hear."

And he hits some more. Some of the balls, indeed, go into the pockets so hard that they bounce up before falling back in. They make satisfying *thocks* each time.

The sound of a game of pool is a beloved musical score, if for no other reason than its familiarity. And not just by those who play the game. Ask someone—anyone—if he or she can summon the sounds of a pool game. They can—and they will always smile when they do. Richard Coe wrote in his 1961 *Washington Post* review of *The Hustler*, "There is . . . an admirable minimum of background music. The clicking balls have a rhythmic melody all their own."

I think my favorite opening to a film about pool is the first couple of minutes of the pool-hustling caper *The Baltimore Bullet*, which came out in 1980 and stars James Coburn and Omar Sharif. The screen is completely dark; the only sound the audience can hear is the sound of pool balls clicking into a rack. No music on the juke-box, no talking, no glasses tinkling, just that soft, melodious clicking. Then the triangular rack comes into view. The camera hovers over it, the balls tightly nestled inside. Someone removes the triangle and someone else breaks up the rack. This is followed by a series of trick shots in which all the viewer sees, besides the ricocheting pool balls, is a cue stick and an arm, and all he or she hears is the sound of those balls dancing. It is pool disembodied, broken down to its essence.

"TRY IT IN THE SIDE," Armand says, figuring if he puts less distance between the pocket and me I might be able to sink the balls harder. At first there's no difference, but then I start to really smack the stick against the cue ball, like I'm boxing. My arm tingles. I don't rest between shots. Armand slides a ball to me, I thwack it in. It makes that sound.

"Ah, you see? You feel that? You feel your arm? You are now hitting with authority. You must do that every time, even when you don't want to make such a powerful shot. Your stroke don't look as pretty right now, but is okay. We work on that. You can be pretty and powerful," he says, raising his eyebrows flirtatiously.

We work on my shooting with authority for a while, then Armand starts setting up shots for me to try. He attempts to teach me how to use draw effectively (this is when you shoot the cue ball far enough below its center that it spurts backward after hitting the object ball). He also tries to teach me how to know with certainty that I'm going to make a shot. Once I can shoot with that much confidence, I will have the luxury of focusing on where to leave the cue ball after the shot is complete.

At one point during the afternoon, Armand goes to the counter to fetch a couple of sodas, and Ted, one of Brownstone's regulars, a spindly, droopy, bespectacled man with an odd, screechy voice and a crazed dedication to pool, gives me the thumbs-up from across the room. "Keep it up!" he squawks, and flashes his crooked smile.

My first lesson with Armand lasts four hours. I don't remember the last time I was that tired. I forget words. I take my cue apart to put it in its case, then absently start putting it together again until Armand takes it gently from my hands.

"We made good progress today," he says. "You're a good pupil. You learn quick. Don't look so unsure. You can do this."

I pay for the table time and we walk outside. It had been glaringly bright when we first arrived, and now it's dusky and mellow. I thank Armand profusely. He shakes my hand and bows. "When do we do this again?" he asks.

I suggest the following weekend. That works for him. I tell him I'll come to his neighborhood this time. He says, "Whatever. I play any-where. I don't mind coming to you again." He's wearing his pointy brown shoes and he looks jaunty as he heads toward the subway, his small frame growing smaller as it recedes.

I arrive home in something of a daze. I pour a glass of water then go into the living room and stretch out on the couch, drowsily pon-dering my afternoon. I feel as if I'm fixing something. I think about what that might be, but before the answer hits me, I fall asleep.

ARMAND COMES OUT TO Brooklyn again for my next lesson, which, as promised, takes place the weekend after our first meeting. We try to play at Park Slope Billiards, just for a change of venue, but it's closed for some reason. So we walk the twenty-six blocks back to my neighborhood and return to the always-reliable Brownstone. Along the way, I pepper Armand with questions about pool players he knows, money he's won, cues he favors. I ask him about his life in Chile. I sense that most people don't interrogate Armand in this way. I don't believe he thinks of himself as an interesting person outside of the grubby pool bars where he hangs out. To be the focus of someone's attention, to have someone listening eagerly to you, in awe of an expertise you never really gave a second thought to, well, this can be quite a tonic. And Armand is drunk with it. He's talkative, bright-eyed, laughing a lot. He's feeling good about himself. The tutorials are clearly benefiting him, too.

Back in the dungeon of Brownstone, Corey gives us the same table as before. Ted greets me warmly as I come down the stairs, tells me to "watch out for this guy," nodding toward Armand and grinning his lopsided grin.

Armand and I begin the lesson the same way we did last time, starting with the basics, Armand trying to get me to "hit with authority." Then he asks me, somewhat abruptly, how I fare with bank shots. I roll my eyes. "Not one of my strong suits," I say. "Frankly, I'm not sure if I have any strong suits."

Armand rubs his hands together. "Good. This I can show you. Is easy. Remember when I first see you play, and I tell you you don't use the cushions?" Yes, I remember. "The cushions are your friends." Armand is a three-cushion billiard devotee at heart. It's what he played in Chile, what he played when he first came to this country, what he prefers to watch as a spectator in his spare time. Pool he likes enough, it's recreation, but three-cushion is art. "I love it," he says to me on our walk across Park Slope. "I *love* it," and he closes his eyes and puts his hand over his heart.

Armand shows me how to calculate where to hit a bank shot. "Make your pool table very small," he says.

"Huh?"

He puts my cue stick across the table so that each end of it rests on each of the two side pockets, like a safety bar. He chooses this line—from pocket to opposite pocket—because, he explains, he wants me to bank the ball into one of these side pockets. Next, he grabs a house cue from the wall and places it across the table in the same manner, but lines it up with the cue ball instead, which is about two feet from the side pockets, near the head rail. So the borders of this imaginary "small table" are the two side pockets on one end and the cue ball on the other. Inside this newly bordered panel of green, resting maybe a foot from the cue ball, on a slight diagonal, is the 8-ball—the ball I'm going to try to bank into a pocket. Armand tells me to find the halfway mark between the two borders of my newly conformed table. That mark turns out to be just to the left of one of the diamonds on the side rail—little insignias stenciled into every pool table for just this type of calculation. I point at the spot and raise my eyebrows. Armand nods. "Yes. There," he says. "That is what you aim for. Hit the cue ball in the center, so that it makes the eight-ball hit that spot on the rail you've just found. If you do it right, the eight will bounce off the rail and roll right into this side pocket." He points dramatically to the pocket. Then he removes the two cue sticks that he placed so carefully on the table. "I hope you took a picture of that," he says, tapping his temple.

I bend down, take a couple of practice strokes, and send the cue ball into the 8, aiming for the spot on the rail that Armand and I have calculated. The 8-ball hits the spot dead-on and rolls slowly toward the side pocket. I haven't hit it very hard, so it seems to take a ridiculously long time. The ball toddles across the table then plops into the pocket. I've just banked the 8. It certainly isn't the first time I've banked a ball, but it's the first time I've actually had a plan, the first time I've picked the exact spot to hit, rather than just wildly estimating and hoping for the best.

Armand's face lights up and he starts clapping. "You see? You see? It's so easy. A baby turtle could do this."

A baby turtle? I don't pursue it.

Armand and I spend the next hour on bank shots. He sets up the 8-ball, I figure out how to bank it in. I'm shooting with incredible accuracy. Even Armand seems a little taken aback. "This shows me you have not been playing to your ability. A true beginner would not keep making these shots. These are hard."

I point out that this isn't a real match and that he's helping me. He nods but doesn't seem wholly convinced. It's true, I finally allow myself to concede—I've come a long way since those early days at Chelsea Billiards. Mark, my first teacher, wouldn't recognize my game.

We finish another four-hour session with Armand bouncing around excitedly and me drained to the point of incoherence. I have to call it a day.

I begin packing up my cue and reflect on the day's lesson, on my blossoming bank shots, on my intense focus without the accompanying self-criticism. I think about how Armand has been able to help me unlock new skills in such a short time. "Armand, have you ever heard of that urban myth about our brain capacity?" I ask. I zip my case and settle it over my shoulder. Armand cocks his head. His silvery eyebrows raise slightly. He waits for a further explanation.

"You know, that supposedly human beings use only ten percent of their brains, that there's ninety percent of our brain capacity we don't ever use, but if we could tap into it, well, who knows, maybe we'd be levitating tables or something." I shrug. "Maybe this theory applies to my pool game. What do you think?"

We head across the room toward the door. I'm being somewhat glib, but Armand's hands are clasped behind his back as we walk. He's thinking seriously about my question.

"Well, I have definitely met many players who don't use their brains when they play pool." He chuckles to himself. We reach the counter and I pay for the table time. Armand pulls the door open. Creamy light spills into the dark vestibule from the street. He looks at me steadily. "But I don't think you're one of them. I think maybe sometimes you use too much brain. And me, I sometimes use too much heart, I get very emotional."

"So what does this mean?"

He's silent for what feels like a full minute. Then he smiles mischievously. "I think it means we make a pretty good team, yes?" He gestures gallantly toward the open door.

Armand is hard to resist at moments like this.

We walk outside. I think about what he's said, about my using "too much brain," and try to decipher it. Despite the sense of liberation I claim to have felt when I first started playing pool, I'm anything but liberated these days. I've imprisoned myself somehow. There's clearly a part of my psyche that I'm not tapping into when I play. I'm wasting a part of me, holding it back. My near-instant prowess with those bank shots demonstrates that something is amiss, that the divide between what I'm capable of and how I'm actually playing is too great. I'm using the same ten percent of my brain that everyone else uses, an A-student trapped in a C-student's pool game. If I can locate and liberate that part of me, the part that can shoot with authority and get the ball to make *that sound*, will my slump be broken for good? Will I win tournaments? Begin dating George Clooney? And if I don't find that part, can I still love the game and be just an ordinary pool player? Will that be enough?

Armand clears his throat, perhaps to reel me in from my thoughts. Once again we find ourselves saying slightly formal good-byes on Flatbush Avenue. Then I remember that I've brought a gift for him. Since he won't accept money (professionals who give private lessons charge anywhere from $75 to $100 an hour), I bought him a nice bottle of whiskey.

"Armand, I have something for you." I hand him a bag tied with ribbon. He opens it and peers inside. "Thank you," he says, smiling broadly.

"I wasn't sure what to get you, but this is to show my gratitude for your time."

"This is great. Because I am an alcoholic."

I'm not sure if he's kidding. He doesn't seem to be. "So, you like whiskey then?" I've never bought a bottle of whiskey before, only ordered the rare shot.

"Yes, like I told you. I am alcoholic, I like everything. Whiskey included."

"Oh." I'm still not sure if he's pulling my leg.

"And I have something for you." This startles me out of my confusion. "I brought you gifts, too."

"But Armand—"

He holds his hand up to stop me. He pulls from one pocket a small box, and from the other a plastic bag wrapped around something thin. I lift the lid of the box. Inside is a wallet, smooth and black and shiny. "South American leather," Armand says.

"Thank you. This is lovely." It appears to be a man's wallet.

"Open the other," he says.

I crinkle open the bag and find three silvery CDs. "I made them for you. You like salsa music?"

"Oh, I love salsa," I say.

"Tell me what you think then. I can make you more."

I feel uncomfortable with the gifts, but I thank Armand.

I walk home, fatigued, my mind a whirl of bank shots and whiskey and salsa music and shiny black leather.

I replay our final parting in my mind: When Armand and I say good-bye after our awkward gift exchange, shaking hands formally again, he says, drawing his bushy eyebrows together as if he's just come to an important conclusion, "What you need now is to play a monster."

The Third Eye

IT'S HARD FOR ME to pinpoint just what type of "monster" Armand is referring to, since most of the players I face across a seven-foot bar table are monsters to me. Maybe that's the point. Maybe what Armand means is that I need to play against—and beat—myself, or the proverbial "demons inside my head" that eat away at my self-confidence when a match takes a wrong turn. That certainly has a neat, psychologically astute ring to it. But Armand, for all his South-American flair and self-conscious references to his fiery "Spanish center," is quite literal when it comes to pool, razor-sharp in his instruction and recommendations. After much rumination, I decide that he means I need to topple someone big, someone who looms especially large to me, and then the curse will be broken and my real game, my fierce, authentic, pool-playing self, will emerge.

But finding this larger-than-life foe is not so easy, since there are so many contenders. Would Trevor qualify? Paul G.? Both are certainly extreme and tortured enough, but I feel compassion for them, not competition. What about Randy Pomeroy, Liz's smug, grating teammate? He's annoying, sure, but he doesn't linger in my consciousness after a match is over. He can be spat out like a piece of chewing gum. Pool halls, pool bars, and pool leagues are filled with such ill-tempered jackasses; they no longer surprise me.

As the weeks pass and I work through the monster conundrum, I realize that I've arrived somewhere new. My sessions with Armand have cracked something open in me. Pool is no longer just about the low-slung jeans, the dark characters, the slaying of dragons. It's no longer about easing loneliness or becoming someone else.

But during this promising awakening, the A-student kicks in. As I begin to fall under the influence of not only the game of pool but also its beautiful equipment and blunt argot, its expanse of quiet, its endless acts of innovation and calculation, I feel a sharp hunger to learn more, to solve the cosmic riddle of how I can improve and excel, to understand where the game comes from and why it's able to hyp-notize so many. Why are some personalities or brains drawn in—instantly—while others can pick up a cue stick maybe once a year, the rest of the time content to swing a golf club, throw a dart, roll a bowling ball, or simply hold a remote control in front of a big-screen TV and ESPN? Why me? Why Sam? Why Alan? Why Liz? I feel I can wrest control of the game from my psyche if I just gather enough of this kind of knowledge—if I ace the test, pitch the perfect idea—when what I really should be doing is sitting breathless in a coat closet, spinning home runs (or rather, brilliant eight-ball shots) out of nothing more than joy and devotion.

Instead, I pull books from the library and articles from the Internet, looking for answers. I subscribe to *Billiards Digest* and buy a billiards encyclopedia the size of a car door. I store it underneath my coffee table. I read accounts of notorious pool characters and wonder if I have anything in common with them. (No, I concede.) This goes on for a couple of months, my desire to excel once again eclipsing my ability to enjoy, until I finally start to wonder how all of this research, as fascinating as it is, is going to help my pool game, or my pool "mind-set." The reason I first fell for the game was that it freed me from my usual approach to school, to career, to relationships, to life. It wasn't about studying, planning, excelling. It was quiet and sultry and intuitive. Why have I turned my back on that? How is looking at a seventeenth-century engraving of gnomes playing billiards (I really did find this in a book) going to get my pool game to "click"? It's not long after this that my thirst for "meta-pool" begins to feel somewhat slaked, as if a fever has broken, and I stop obsessing, for the time being at least, about what it all "means."

This brief, monomaniacal foray into billiards lore and minutiae doesn't influence my play—for good or for ill—or my team's place in the league standings. We always seem to miss a playoff berth by just a few points. A couple of matches here and there, and who knows, maybe we'd be on our way to Vegas. But it never happens. Sam seems resigned. Valerie doesn't care; she's in it for the Monday-night haul, not the Big Glory, though I'm sure she'd be happy to come along for the ride, should we make it that far.

I'm content for us to finish in second or third place, since my preoccupation is still mostly with my own game. One night at the bar, as I'm nervously awaiting my match, Armand saunters in, smiling, wearing his trademark elfin shoes. He's still clean-shaven. Our schedules have been at odds lately, and I haven't practiced with him in a while. I'm losing less frequently since our lessons, but my wins, when I get them, are not decisive. They're clawed out of the ground, stubborn weeds resisting the pull from a flower bed. His presence takes me by surprise.

"Hey there," I say uncertainly as he approaches. "Are you playing tonight?" I'm pretty sure Armand is not a member of the team we're up against, so my confusion is mounting.

"No. I come to see you."

"Me? What about?" Do I owe Armand money? He said his lessons were free. I haven't made that up, I'm quite sure.

"No, I come to *see* you. To watch you play. I want to see how my pupil is doing."

"Oh."

Armand sees the panic in my face. "Heather, I am not here to judge. Just to watch. You're going to kick ass." He makes a little fist and pumps it in the air, grinning. I smile weakly and begin to unpack my cue. I'm beside myself. I don't want Armand watching me shoot. I believe him when he says he hasn't come to judge me. That isn't the problem. *I* will judge me. I know I'll try to impress the man who taught me never to play to impress. Those three letters: E-G-O. For a moment, I hate him.

"I'm going to get a drink," Armand announces. "Can I get you anything?" I shake my head. "Not even a beer?"

"No, I'm fine."

"Not even a teensy, eensy, little tiny beer in a thimble—"

"Armand."

"Okay, okay." He puts his hands up in surrender. "I'm just trying to relax you." He walks off toward the front of the bar, where the drinks are served.

My match starts about five minutes later. I'm playing a portly guy wearing a tattered Yankees baseball hat who likes to bring his bulldog to his matches, but our bar doesn't allow animals, so he's looking a little lost. He breaks the rack, but nothing goes in, so it's my turn. As I take in the spread of balls on the table, I notice Armand standing in the doorway, holding a shot glass of whiskey, also taking in the spread on the table. His eyes meet mine for a moment. He raises his eyebrows, smiles, and brings the glass to his lips. I look away. My stomach churns and I heave a loud, exasperated sigh. I see a nice shot on the 7, go for it, and miss. I back away, giving my opponent room. When I look around the room, Armand is nowhere to be seen.

Mr. Bulldog and I go four games—I win one, he wins three and thus takes the match. He even executes a difficult massé, which is one of Sam's favorite shots. (A massé is performed by raising the butt of the cue to an extremely high angle—usually more than forty-five degrees—and "striking the cue ball from above." This puts severe English on the ball, causing it to curve sharply as it rolls along the table. Mike Shamos provides a wonderfully detailed description of the shot and its history in his encyclopedia.)

I return to the high table around which my teammates are sprawled and lean my cue against the wall, looking for my purse. And then Armand appears, as if conjured like a spirit.

"I see that I make you nervous, so I go to the front," he says. I find my purse and begin to rummage through it, pretending to look for something. Now might be a good time for that beer, I think.

"Do you like the CDs I give you?"

"Huh?" I turn around and face him, annoyed.

"The salsa CDs. Do you like them?"

"Oh. Yes. Yes, I do. Very much."

"I can make you some more."

"That's okay, Armand. You don't have to do that."

"It's no trouble." He gazes at me expectantly. "So, how did you do?"

"I lost."

"Ah, that's a shame. But not to worry. Next time you'll win. I know this."

I shrug.

"You know, you need to get over this thing you have about playing in front of people who are interested in your game. People will always study your game. They will always watch. It's how you learn. You should be studying theirs, too." He pauses, then says, "You know, you can do a massé, too, if you try."

I nod meekly. I'm behaving like a fool. "Armand, you're absolutely right."

"So you'll try then? You'll let the world watch you, just a little?" His eyes twinkle.

"Yes, I'll try."

"Good. And don't forget to watch back." He wags a finger at me. "I won't forget."

THE PARADOX OF POOL is that being good at it is so solitary, and yet when you win big, all you want to do is share the feeling, even if it means simply screaming into the night air. I have a tendency to forget this when a match doesn't go my way and I turn inward, as when I lose to Mr. Bulldog in front of Armand.

Bar pool is made up of loners collected into a group. I play on a "team," but my match is against one person and its outcome rests entirely on my shoulders. There is a heavy, painful, utterly delicious burden in that. But once you play in a league long enough, you're sharing that burden with everyone, whether you want to or not. As Armand said, you watch, but you have to accept that you're being watched as well. It's a two-way street. I chew on this while observing the other players shoot after my match with Mr. Bulldog, listening as they swap dramatic tales from the front lines between breaks, dissecting earlier matches shot by shot, all of them leaning forward when they speak, alive with tension and excitement. Another line of dialogue from *The Color of Money* comes to me: "Pool excellence is not about excellent pool. It's about becoming someone," the older, wiser Eddie Felson says. I have to smile. I realize my loner-in-a-group theory has a few kinks.

Despite its outer stillness, there's a posturing and hyperbole that wind around a pool match like a hot coil, a danger and sexiness to the game, a certain flash and theater that you don't often find on, say, a baseball diamond in the Midwest. I can go on and on about the intellectual thrill that baseball gives me, but it sure doesn't make me want to slither into a pair of black leather pants or walk into an unknown bar on a rainy night, thinking of Westerns. I can read all the encyclopedias I want, but the truth is, pool is as much about ambience and—

Armand is right—an audience as anything else, at least some of the time. And you must learn to conquer that gaze so you can revel in it rather than be doomed by it.

I believe the game's theatricality, its sense of atmosphere, comes from movies. Pool has been played on film for more than a century. Watching it on a big screen, or even a small one, is mesmerizing: the graceful, sinewy bodies, the smoldering looks, the elegant click click of a game. It's hard not to have these cinematic associations come into play when you're in a real pool hall, watching real games. (As someone who regularly inserts fantasy scenes of *The Hustler* into her own losing matches, I have some authority on this subject.)

I've never played a game of pool (or watched one in a bar) in which one of the players, if not both, doesn't have something to prove. There's always a proverbial little guy, and often a bully; there's an undercurrent—and an underclass—in every game. Pool is a Western. It's 1930s Chicago. It's immigrant New York. It's about bravado, about having confidence that maybe you shouldn't have. It's wit demonstrated through action—the core of moviemaking. Pool feels, despite a long history that springs from somewhere far away, utterly American. This is, I believe, what we're meant to see, feel, and intuit in movies about pool. It's what we're meant to experience when we watch a professional nine-ball tournament on ESPN, too.

It's true that when I'm shooting a game of pool, every once in a while, if the table is going a certain way, and if I am in a certain mood, and the light and air and crowd are arranged just so, for a moment, I am Johnny Bench. I am as tall and powerful as those young softball titans from my summer girls' league. I am as tortured and irresistible as Paul Newman. How could I forget?

I ASK ARMAND IF he wants another whiskey—"Always," he says—so I walk over to the bar and buy him one.

Transformation

Armand's little lecture has a powerful—and therapeutic—effect on me. I feel grateful, and I feel calm. I realize, in a corny, there's-no-place-like-home sort of way, that I don't need to seek out a connection with the pool players of the universe to feel like one of them, that I don't need to have my connection to the game explained or validated by "texts," that there may not be any higher truth here. What I do know is that I am happy to be at the tables I've come to know, with the people I've come to know, whether they're watching me or not. I don't feel as though I'm fighting anyone anymore—not Wally and his hillbilly charm; not blonde, silky Melanie and her icy condescension; not the players who defeated me during my slump and the superstitions I developed as a result. I don't even feel like I'm fighting myself, for a change. On the flip side, I no longer feel particularly sexy or overheated, as when I hip-swung and hair-tossed through the pool bars of Manhattan while playing for Paul G.'s team, my new cue pulled out of its case week after week like a trophy from my affair with Roger.

The intensity, the frustration, the sex, the sizzle—all of these feelings have, over the past several months, evaporated like mist. The drama and exhilaration once again come from the sixteen balls and the green cloth, nothing more. And yet I also no longer feel lonely. The empty, out-of-place feeling that plagued me during meaningless Midtown lunches as a woman forging a career in New York seems to have evaporated as well. Now I just want to play my game. And, of course, win.

But I'm not allowed to exist in this blissful state for long.

I show up at the bar one Monday night for our regular match. Alan has just returned from an extended trip to Las Vegas, where he was a paid referee for a huge national amateur pool tournament held at the Riviera Hotel & Casino. (He spent months studying to become officially certified and has been angling for just such an assignment for a long time. His goal is to referee for the pros.) Alan mentions how hard it was—impossible, really—to find a table in the casinos available for non-tournament play. There are so many rules and re-strictions now, he says.

"That's because everything good gets ruined," Sam interjects. This seems to be the essence of his life philosophy, which he expounds upon that night, between pool matches.

What has set him off is not Alan's Vegas travelogue, but the "new and improved" Chelsea Billiards, which Sam visited recently and which is now saddled with the ostentatiously clever name Slate (referring, of course, to the layer of slate inside a pool table). The poolroom still looms along the eastern border of Chelsea, still vast, but newly plush, with a checkerboard of pool tables both upstairs and downstairs and a trendy "club scene" atmosphere. The puny bar on the ground floor where I picked up the auspicious pool-school flyer four years ago has been replaced with a much bigger and swankier bar, one better able to serve the slew of pool-happy, apple martini–drinking investment bankers who frequent the place now.

There's a heavily muscled bouncer at the door, and inside are a full-service restaurant with sexy waitresses, a "cocktail menu," swirling dance lights, thumping, contemporary rock music so loud it makes you wince, and wide, curving stairs the size of dining tables that take you to the poolroom's different "levels." The place has become a huge success. I went in one time after the renovation but didn't even make it to the stairs before turning around and walking out.

"It's a nightmare," Sam says, shaking his head, still a bit shell-shocked at the state of one of his old haunts. I'm told that pool school still operates out of the basement on Monday evenings and Saturday mornings, but I haven't been able to bring myself to visit. I don't think the place has been ruined, though, the way Sam does. I think it's just become something else.

"LO MEIN? YOU'RE KIDDING."

"Sadly, I'm not."

Liz and I are eating burgers after playing pool for a couple hours at SoHo Billiards. She's telling me about running into Roger at The Wrong Side a few weeks ago. He stumbled in with lo mein hanging in long, crusty strands down the front of his shirt. He'd thrown up on the way over, he said. Liz had seen him a couple weeks before that, too, she tells me, and he'd sat in unfocused silence, vacantly watching her pool match against an old teammate of his. That time he'd been hanging around the bar since the afternoon. He'd been waking up in strange places, he told her, most recently on Big Tony's couch in Queens. They'd been "partying" in Atlantic City, or Foxwoods, he couldn't remember which. That night he'd spilled two drinks, one on Liz and one on himself. He bragged to Liz, pressing useless paper napkins against his wet shirt, that he was seeing a "hot nineteen-year-old." Which answered any questions I may have had about his status with Shelly. He still lived in the same apartment—Liz had asked him. Shelly had moved out a while ago.

"Jesus. Is he working?"

"I asked him that this most recent time, since he appeared to be in such a state, with the lo mein and everything. He said he hadn't been in the office in a while, that he was 'taking some personal days.' I guess his co-workers have been calling his apartment and his cell phone, looking for him. When I asked him if his boss knew he was taking this 'personal time,' he said, 'Well, he does now,' and then started laughing hysterically." She shakes her head, her dark eyes sad.

I haven't seen or heard from Roger since being ousted from Paul G.'s team, which happened more than a year ago. He stopped showing up at league pool, Liz says, though for a while there were raucous "Roger sightings" around town that her teammates would report to her in vivid Technicolor. Sometimes she would pass these snippets on to me, when she felt it was no longer painful for me to hear them. But I haven't heard any stories for quite some time.

Liz continues to run into Roger even though he's fallen off the radar because he occasionally haunts the pool bars in her division, mostly because he's friends with Big Tony, who used to play on Liz's current team. Tony shows up every once in a while to hassle Liz's captain, and Roger sometimes follows. Although kept on a tight leash by his wife, Tony likes to have a male buddy around with whom he can "get into trouble," and he's so arrogant and intolerable most of the time that someone much younger and half in the bag is the perfect— and only—match for him. Unfortunately, Roger fits that description. It's a dangerous friendship, born of convenience on Tony's part and desperation on Roger's.

"He looked really bad this time," Liz says, referring to the most recent run-in with Roger, when he showed up covered in lo mein. "When I saw him that first time, when he spilled the drinks, he was just really loud and drunk and being silly, bragging about this girl he was seeing. But this time he seemed really down. He barely spoke. He told me he'd had to go to the emergency room a few days ago.

He said he'd been out partying, but he couldn't drink because his stomach was killing him, and then I guess he started throwing up blood." I wince.

"So he went to the hospital and they found out he had a bleeding ulcer. They wanted to keep him overnight, but he refused, so I guess they gave him some medication and he left. He said he's not supposed to drink for a while, and that that lasted about two days. Which was pretty obvious, considering he was telling me this with lo mein falling out of his breast pocket."

We pick at our burgers, no longer hungry.

"So we don't know if he's still employed," I say. "He really claims that he's just taking a few personal days?" Other than my sudden loss of appetite, I'm numb.

"Yeah, as I said, I asked him about that and it was unclear. He said he was thinking of quitting, that he hated being a lawyer, but I got the feeling the quitting had already been taken care of for him."

"So he was fired?"

"I just don't know, but it did not sound like he was going to the office. Any office."

"What about Shelly? Does she know about this?"

"I don't know. I didn't get the feeling they were in touch."

We sit in silence. A waitress comes by and asks us if everything is okay, which strikes me as a cold and preposterous question.

Liz says Roger spent Thanksgiving by himself, and that he seemed depressed about it. He'd mumbled something about dreading New Year's Eve, but he was fairly incoherent. She says he looked gray and waxy, and that he smelled awful, like milk that had gone sour. He'd held a large gin and tonic in his hand but wasn't drinking it.

This had all been a few weeks ago, and she hasn't seen him since, or heard about him from anyone. We sit quietly, pushing our fries around. I'm working up the courage to say what neither one of us wants to say.

"Do you think he's alive?" I finally ask. Liz sighs heavily and looks at me, her gaze full of compassion.

"I don't know. I was wondering the same thing." She sips from her water glass. "You know, I even asked Tony about it. I saw him not long after I saw Roger, and I know they've been partners in crime lately, going around to bars, Tony popping his painkillers and complaining about his pool team. They've been going to casinos, too."

"What'd he say?"

"Well, you know Tony, sensitive guy that he is. He got all disgusted and said that he had no idea what was going on with Roger, that he never seemed to want to hang out anymore, that he was a mess."

"Tony said that Roger was a mess?"

"Yeah, I know. How bad off do you have to be for Tony to pronounce you incurable?" A guilty silence drapes over us. The waitress seems to know to stay away. I prod Liz to continue.

"Well, Tony says that Roger's been babbling about wanting to travel, wanting to go to Europe, so his verdict is that that's where he probably is."

"That seems unlikely. I can't imagine him even being able to get on a plane, from what you've told me."

"I know, I agree, but that's the last Tony heard from him, these big European plans."

We're back to the original question. Finally, Liz says, "I think we would've heard if he, well, you know, if something had happened."

"You mean if he's dead." I have a need to say the word out loud, just this one time.

"Yeah."

I hope Liz is right. Even in the strange, dark, fractured network made up of dubious characters like Big Tony and Trevor and Paul G., someone would know if Roger was no longer alive, and word would spread. I stare at an empty table near us. Liz stares at her water glass.

I try to muster some optimism. Maybe Roger has finally hit bottom and is in rehab somewhere. I cling to this thought. It gives me hope.

Or maybe he's in Moscow or Marrakech or Barcelona, looking at art and gazing up at a vast, blue foreign sky. Or maybe he's driving around Paris, taking in the buildings, tall and ancient and ornate, their structures solid, their histories and their futures unquestioned.

Monster

WALTER MITTY, THAT SAD, funny fantasist made immortal by James Thurber, is a commander of a Navy hydroplane, a world-famous surgeon, the greatest sharpshooter in the country, a fearless wartime pilot who could down several brandies and still take on the Jerries, and a principled man ready to face his executioners with nothing more than the flick of a cigarette. In Thurber's *The Secret Life of Walter Mitty*, he is all of these people in the space of one car ride and a subsequent shopping excursion, intermittently brought back to reality in painful bits and pieces by his nagging dullard of a wife. Mitty says to her memorably, after being roused from a reverie by one of her exasperated tirades, "Does it ever occur to you that I am sometimes thinking?"

Pool has created a quiet space for me where I can be "sometimes thinking." There is no Mrs. Mitty to interrupt me. The game itself, as well as the weekly league matches, the practicing, the war stories swapped with Liz, even the melancholy side trip with Roger, has provided an extra charge to my already active fantasy life; pool has enabled me to take the fantasies one step further, helping me to create, creepily and excitingly, that alternate persona I was searching for while I was working for Larry and peering into poolroom windows.

My pursuit of pool excellence is not some figment, however, a story lodged deep in my mind, enacted only in private in some secret world of my invention; it's now out in the open for people to see. But it is also, in its own way, still a complete fantasy. I will never be Jeanette Lee or Fran Crimi or even Melanie, just like I would never be Johnny Bench, but the pursuit—and the rich fantasies that go along with it—remains delicious.

Americans are bred to pursue, to look only forward, to *keep at it*. But reaching the goal isn't always the answer. The quixotic journey is, as the self-help books and bittersweet coming-of-age novels tell us, where the character-building and the heartbreak and the fun lie. Sometimes actually reaching the goal leaves nothing but a large, sad crater behind.

But sometimes it leaves a mountain.

WHEN I WALK INTO the bar one Monday just after the air starts to turn cold, when people have begun to shiver as they smoke in tight clumps on the sidewalks now that smoking has been banned from the bars, taking quick puffs between their muffled conversations, trying to finish the damn drag as quickly as possible so they can get back inside, when I take note of this change of season and walk into the bar, and see Big Tony in a far corner showing some moke his new digital camera, I know the night is going to morph into something wildly different, something strange and enervating—and possibly exhilarating beyond my wildest dreams.

It's late 2003. Tony has been a 7 for well over a year now; I haven't seen him in almost as long, not since I played for Paul G.'s team. With Melanie, my pool-school nemesis, appearing in sports magazines and no longer deigning to grace any of the league bars with her presence, he's the only villain I can create, the only one I've been able to hold on to. The only one worth beating. I've missed him.

It's childish, of course. But it's also logical: If I can beat someone who, by his designated rank, is considered among the best—even if he's the best only in our narrow little world—then my pool obsession will no longer be confined to my Walter Mitty imagination. Big Tony is my monster. Armand told me to find him, and there he is. Waiting.

I've watched too many movies at this point, read too many books, tracked down too many teachers and scholars and fanatics. I know it won't happen the way I've seen, read about, or imagined.

But that doesn't mean it won't be sweet.

"HEY, HONEY, HOW YOU DOIN'?"

"Tone, how're *you* doing? I heard you were down for the count." I try to conceal my excitement at seeing him.

"Ah, don't believe that crap. I'm on two different teams now. I'm playing mostly out on Long Island these days—I've had enough of this Manhattan shit. But every once in a while, you know, I'll play for a team downtown and maybe show up for a match or two. See, the problem is the league rules just make it impossible for a guy of my ability."

A guy of his ability. I wish Liz were here to listen to this.

"So, are you playing tonight?" he asks. His face hangs like a coat. His smooth skin is creased, as though maybe he took a nap in his Land Cruiser earlier. He's wearing a faded jean jacket, and his hair looks different, puffier, the ends curling under in little dark cylinders. Good God, has Big Tony gotten a perm? I keep my face serious.

"Well, if Sam puts me up, I'll play. I don't know if he will yet."

"See, that's what I hate about league. Why'm I gonna come out if I'm not gonna play? God, that pisses me off." Tony is leaning against a ledge that runs along the wall in the back of the bar. People sit their beers on it and sometimes lean their cues against it, until one of them inevitably clatters to the floor, and then people grab their sticks and find safer places for them.

"Yeah, I remember your philosophy, Tony."

"Well, I hope you get to play tonight. You get 'em, killer." He turns to the man next to him, a sawed-off guy in baggy jeans and a hockey jersey, and says, holding up his digital camera, "So, this is a good one. I been taking pictures constantly. They come out great. I can e-mail 'em to you."

"I want to get *you*," I say.

Tony cocks his big shaggy head. "You want me to take a picture of you?" He holds the camera up to his eye and points it at me.

"You said go get 'em, and I said I want to get you. I'm going to ask Sam if he'll put me up against you tonight. I've been bugging him all season to throw me up against a six or a seven." I feel my mouth going dry. I'm not feeling particularly cocky, but I know the odds of my getting this opportunity again are slim, and the only way to engage him is to issue some challenge that plays to his machismo.

Tony puts the camera down. "You're joking, right?"

"Why would I be joking?"

His shoulders shake in silent laughter. He rolls his head at me like a junkyard dog. "What'd I ever do to you? We don't have no beef. That league crap from way back, with Roger? That wasn't me, man. You know, it was just . . . the situation. You don't want to play me, honey. Really. Tell Sam to put you up against someone else, a four or a five maybe. I mean, I know you've played me before, but that wasn't real or anything. That was just practice."

"Well, if it wasn't real, then that means your beating me wasn't real, either."

A waitress walks by carrying a tray of empty bottles and glasses. "She's got ya there," she says, sliding by without stopping. I could've kissed her. There's no way he'll turn me down now.

Tony stares at my face, his brown eyes peering out from thick, hooded lids like two bugs under a rock. Then he shakes his head. "You believe this?" he says, turning again to his pal, who's glassy-eyed with booze and not really paying attention.

He turns back to me. "Okay, I'll play you. Tell Sam to put you up. And I'll tell my captain. You know me, I'll play anybody. I always wanna play. But if I was you, I wouldn't take it so seriously. And anyway, if you really wanted to play, *Jeanette*"—he pauses acidly, letting his sarcasm dangle in front of me—"you'd play me straight pool, or even bar rules. League is for sissies."

I am thirty-five years old, and I am in a bar listening to a middle-aged man with a perm call me a sissy. Yes, it has come to this.

"I'm not an idiot, Tony. You're a million times better than I am. I need to play you in a league match because I need the handicap. And of course I need the W on the score sheet."

"You're killin' me here!" He slaps his thighs, which rest plumply against the wall, filling his jeans to the breaking point. His legs look like two duffel bags stuffed with laundry.

"So is that a yes?"

"Hell, yes, it's a yes. We'll have some fun, you and me. Hey, you wanna go now?"

"I need to find out what Sam wants to do, if he'll even agree to this," I say, buying time, my stomach rolled into a tight little ball.

"Hey, whenever. I'll be here all night, hon." He shakes his head again and nudges his pal, smiling. His teeth are straight and white. I wonder if he's had them bleached.

I wander over to where Sam is sitting, the rest of my team draped around the nearby tables, watching the match in progress.

"So how's it looking, cap'n?"

"Ah, well, I'm not sure if I'm gonna need you tonight. I think I'm going to play Valerie, since she didn't play last week."

"Well, I may need to play."

Sam looks up from the clipboard and raises an eyebrow.

"I think I may have just done something really stupid, and really egomaniacal."

"Oh?"

"Did you notice Tony over there in the corner, showing off his new camera?"

"Yeah, I wasn't sure if he'd be put up tonight. Sometimes he likes to leave early."

"Well, he's sticking around. I just challenged him to a match."

"Really? You 'challenged' him?" Sam makes little quotation marks in the air with his fingers.

"Yes. Really."

"Well, that's interesting. Why?"

"I don't know. Because I'm an idiot. Because I enjoy pain."

He rubs his beard thoughtfully. "So when are you going to play?"

"Well, that's up to you, I guess. I mean, you have been promising to put me up against someone ranked much higher."

"Yeah, I did, didn't I?" He studies the clipboard. "Let me think about this."

I leave Sam to sort out life's mysteries and my pool needs.

I wish I could say that the bar began to move in slow motion, that I was in the center of a vortex of light and color and jubilant noise, that Tom Petty's "American Girl" boomed out of the jukebox at just the right moment, or that an old boyfriend walked in just in time to see me bank the 8, but that's not how it is.

First, Sam has to figure out when to put me up. I see him talking quietly to the captain of Tony's team, who listens and looks amused. This means I have to stand around, agonizing, watching my team-mates play their matches and trying not to worry about the ridiculous drama I've thrust myself into. I can tell Sam thinks it's "cute," my little tough-girl challenge. Tony, on the other hand, seems barely able to remember our exchange, just wanders aimlessly around the bar, occasionally distributing unsolicited advice to some poor sap playing pool on one of the other tables. He finally puts his camera away and his friend disappears. He flirts absently with the waitress, who shows him some of her tattoos after repeated requests. He paces the bar, goes outside once to check on his car, then comes back, looking irritable, as if he's ready to leave.

"Tony, where are you going?"

"I was thinking I might drive out to Long Island."

"But what about our match?"

"What match?"

Is he kidding?

"Tony, for chrissake, do you remember our conversation? We're supposed to play—"

"Oh, shit, yeah." He puts his chin in his hand and nods, like it's slowly coming back to him. "Well, let's get this show on the road." I'm nothing more than an item on Tony's to-do list.

Valerie plays and wins her match and goes outside to smoke a cigarette. Alan leaves for the suburbs. Dennis, a new 4 on our team, is playing the current match, against a tiny Asian woman who I think might kick his ass.

I'm right. Although Dennis plays extremely well, the match is over quickly. And then Sam says the magic words: "Heather, you're up. And they're putting up Tony." It's happening. Now.

Tony, of course, is MIA. I find him at the bar in the front, talking about football with a guy he just met. "Tony, we're up," I say. He flicks his eyes at me, then back to his new compatriot, and says he'll be there in a minute. I return to the back room, pull my black, cylindrical case from under the table where Sam is standing, and start putting together my cue.

Sam nods. He tells me he's there for "consultation."

Tony lumbers over a few minutes later. I've already shoved the quarters into their slots on the side of the pool table. It's a buck-fifty to play one game, what Sam calls "poolway robbery."

"So let's get this show on the road," Big Tony says again.

We bend over one end of the table, taking some practice shots, side by side like workers on an assembly line. Then Tony says, "Ready?" I nod, we both shoot, and I watch as my 12-ball slips across the table to the far rail and rolls lazily back to me, coming to rest an inch or two closer to the head rail than Tony's 14. I've won the lag. Well, at least you've won something, I think, and try to look nonchalant while Tony racks the balls. Then I break—pitifully. I don't use my hips as Katya has taught me. The balls move meekly, staying for the most part in a little puddle.

"Jesus, did anything even hit a rail?" Tony asks derisively. Four balls have to hit a rail for the break to be good. I count and exactly four hit.

"Okay." Tony sighs. So far, this is not turning out to be fun.

Tony studies the table and picks his first shot. He decides to go for the low balls, or solids. He makes four in a row, then misses. I am so rattled, and I so regret suggesting this stupid match that I miss an easy shot on the 12. Tony's turn again. He doesn't have much but manages to cut in his 2. Then he safeties me. I'm honored that he even thinks he has to play defensively. I have nothing, but I manage to nick one of my balls, so I'm not fouled. Then Tony finishes up the game, sinking his remaining two balls and plunking in the 8 in about thirty seconds.

I rack the balls, feeling helpless. I'm finally playing a 7—playing Big Tony, of all people—and I can barely breathe, let alone sink a ball. Unless I get ahold of myself, this will be over in half an hour.

Tony breaks, and the balls scatter; two low balls go into the pockets. He's solids again. He picks up his pace, no doubt thinking about his drive to Long Island, and runs the table until he gets to the 8, which is, thankfully, blocked by one of my balls. He sends the cue ball into a rail, where it bounces off and slides in a clean line to the 8, hits it softly, and comes to a stop nearby. My turn: I make two balls then miss a straight-on shot. Tony is able to bank in the 8, and game two is over. He needs four more games to win.

Sam walks by me. "Relax," he says, and rubs my shoulder. At this point, relaxing feels more like rolling over and whimpering for my mommy, so I remain keyed up while I rack again. The third game unfolds pretty much like the previous two, until Tony's final shot, when he does the unthinkable.

Perhaps out of overconfidence or boredom or both, he sinks the 8 without putting the cue ball on enough of an angle, and so it follows the black ball into the pocket.

Tony has scratched on the 8. I've just won a game.

He blinks in surprise and curses under his breath. I watch, still stunned, as he angrily pushes in his quarters and begins to rack the balls. Sam smiles and gives me the thumbs-up sign. Valerie is back from her smoking break and looks at him questioningly. I see him lean in and whisper something to her. "Really?" Her face lights up and she gives me a thumbs-up, too.

I exhale slowly. Everything has just changed. Tony still has to win four more games; but now I have to win only one. All I have to do is beat him once, just one game, and this will be over. The scratch was certainly unexpected, but what do I care? He made a mistake, and I've been handed a win. That's what happens sometimes.

"The balls roll funny for everybody, kiddo."

I BORROW SAM'S BREAKING CUE and get a slightly better spread than the miserable break I made earlier. It's not great—I don't sink anything—but it's at least less embarrassing.

Tony is angry. He's stripes this time. He sinks two balls and then misses a third, one he should've made. The momentum has shifted. I have a psychological advantage here, and I know I need to cling tightly to it. I examine the table and see I have a shot on the 4, followed by a shot on the 7. I bend down calmly and stroke in the 4. Then, miraculously, I put in the 7, too. The shots aren't pretty—I'm too nervous—but I'm not concerned with appearances. I have a look at the 5 now. I shoot too quickly and jump up before the shot is over so I miss, but I get lucky on the leave. Tony doesn't have much. But then, Tony doesn't need much.

Tony is able to sink a ball, but he doesn't have a lot of options after that. It's already my turn again. I realize it's time to start playing defensively. I aim for my 5, not because I have even a remote possibility of sinking it, but because putting the cue ball near it will make the table much more difficult for Tony.

Tony, meanwhile, has his lips pressed together in a thin, furious line. He escapes from the trap I set for him, but he doesn't pocket anything. He doesn't leave anything for me, either. The game goes on like this for a while, the two of us picking at each other in silence, occasionally pocketing a ball. But Tony gets to the 8 first, sinks it— without scratching this time—and wins the game. I have only one ball left on the table. Progress has been made.

I feel slightly nauseated as the knowledge hits me: *I can win this.*

"I'll be back in a sec," I say, and head for the women's room.

I don't have to go to the bathroom. I do, however, need to calm the hell down. I feel my pulse racing. I slip into one of the stalls, lock the door, put the toilet lid down, and sit down on top of it, trying to regulate my breathing. I'm sweating. The stall is rancid—it's a bathroom in a bar, what am I thinking?—so I stand up, let myself out, and begin pacing in front of the sinks. I don't want to look in the mirror, though I suppose it would've been an appropriate time to address myself, Travis Bickle–style. "You talkin' to me? Huh? You talkin' to me?" The soundtrack from *Rocky* would've been a nice touch as well. I could've danced around, my head down, bopping back and forth on the balls of my feet, tiny, clenched fists punching the air. A visit from Tony Robbins would've been helpful, too, his Pleistocene-era chin looming over me like a highway overpass as he bellows motivational catchphrases: "Who can change your life? Can your boss change your life? Your accountant? Your pool opponent? No! *Only you can change your life!*"

This is insanity.

I pace some more, muttering, "Calm down, calm down." Then I wash my hands, which means I have to look in the mirror. I appear as I always have, with the exception of the excited, deranged gleam in my eyes that I doubt anyone but me would notice.

I walk out and see a visibly annoyed Tony with his arms folded, waiting, his mouth curled into an impatient sneer. I realize that now I have to go to the bathroom.

But I rack the balls instead, and Tony slams into them, an explosive break that sends the cue ball flying off the table.

"Take it easy," someone calls. Sheila, the waitress with the tattoos and the smart mouth, hands Tony the cue ball, which has just rolled by her. He gives it to me without comment. It's my shot. I can put the cue ball anywhere behind the line. Westward ho.

I notice that Dennis and Val are still there, even though their matches are over, lingering, watching my match unobtrusively, trying not to distract me but smiling encouragement when appropriate. Sam sips from a "superpint" of Guinness, one of three that he lines up on his bar table. They look like miniature grain silos. He's watching the game, too. Tony's runty friend, the one who was vaguely interested in the digital camera earlier, weaves out of the men's room and plunks himself down on a stool. "Less'go, Big T!" he calls, the only idiot who would ever openly root for Tony. It's like rooting for Goliath.

Another painstakingly slow game follows, full of defensive parries. I am determined to outwait—and outwit—Tony. He's made one mistake, he might make another.

This time, I get to the 8 first.

I'm in a terrible position, but I don't care. That I have even made it to this point is almost incomprehensible. Dennis, Valerie, and Sam huddle together, as if gathered around a bonfire. I could be wrong, but the din in the room seems to have softened. Gazes have shifted to our end of the room. The jukebox is in the process of changing songs, so the bar has become unnaturally quiet. I feel the anticipation.

I stare at the 8, lounging in front of the head rail, dead center. It's almost a ninety-degree cut to get it in the pocket—and an almost surefire scratch. I don't want to risk it. My other option is to try a long bank shot, to the opposite corner. I never succeed with those shots. But wait. That's not true. I think of Armand then. *He taught me how to do this.* He even marveled at how quickly I followed his lead. Damn if I'm not going to try the bank.

I look at the table and try to calculate where I need to aim the cue ball, just as Armand showed me. I locate what I think is the right spot. I take my time, bend down slowly, stand up, bend down, stand up again, keep doing this until I'm less jerky, then I shoot the cue ball, hard. It hits the 8 dead on, slamming it against the rail, and I watch as the gleaming black ball sails back down the length of the table. It hits a few inches to the left of the corner pocket. The right idea, but not even close. Still, I feel energized.

Tony has two balls left on the table, which he puts in easily, then the 8. I notice how carefully he's shooting now. He sinks the 8 quietly. It's now 4–1. I'm running out of games to squander.

I rack the balls while Tony goes to get a beer. When he comes back I excuse myself and go to the ladies' room again. Valerie flashes me one of her brilliant smiles as I walk by, and widens her Elizabeth Taylor eyes. "You're doing great!" she squeals, trying to keep her voice low.

"Thanks," I say, forcing my own smile.

Tony is already swinging back with his cue, readying for another of his thunderous breaks when I return. The balls zing every which way—one of each kind goes in—but once again, the cue ball leaps off the table and bounces along the floor. This would never happen on a nine-foot-by-four-and-a-half-foot table, only on a bar table.

"Jesus!" Tony says, and chortles to himself.

I pick up the cue ball, which has landed near Big Tony's friend, who seems not to have noticed. I stand with the ball in my hand and stare at the table. It's open. The whole world is open.

The jukebox is cranking again, a song by—Jesus Christ, is that Devo? What century is this?—and some people are yelling and whooping by the dartboard, and Tony is murmuring to his friend, who remains drunk and oblivious, and I torture myself over which shot to take, which ball to choose, a stripe or a solid, trying to figure out which one Tony wouldn't want me to choose, and finally I place the cue ball on the table and shoot at the 11, which I pocket, then try to make the 14 and miss, and now it's Tony's turn.

Any consternation he might have been feeling earlier seems to have vanished. He's back to being relaxed, sure of himself. But I can wait. *Just wait him out*, I think. *Do something to piss him off.*

And I do. When it's my turn again, even though I have a shot on the 10, I don't take it. I safety Tony instead, nudge the cue ball next to my 13, which gently pushes the 13 into his 3. He gazes at the table through slitted eyes, then shrugs one shoulder, annoyed, like a slumbering lion who's just been bitten by a fly.

He untangles himself from the nest I've left him in, but that's about all he does. My turn again. I miss my shot, and Tony takes advantage, sinking four of his balls, *plunk, plunk, plunk, plunk*, the last one a beautiful slice that sends his object ball bouncing off one of mine and into the pocket, simultaneously breaking him out for his next shot. It looks like the game might be over.

And then my waiting pays off. Big Tony makes a mistake.

Thinking, like those of us watching, that he's going to run out the rest of the balls, he makes his next shot too quickly and misses it, just plain misses the pocket, stranding his 7. It's my turn again, and since he's sunk so many of his balls, he's cleaned out the garage a little, giving me ample space to park the car. I have a shot. No, I have several shots. And so once again, everything changes.

Of course I've been in this situation before, and the seesaw of momentum can easily rock back to Tony's side with the misguided click of one ball. I look at the table, and at the other two tables as well, which sit unused and lonely. Without a spread of balls on top of them, all of the flaws in the cloth are exposed. The tables look forlorn, naked. I find myself thinking—naturally—about *The Hustler* and a vivid line one of the characters says early in the movie. He remarks that a poolroom looks like a morgue and "those tables are the slabs they lay the stiffs on." I look back at the colorful splay on my own table. I am still alive, I remind myself. I concentrate on quelling the flutter in my stomach, the tremble in my bridge hand. I am not ready to be just another stiff.

Big Tony mumbles something about how long I'm taking, so I step up and shoot the 12.

Don't think.

I go for the 13 next.

Don't think.

The jukebox thumps—I don't recognize the song; I won't recognize any song for a while—and I circle the table, don't take my eyes from it, won't look at Tony or Sam or Dennis or Valerie, won't acknowledge Sheila, the waitress, who asks if anybody needs anything, won't pay attention to Tony's drunk friend in the hockey jersey, whose lips are moving, as if he's singing along to some tune only he can hear.

Go, just go.

I poke at the 10 and it doesn't go in, but I get lucky—yes, *I* get lucky—and the cue ball rolls haphazardly to a place on the table that ties Tony up but good.

I stand apart from everyone, my breathing shallow. Tony's hair looks like the landscaped pacasandra in my mom's front yard. His face appears slightly askew as he peers down at the table. *Fuck*, he's thinking. *How'd I get here?* I know his mind is absorbing everything, calculating angles I can't even fathom. He bends slowly, adjusts his feet a little, and fixes his taut, myopic gaze on the 7 he inadvertently abandoned in the previous inning. He's going to put it in, then go for his 3, or do something else that I haven't thought of. I still have one more game after this one, one more chance, but I know Tony will hammer me if it comes to that. He'll never let me get this advantage again. He realigns his face. It's tight and mean as he draws back his cue and pocks his 7, which goes into the pocket. He turns to the 3 next—so I'm right—and rocks his cue back and forth like a violin bow, then releases it, and I watch it strike the cue ball, which rolls right into the 3, and then I watch the 3 glide silkily toward its destination, the inviting corner pocket opposite the one where he just put the 7, watch first in surprise, then in exhilaration, then in fear as the 3 softly nicks the corner of the pocket and for a moment appears to hover over it, then taps the other corner and comes to a precarious rest on the edge. It doesn't go in.

It doesn't go in.

The 3 sits on the lip of the pocket, a plump, red-frocked opera singer waiting to belt out an aria. I stare in disbelief.

"Oh, what the fuck," I hear Tony say. He turns away, as if he's just witnessed a gruesome car accident. Which in a way he has.

"What the hell was that?" Tony's idiot friend asks.

"Hey, shut up," Tony says. Then he smiles grimly. "You believe this?" I don't know if he still thinks he can win—knowing Tony, I'm sure that was never in doubt—or if he's simply amused by the concept of losing, but for a moment his anger fades and he seems almost entertained. I stop myself from looking at him.

As much as I would love to have the game come down to my own prowess—my brilliant stroke, a near-impossible bank shot, an instance of perfectly applied English that sends a ball curving in a dramatic arc—the truth is that it comes down to Tony's mistakes, and to the very undramatic act of my waiting for them.

And the beauty of it is: It doesn't matter. The victory still feels like finding a hundred-dollar bill on the ground.

I methodically sink the 14 and the 15, then make a defensive shot, then watch as Tony pockets the Judas 3, which leaves him in a lousy spot to attempt the 8. But he tries anyway, marks the pocket he's aiming for by placing his Bic lighter right next to it on the rail, knowing that he won't make it unless the laws of physics have been overturned. He tries instead to leave the cue ball somewhere messy, but it's hopeless. The table is mine now. I take my time and pot in my remaining ball, leaving the 8 within my reach. It isn't a slam dunk—I could miss. Hell, anyone can miss the 8, even if it's right in front of a pocket. It's the demon ball, the black devil, a "diabolical little pisswad," as Roger once called it while trying to comfort Trevor, who'd clutched.

So, taking nothing for granted, I gulp great lungfuls of air and stand motionless, just stare fixedly at the 8-ball for a minute. Then I bend down and examine its position, and the position of my cue ball, and the rest of the lonely expanse of table, and realize that I can't possibly scratch, that the shot isn't all that difficult. I don't go so far as to think, *Who cares if I blow it? I've done so well already, and that's enough.* Because it won't be enough. So I shove Sam and Alan and Valerie and Dennis out of my mind; close the door on Roger, and on Paul G. and Trevor, and on Mexico and Chelsea Billiards; erase Hector Silva and his pickup lines; hit the mute button on Honey; close the lid on Melanie, and on Armand and Jeanette Lee and Wally and his hillbilly jokes; unplug Travis Bickle and the *Rocky* theme song and Tony Robbins and Paul Newman; think briefly of Liz—what a story I'll have!—and why not, think of Johnny Bench, too, then finally feel ready to draw back my cue, my emerald-green McDermott, fifty-eight inches, eighteen ounces, and make the most ordinary, most unheroic, most unremarkable shot on the 8-ball, and then listen as it makes the sweetest sound anyone's ever heard when it drops into the pocket.

I remember hearing a roar—worrying, even, that it's me, victim of some long-in-the-making psychotic break—but it's Valerie and Sam and Dennis, who've been watching intently and who understand the gravity of what has just happened and have no choice but to scream.

I don't move, just stand where I am, as if I'm swaying in a breeze. Then Tony comes over. He's unscrewing his cue stick and he puts his hand out. "You believe that with the 3?" he says. "I don't know about the roll on this table." We shake hands and he says, "But you played good, you played good. You gotta admit you got lucky, too." Yes, I did. Then I think of something.

"Tony, can I buy you a drink?"

"I gotta get out to Long Island," he says, the match already gone from his brain.

"You sure?"

"Yeah. But thanks. Some other time." He winks at me, zips up his cue case, and walks out of the bar.

I turn to my comrades, who are whooping and clapping and grinning crazily. I hug Valerie and Dennis and Sam tightly, in quick succession. "You kicked ass!" Valerie yells. My arms are shaking.

I wander around the bar, somewhat dazed, my insides ablaze. Sam buys me a beer that I don't really want, but I know having a drink bought for me is part of the ritual. I figure I'll take a few token sips. I call Liz from my cell phone and leave her an ecstatic message: "You will never believe what happened tonight . . ." But I know that she will.

I AM STILL A 2, a remnant from my slump, but I will go up to a 3 next season and will win enough games to start dreaming about becoming a 4. My team will change, with people leaving because of conflicting schedules and complicated lives, and new people will replace them, but Sam and Alan will remain, practicing straight pool during the week at Alan's house and doling out advice to the rest of us every Monday. Valerie will eventually switch to Sam's Tuesday-night team, where she'll keep on glowering at anyone who tries to tell her what to do. Liz and I will continue to play on separate teams, exchanging our ritual pool postmortems via e-mail the day after our matches. She'll dip down to a 3 briefly, then ascend to a 4 again and stay there for good, consistently mowing down her opponents, making them pay. Dennis will turn into an excellent coach and will help me through some tough matches, though there certainly won't be another one like the match with Big Tony. Tony, meanwhile, will quit and rejoin his Manhattan team three more times, finally leaving for good and committing fully to his league on Long Island, where a guy of his ability can enjoy himself. He'll show up at tournament qualifiers from time to time and play well. I will not run into him in a bar again.

Armand will retreat into the world of three-cushion billiards and pool-table repair. He'll retire from the APA and show up only occasionally at the pool bars he used to frequent. When I see him, he'll ask me about my game and if I'm still enjoying my salsa CDs. He'll sip from a shot glass of whiskey and will still be wearing his pointy, caramel-colored shoes.

As for Dawn of the Dead, which hired me then fired me, the team will finally fall apart completely. Gary will go on "hiatus" and never return to the league, throwing his punches somewhere other than in pool bars. Paul G. will "resign" to work on some deals he has brewing. He'll continue to live with his mother and get a new job pushing copier products, and he'll still talk loudly about his big plans. The remaining players will join other teams or fall into their own darkness, succumbing to addictions or to life's disappointments or both, with the exception of Ricky, who will move to L.A. to try to become a movie star.

Trevor will get drummed out of another East Village bar and will eventually leave town altogether, a geographical change I'll hear about only because of his return. He'll leave a strange message on Liz's cell phone one day, almost two years after we played on Paul G.'s pool team together. He'll tell her that he's returning to New York and wants to "reach out," that he's been going through his address book, dialing up old friends, so he thought he'd give her a ring. He calls Liz "Kelly" in the message. He doesn't leave his number, and he never calls back.

As for Roger, his phone number will go out of service and he'll start to recede from my psyche, but then, quite unexpectedly, I'll run into him one night at his old stomping grounds, the small pool bar next to his apartment building.

I'm ready to begin a match there, on the bar's lone pool table, when Roger walks in from out of the rain, just like he did the first night I saw him, at the Ace bar in the far East Village, when I was searching for a new pool team after my ignominious breakup with Wally.

Roger doesn't see me at first; he just leans on the heavy bar and chats with the bartender, a young woman in a tight tank top and ripped, faded jeans with whom he seems to have a familiar, relaxed rapport. I approach the pool table silently, not sure if I want Roger to turn around. But eventually he does turn, and he notices me. His eyes widen for a second, and then he says, rather casually, "Hey, there," as if we still see each other every week. When it's my opponent's turn and I step back from the pool table, Roger leaves his freshly poured drink on the bar, comes over, kisses me on the cheek, and asks me how I am. I say "Good," and that's it until I'm done with my match.

We stay at opposite ends of the room as I pack up my cue—the one Roger bought me. I say nothing to my teammates about who he is. Then I inhale deeply and walk over to him. He turns so that he's looking at me sideways while leaning on the bar. His grin is as easy as

ever, but there are deep grooves in his face. He looks older, his eyes
tired. He's wearing a loose short-sleeved, button-down shirt in pale
yellow, something an old guy might wear on a cruise. He tells me,
after various platitudes have been exchanged, that he's moving back
to California. A relative of his out there owns some land somewhere,
and he's going to help develop it. He spent the last several months—
and all of his money—traveling around Europe with "this chick" he
dated for a while, a flight attendant who was used to nice hotels and
easy, last-minute access to big planes. "She drove me nuts," he says.
"And I spent all my money. We're talking tens of thousands of dollars." But he just sold his apartment—the closing is next week—and
he's going to be flush again, hence the move out west and the new
business venture.

"I'm gonna sober up," he adds, casting his eyes downward.
"That's part of it, too."

"This is good to hear, Roger."

"Well, you know what they say about California and New York,"
he says. No, I don't.

"If you live in California too long, you get soft. If you live in New
York too long, you get hard. So you should alternate between each
place about every five years. That means I'm due. Overdue."

"Well, God . . . I mean, good luck and everything."

"Thanks." He looks around the bar for a minute, then back at me.
"I'm selling most of my stuff and driving out next week. I haven't
driven cross-country in, like, a decade."

"I'm glad I saw you, then."

Roger nods. "You leaving soon?" he asks, indicating the door.
"You wanna split a cab somewhere? Do you still live in Brooklyn?"

I stammer around and then say, "I do still live in Brooklyn, so I'm
heading east and then downtown."

"That's perfect. I'm going the same way. I thought I'd stop by
The Wrong Side and see who's there." Paul G. and Gary and Trevor

float into my mind. I don't need to see them, but I can certainly share the ride.

Roger settles his bar tab, and I say good-bye to my teammates without offering any explanation of who I'm with or where we're going. Roger and I walk outside into the slanting rain.

"Holy fuck," Roger says, looking up at the wet sky. I flick open my umbrella. We walk for a bit, then see a taxi stop and someone get out. We run up behind the car. Roger yanks open the door and we slide inside. I tell the driver we'll be making two stops.

"Relationships are tough, man," Roger says, apropos of nothing.

"I know." I sigh. I clutch my cue case against my stomach. The cab is moving at a good clip now.

"Shelly has a new boyfriend, some hot, humorless dude, and he's totally jealous of me. It's nuts. I'm just this unemployed jerk. And he's this musclehead; he could pound me into the ground with one fist. I don't get it. Shelly and I are just friends. But we've got a long history, too, you know? Histories are important. Memories are important. You don't just wash them away."

I watch Roger's profile in the flickering darkness of the cab.

When we get within a few blocks of The Wrong Side, Roger tells the driver to let him out, he wants to walk. He offers me money for the fare, but I decline. Then he grins.

"So how about this, huh? What're the odds?"

I shrug.

"Well, take care of yourself," he says.

"You too." We smile at each other, and he gets out.

A couple of weeks later, I learn from Liz that Roger, on his way out of town, pulled up in front of the bar in a huge rented truck, what was left of his belongings packed up inside. It was late, near midnight. He left the truck in the street and ran into the bar for one last drink before he hit the road. When he came back out, the truck was gone. It had been illegally parked—abandoned, really—so a cop had

had it impounded, taken to some faraway lot in the hinterlands. Roger would have to find the vehicle and pay to have it released before he could leave the city.

That's the last I hear of him. But I still wonder about him sometimes and hope that he's okay, developing land, living somewhere soft. He needs the cushion.

THE EPILOGUES OF MY pool comrades are, of course, far from my mind as I look around the bar, the astonishing victory over Big Tony still fresh on my skin. I'm feeling less tingly now, but my chest is full, as if I'm going to burst. I remember feeling that way right before my birthday parties when I was a little girl, and also on the day I cracked that ball out of the softball diamond in my first summer girls' league game. And I remember feeling this same way every time Johnny Bench came to the plate, even as he got older and the Big Red Machine was no longer in its prime.

Now that the league match is over and Tony and his teammates have departed, other bar patrons move in and take over the pool tables. I watch as Sam shows a comely young woman how to set up a bank shot. Valerie is laughing, her mouth open wide, after a rumpled, sexy-looking man with five o'clock shadow and what can only be described as "bedroom eyes"—smoldering, heavy-lidded, hungry—whispers something in her ear as he passes her on the way to the men's room. She's nothing but teeth and earrings and long, dark hair as she lets loose a throaty rumble, then gives the man causing her to laugh the finger before sauntering to the chalkboard to add her name to the list of people who want to play pool. Dennis smiles at me from across the room and shrugs.

I sip the beer Sam bought me, and after what seems an appropriate amount of time has passed, I put my coat on, pack up my things, and say my good-byes to my teammates, who are now engrossed in "social" games of pool or else are preparing to leave. I walk through the bar alone, then out onto the street, the icy air hitting me like a door, and keep my eye out for a cab that will take me to Brooklyn. I'm content to walk for a block or two in the cold. The night is clear and crisp. I feel like shrieking some exultant sound into the wind, but I just smile to myself instead. A yellow cab rolls by, and I stop it and climb inside, balancing my cue case on my lap.

The driver is young and energetic, from Pakistan, he tells me later. I give him my address. He turns around and grins. "This is my very first fare to Brooklyn!" he exclaims. It's only his third day on the job. I offer directions and encouragement, since he will need both.

We chug over the Manhattan Bridge. The city lights sparkle in the cold. I peer into the windows of some of the buildings as we go by. The cabbie chatters about driving in the city. He asks me if I had a good day today.

"Yes. I had a great day, actually."

We make it safely to my neighborhood. I have him drop me off on the corner of my street and Flatbush Avenue, and then make sure he knows how to find his way back to Manhattan, putting my hand up, part wave, part salute, as he drives off.

I stand on the street corner in front of Brownstone Billiards and wait for the traffic light to change. I find myself looking for the kid in the baseball hat, hoping he'll come by again with a slice of pizza and ask me if I've won, if I'm any good. But he doesn't appear. No one comes by. The sidewalk is empty.

I cross Flatbush and look back at Brownstone's sign, with its little cartoon rack of pool balls. The sign is perched above the poolroom's wooden door, high above the street, its white light shining and winking like a cluster of stars.